POVERTY IN AFRICA

A geographical approach

ANTHONY O'CONNOR

Belhaven Press
(a division of Pinter Publishers)
London

First published in Great Britain in 1991 by
Belhaven Press (a division of Pinter Publishers),
25 Floral Street, London WC2E 9DS

British Library Cataloguing in Publication Data
A CIP catalogue record for this book is available from the British Library

ISBN 1 85293 087 X (hb)
1 85293 088 8 (pb)

Typeset by Witwell Ltd, Southport
Printed and bound in Great Britain by Billing & Sons Ltd, Worcester

Contents

List of maps

List of tables

Preface

This book is intended for those without extensive knowledge of tropical Africa who would like to know more about it, and especially about its poverty. The focus is on the present rather than on the past – on what causes Africa to remain poor, rather than on past circumstances which may have contributed to its poverty but which are facts of history that cannot now be changed. The focus is also on circumstances internal to Africa rather than on the features of the global economic and political system which undoubtedly contribute to Africa's problems and may even make some of them impossible to resolve. Even with these severe limitations we have a long agenda for a short book.

I have thought many times while writing, should not someone from Britain mind his own business? Should not this book be written by someone in Africa? But no-one in Africa seemed to be doing it: and in some ways presenting a near-continental view may be more difficult for a resident of one country than for an outsider. Probably few people from Africa have both had the opportunity to work in four different African countries and had the time subsequently to write books. I only hope that most people in Africa who read the book will forgive my intruding into their affairs, especially in a way that is less flattering than when I was writing about African 'development'.

It needs to be made clear, however, that this *is* an outsider's view, with all the limitations implied. It should also be made clear that the book aims to inform and to aid understanding, but not to prescribe. It does not offer solutions to the problems of poverty. Indeed, it would be improper for a university teacher in Britain to propose, uninvited, what should be done by policy-makers in Africa; and even more improper for students outside Africa reading a book like this to think that they could do so. It is certainly intended mainly for students rather than for 'practitioners': but in so far as it is read by decision-makers in or concerned with Africa, or by students in Africa who will have some influence in these matters, I hope that it may assist them in making better-informed decisions.

To me, as probably to most of you, both the extent and the intensity of poverty in Africa seem quite intolerable. Yet there is very little that I can do about it – except to write a book like this, in case in some slight and indirect way it helps. Even this could not have been done without much advice, encouragement and support from Iain Stevenson at Belhaven; from colleagues in the Department of Geography at University College London, including the cartographer, Louise Saunders; from other colleagues at the School of Oriental and African Studies; and especially from my family. To all, I am most grateful. Let us all hope that it will soon be possible to write about Africa rather more cheerfully.

London
July 1990

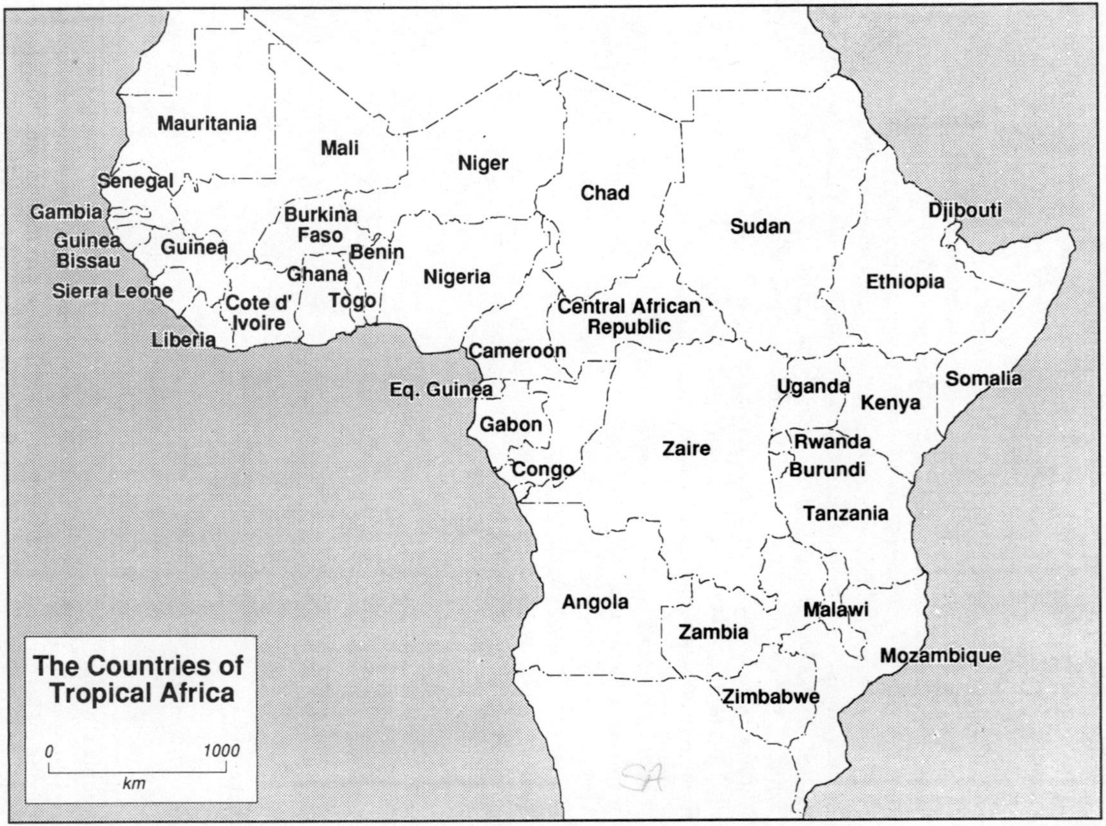

Map 1.1 The countries of Tropical Africa

1
Africa and poverty

'To think of Africa is to think of poverty.' This statement, agreed by a group of British students in 1988, is of course not true for most people who live in Africa, although people all over Africa are becoming more aware of their relative poverty in comparison with people in most other parts of the world. Nor, probably, was the statement true for most outsiders in the 1950s or 1960s, though poverty might have been included among their images of Africa. Increasingly it *is* now true for such outsiders, especially those in the rich countries who saw something of the mid-1980s famines on their television screens.

The fact that a special session of the United Nations General Assembly in 1986 was devoted to 'the critical economic situation in Africa' indicates that this image extends from concerned individuals to national governments and on to international organizations. Sadly, those governments outside Africa which have the power and the means to do something about the situation have not actually shown much inclination to help – certainly not by considering basic changes in international economic structures. The national governments also, of course, include those within Africa. All of these have many concerns other than poverty, but most of them are having to give increasing priority to their economic predicament and its implications for people's welfare.

Our concern in this book is with material poverty – with low levels of income, whether in terms of cash or of subsistence production, and therefore low levels of consumption of goods and services. This is reflected in diet, among other things, so that both undernutrition and malnutrition are aspects of material poverty. So is the related issue of ill health, with which we can link low levels of education, since funds can be spent on these services as an alternative to goods, whether by governments or by individuals.

It should be made very clear at the start that no cultural or spiritual poverty is implied, although these matters may of course be equally relevant for human happiness. What much of Africa lacks in material terms it partly makes up for in these other ways. Many people who certainly seem poor by global standards evidently manage to enjoy life just as much as many people in richer societies elsewhere. For many others, however, and probably for an increasing number in recent years, this is not so. For these people, in the Sahel, in Ethiopia, in Zaïre, or in Mozambique, no amount of cultural richness can compensate for their extreme and unrelenting deprivation in material terms.

Forty countries and five hundred million people

This book is concerned with tropical Africa rather than with the entire continent, for in human terms this is a much more meaningful entity. Both culturally and economically the countries from Egypt to Morocco are quite distinct from tropical Africa, and Egypt and Libya at least are in every sense part of the Middle East. With respect to the majority of its people there is less reason to exclude South Africa; but it is highly distinctive in many ways, including the nature and causes of poverty there. In aggregate economic or welfare terms, South Africa resembles Brazil far more than most African countries, while in terms of the sharing of wealth and welfare it forms an all-too-exact microcosm of the world as a whole. The countries in between, from Mauritania in the north-west to Mozambique in the south-east, have much more in common, and at least some generalizations can be made that apply to all of them.

Strictly speaking, Botswana, Lesotho and Swaziland lie outside tropical Africa, so while much of what is said does apply to them they receive little specific attention. A recent geographical study that does give much attention to them is Morag Bell's *Contemporary Africa* (1986). Partly due to my total ignorance of it, Madagascar is not covered at all; nor are smaller islands such as Mauritius, some of which have far more South Asian than African characteristics. Otherwise, we are concerned with more or less that area to which the label 'Sub-Saharan Africa' is increasingly being given in official publications.

In approaching tropical Africa from a geographical perspective we should be equally concerned with the common features that distinguish it from other areas and with the substantial variations between one country and another. We shall see how far we can generalize, but we must also consider carefully just how widely such generalizations really apply. The variations are of course not only from country to country, and in many ways the nation–states, most of them entities imposed on Africa by the colonial powers, are not the most appropriate units for analysis. Some attention must therefore be given to regional variations within countries, especially the larger ones such as Ethiopia, Sudan and Nigeria.

At the same time, we must recognize that poverty is really experienced by families and by individuals rather than by countries or even regions. It is individual people who may die of starvation, not entire nations. Throughout the book our concern is really with the people of tropical Africa, or with the great majority of them, even when points are made in terms of the whole region or of its component countries.

The African condition

Material poverty, by international standards, is undeniably a feature of most parts of tropical Africa. It has most of the world's poorest countries, whatever criteria we use for measuring this. In tables produced by the World Bank, based on Gross National Product per capita, African countries occupy fifteen of the twenty lowest places. In tables produced by UNICEF, based on child mortality, they occupy seventeen of the lowest twenty places. Tropical Africa also has many of the world's poorest people, even though the absolute number below any given income level may be higher in Asia.

The most striking and disturbing contrast with south and east Asia is that no improvement is taking place. There was genuine economic development across most of tropical Africa in the 1960s, with rising average incomes almost everywhere, and with some benefit being felt by the majority of the population. But with the exception of those countries that have had oil to export, notably giant Nigeria and tiny Gabon, the situation changed considerably in the 1970s. Economic growth then only just kept pace with population growth in most countries, and failed to do so in some, so that there was no longer any rise in income for most people.

The 1980s have witnessed a further shift in fortunes, as average per capita income across tropical Africa has fallen year by year. Infant and child mortality rates which had continued to improve through the 1970s are now no longer improving. For most people material conditions by 1989 were worse than they had been ten years earlier, and for very many they were worse than they had been for their parents twenty-five years earlier. One of the most influential books on Africa to appear during this period, written by Lloyd Timberlake (1985), was appropriately entitled *Africa in Crisis*. Although it was prompted by the 1984/5 famines, it stressed that the problems were basically longer-term in nature, and the book was reissued three years later with little change. Other long-term problems, essentially of a political nature, had been eloquently indicated by Ali Mazrui in 1979 in a book whose title has been used for this subsection.

In many countries the steepest decline in living standards came in the drought years of 1983 and 1984, since when there has been a partial recovery. In Nigeria it came later, with the sharp fall in oil prices in 1985 and 1986. The worst conditions, including famine on a massive scale, have occurred first in Ethiopia and then in Mozambique. In Sudan, famine on the Ethiopian scale was averted by a more effective relief operation in the west of the country, but then struck largely unrelieved in the war-torn south. Perhaps to avoid total gloom we should note that in a few countries, notably Ghana and Uganda, conditions in the late 1980s were better than in the 1970s, and that a few others such as Cameroon and Zimbabwe have fared much better than most throughout this period.

The specific aspect of long-term economic decline which has received most attention outside Africa is the fall in per capita agricultural production that has taken place in most countries, and especially the fall in per capita food production which has necessitated rapidly expanding food imports. Since the great majority of the people of tropical Africa are engaged in agriculture this is indeed the central problem. However, it should be noted that although all data on the subject are highly unreliable, it is very unlikely that food production has fallen in absolute terms over any sustained period, as is sometimes suggested. We might also note that the small manufacturing sector has fared no better, with many factories working far below capacity throughout the 1980s; and there is ample evidence of decay in other sectors of the economy such as transport.

In contrast to a country such as India, most African countries have a monetary economy that is to a large extent externally orientated, and the economic crisis of the 1980s includes the building up of massive external debts which many of these countries are totally incapable of repaying. Partial repayment has been consuming a large share of their export revenues, while these revenues have actually been falling as a result of ever-lower commodity prices on world markets. This means that, by the late 1980s, imports into tropical Africa had had to be cut back to only about two-thirds of their 1980 volume. Again, of course, conditions differ greatly from one country to another. The debt crisis is particularly severe in Nigeria and Côte d'Ivoire, which perhaps do have the resources to escape from it; in Zaïre, which has the resources but seems quite unable to mobilize them; and in Zambia and Sudan for whom it is hard to see any escape route. Ironically, the countries with least debts are those such as Uganda and Chad, to whom no-one has been very willing to lend.

Prospects for the 1990s

An economic downturn in the 1980s would not be so serious if it were demonstrably only temporary. Unfortunately, this is not so. Some of the conditions that have contributed to the decline are likely to persist or even to intensify. Few long-term predictions for Africa are for continued steep decline, but few are for rapid economic improvement either. The general consensus both inside and outside Africa is that various tough measures now being taken in many countries should arrest the decline, but that more or less static levels of income and welfare are the best that can be hoped for over most of tropical Africa through the 1990s. This was the scenario presented as early as 1980 in the *Global 2000 Report* to the US President, and it is now endorsed by the World Bank and by various United Nations bodies including the UN Economic Commission for Africa. The latter body has in fact criticized a 1989 World Bank report on Africa as being over-optimistic.

In 1986 the United Nations formulated a Programme of Action for African Economic Recovery and Development (PAAERD), based on the African Priority Programme for Economic Recovery 1986–1990 (APPER) prepared by the Organization of African Unity. But full implementation of this depended upon both political stability within African countries and greatly increased economic assistance from the rich countries. Instead, civil wars have continued in several parts of Africa, and net inflows of finance to Africa from overseas have fallen substantially.

We must *hope* for improvements in both directions in the 1990s, and indeed all who have any influence must strive for them: but there is really no reason to *expect* any improvements. Political strife may remain just as intense as ever, and the richer countries of the world will probably remain just as mean and self-centred as ever. Similarly, there is no reason to suppose that severe drought will not recur in the 1990s. It is increasingly clear that the 1960s constituted a very exceptional period for tropical Africa, and that it was not realistic to expect the economic development then occurring to continue indefinitely. At that time 'Development Plans' were being produced in almost every country, but this is no longer the case. Now, more countries have stabilization or recovery programmes as well as the structural adjustment programmes that are a condition of International Monetary Fund assistance. Today, realistic plans must assume that poverty will persist to a very large extent, but also that something can be done to help those in greatest need and to make certain selective advances when and where circumstances are favourable.

In search of understanding

This book provides no prescription for the elimination, or even the reduction, of poverty in Africa. It would be highly presumptuous for a British academic to attempt this. It does not even provide a full explanation of the region's poverty. But it does indicate some of the factors that contribute to the situation, and seeks to aid understanding of the issues involved.

There is in fact very rarely a clear and simple explanation for even one particular aspect of poverty. Some writers do insist that there is one *real* cause, such as the harsh natural environment, or runaway population growth, or bad government, or the evils of past colonialism, or the present greed of the rich world. An alternative view is that all these factors are equally real, and that all are partially responsible, even if not equally so, and even if some are more significant in certain areas than in others.

It is proposed here that most poor people in Africa are poor because of a whole range of circumstances operating together. These are environmental and economic and social and political. Some are rooted in the past, while others are very much features of the present. Furthermore, they operate at a wide variety of scales – global, continental, national, regional, local, and even personal.

It is also suggested here that the relative importance of the various factors does differ greatly from place to place. Poverty that intensifies into famine may in one area be very largely the result of persistent drought, while in another area it may have nothing to do with drought. Even the relative importance of the different scales of analysis may vary spatially. In one place global factors, such as falls in commodity prices, may be of critical significance, while in another place a local epidemic or a local conflict may have caused people to be especially poor.

This means that the most appropriate set of policies to alleviate poverty must also differ from place to place. For instance, growing cash crops for export markets ought perhaps to be phased out in certain areas but vigorously promoted in other areas. But almost everywhere there is a need for action on a wide range of issues rather than on just one or two. And action is urgently needed at a variety of levels, including both local and global as well as the national level on which all the emphasis is so often placed. However desperate the need for action in these terms, it must be based on a clear understanding of the issues. At a very introductory level, a book like this may help to contribute to such understanding.

2
Poor countries

It is in many ways easier to discuss poor countries than poor people, especially for those who are themselves far from poor. This book is written by someone who has some first-hand experience of living and working in poor African countries, but with no experience of what it is like to be poor as an individual or a family. Most parts of the book therefore deal with national aggregates, or even the general tropical African situation, rather than with poverty as experienced by individuals. This chapter does so quite explicitly, but we should still try to remember that it is the people behind the national aggregates who matter. In a sense, discussion of Tanzania as a poor country is just a convenient shorthand for what we should be saying about the living conditions of 25 million children, women and men.

Discussions of poor countries are usually partly based on statistics submitted by their governments to the United Nations, to the World Bank or to the IMF, or on estimates made by such organizations. All are subject to a wide margin of error, for in general the poorer the country the less able it is to gather accurate statistics; but throughout this book our concern is with broad orders of magnitude rather than with precise data – which must in any case relate only to a particular year. The most widely used set of figures is that for national income, or more specifically Gross National Product, normally related to population size. These can usefully be supplemented by other economic indicators such as per capita commercial energy consumption, for which relatively reliable figures are often available.

Also highly relevant for an examination of poverty are data for such matters as life expectancy or infant mortality. These have sometimes been used for all countries of the world to produce a Physical Quality of Life Index, or a comparable aggregate measure, on which countries may be ranked rather differently from their GNP rankings. In global terms the most important case is China, whose per capita GNP is officially recorded as similar to the African average but where life expectancy and infant mortality are both vastly superior.

All these data, of course, provide only national averages and trends. They give no indication of the range that exists around the average in terms of either regions or individuals – for which only few and highly unreliable figures are normally available. This chapter is based on such national averages, but some attempt to disaggregate further is made in the chapter following.

National income

One reason why all data for national income, Gross National Product or Gross Domestic Product in Africa (as well as in China) must be treated with caution is that they must attempt to include a vast amount of subsistence production. The volume of this is never known, and its value can only be subjectively estimated. Subsistence services present an even greater problem. Even the volume of commercial production of many items may not be known with any accuracy, especially those sold in local markets – or smuggled out of the country. Then there is the problem of expressing the value in terms of a common currency. This has become much more difficult in recent years, as many African currencies have become grossly overvalued in relation to the dollar and as many substantial devaluations have taken place. Some of the changes in the rankings of individual countries in the late 1980s must be explained by such devaluations rather than by sudden changes in national fortunes.

As an indicator of wealth and poverty the figures have to be expressed in per capita terms, and there are many African countries in which the total population is not known at all accurately. Thus the 1984 census in Ethiopia counted 42 million people when previous estimates had been around 35 million. All per capita figures for the country had to be adjusted accordingly, pushing the country to the very lowest place in world GNP rankings.

A new set of GDP estimates is currently being prepared by the United Nations. These differ greatly from previous figures because of a very different methodology, and seem more realistic in most cases. But as yet they are available for only a selection of countries, and so are not used here. In any case, the data more readily available to us *are* of use as general indicators, and are valid for international comparisons within Africa. They also usefully indicate the direction and extent of change over time.

If one accepts a crude division of the world into two groups of countries,

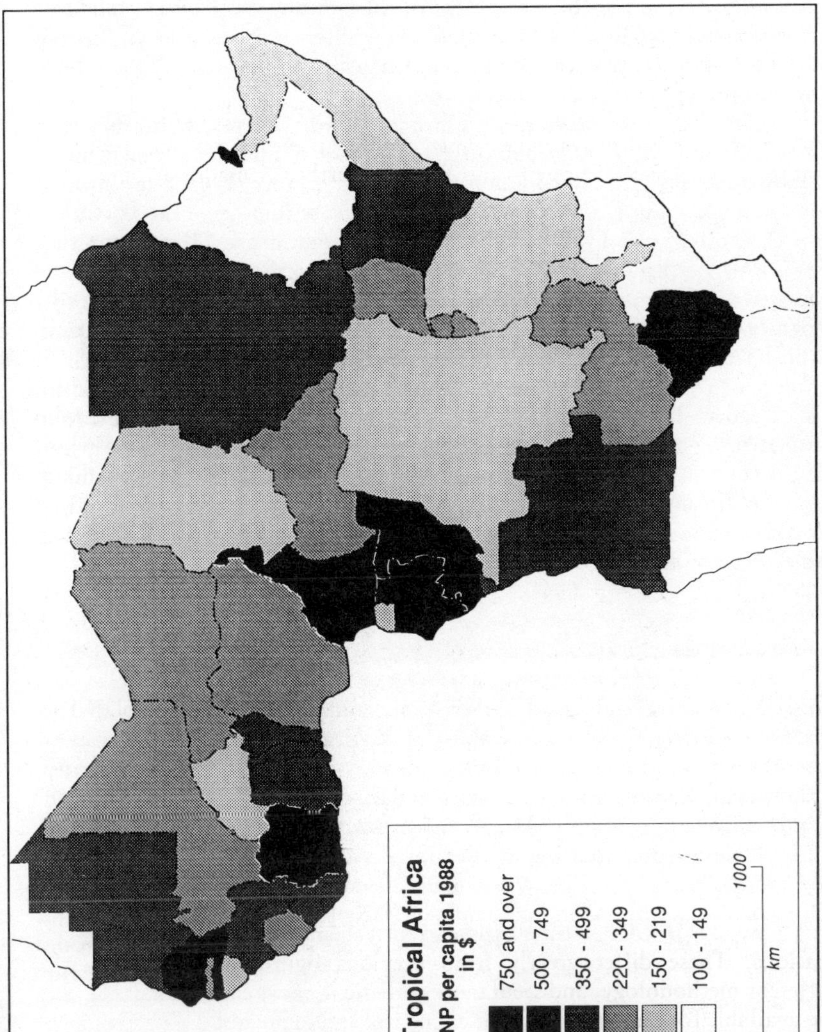

Map 2.1 GNP per capita, 1938

variously labelled developed and less-developed, rich and poor, or (following the 1980 Brandt Report) North and South, then all tropical African countries, with the possible exceptions of oil-rich but tiny Gabon, fall very clearly into the second group. For those who prefer to think of First, Second and Third Worlds, tropical Africa unequivocally forms part of the Third World in income terms as in most other respects.

I suggest that these categories are in fact grossly over-used, and that for instance Argentina, Angola and Afghanistan, or Chile, Chad and China, actually have very little in common. It may be far more realistic to think in terms of a spectrum from richest to poorest, rather than in terms of two or three clear categories. In these terms we can say that nearly all the countries of tropical Africa lie far towards the poorer end of the spectrum.

A useful compromise, now widely adopted by the United Nations, is the recognition of a group of thirty to forty 'Least developed countries', which all do have much in common. Most in the group are African, and a clear majority of the countries of tropical Africa would normally be included in this category. Recent World Bank publications have similarly identified thirty-five to forty 'Low-income economies', most of them African; thirty-five to forty 'Lower middle-income economies', in which the remaining tropical African countries are included; and about twenty 'Upper middle-income economies', which include South Africa. The data for Map 2.1 and Tables 2.1 are drawn from these publications.

Specific countries

Ethiopia, Somalia and Chad are certainly among the poorest of all the world's countries, however unreliable the statistics may be. GNP per capita was estimated at only $120 to $180 in the late 1980s, and the vast majority of their people are very poor by any standards. In southern Africa incomes are probably equally low in Malawi and in Mozambique, with the situation in Mozambique deteriorating as that in Malawi has slightly improved, at least in relative terms. The World Bank also quotes a figure of $170 for Zaïre in 1988, for although that country clearly has more pockets of wealth, these are not yielding income to most of its people, and the GNP figures do not include the interest on the funds drained away into its leaders' Swiss Bank accounts.

For rather more than half the countries in tropical Africa the per capita GNP estimates for the late 1980s were between $250 and $350, comparable to India but far below any Latin American country apart from Haiti (which shows many African characteristics). Just six countries have substantially higher figures that make them all rather special cases. Per capita income was

Table 2.1 Population and per capita GNP, 1988

	Population (millions)	*Per capita GNP ($US)*	*Earlier 1987 GNP figure*
Angola	9	?	(500)
Benin	4	390	(310)
Burkina Faso	9	210	
Burundi	5	240	
Cameroon	11	1,010	
Central African Rep.	3	380	
Chad	5	160	
Congo	2	910	
Côte d'Ivoire	11	770	
Ethiopia	47	120	
Gabon	1	2,970	
Gambia	1	200	
Ghana	14	400	
Guinea	6	430	(350)
Guinea-Bissau	1	190	
Kenya	22	370	
Liberia	2	?	(450)
Malawi	8	170	
Mali	8	230	
Mauritania	2	480	
Mozambique	15	100	(170)
Niger	7	300	
Nigeria	110	290	(370)
Rwanda	7	320	
Senegal	7	650	(520)
Sierra Leone	4	?	(300)
Somalia	6	170	
Sudan	24	480	(330)
Tanzania	25	160	
Togo	3	370	(290)
Uganda	16	280	
Zaïre	33	170	
Zambia	8	290	
Zimbabwe	9	650	
TROPICAL AFRICA	440	330	

Notes:
Countries with less than ½ million people are omitted.
Where figures are given for both 1987 and 1988 the large differences represent revisions rather than real change.
Sources: World Bank, *World Development Report* 1989 and 1990.

thought to be around $600 to $800 in the late 1980s in Senegal, Côte d'Ivoire and Zimbabwe, and above $900 in Cameroon and Congo – which is comparable to several Latin American countries such as Honduras and Guatemala. Gabon, with large oil revenues and a very small population, has a much higher figure still, possibly over $3,000, though this depends on whether its population is assumed to be under one million or substantially more. This is a case where an average figure is particularly misleading, for many people in Gabon have a standard of living no higher than in most parts of Africa.

Commercial energy consumption (Map 2.2) can be measured far more precisely than GNP (though of course subsistence fuelwood use cannot), and it gives a useful indication of the extent of commercialized economic activity taking place. The rich countries consume about 5,000 kg. of oil equivalent per head per year, while the average for poor countries is around 400 kg. This is also the figure for countries such as Zimbabwe and Zambia, but only 150 kg. per head is consumed annually in Nigeria despite its oil resources, and only 60 kg. in Sudan, 40 kg. in Tanzania and 20 kg. in Ethiopia.

Although our data sources often tie us to countries as the basis for discussion, we should always remember that these are very arbitrary units. Thus, if we were mapping income levels in West Africa we should obtain a much better picture of reality if we had separate figures for each of the twenty-one states of Nigeria – many of which are larger in population than neighbouring entire countries. If the data existed they might show that the 7 million people of Borno State of Nigeria have a much lower per capita income, and a much lower commercial energy consumption, than the 7 million people of Niger Republic to the north.

Economic growth, stagnation or decline

The poor countries of the world are sometimes labelled 'The Developing Countries', but that term is surely not appropriate for tropical Africa in the 1980s. 'Development' is, of course, by no means the same thing as economic growth, since even its economic dimension involves more than just growth, and since it also has social and political dimensions. But however defined, development is extremely difficult to achieve without economic growth, and indeed without rising per capita incomes.

Per capita incomes did rise throughout most of tropical Africa in the 1960s, and the pattern was discussed in detail in an earlier text (O'Connor 1971, 1978). The GNP growth rate for the whole region was estimated at 4 per cent per year, compared with a population growth rate of 2½ per cent. Economic growth lagged well behind population growth only in Chad,

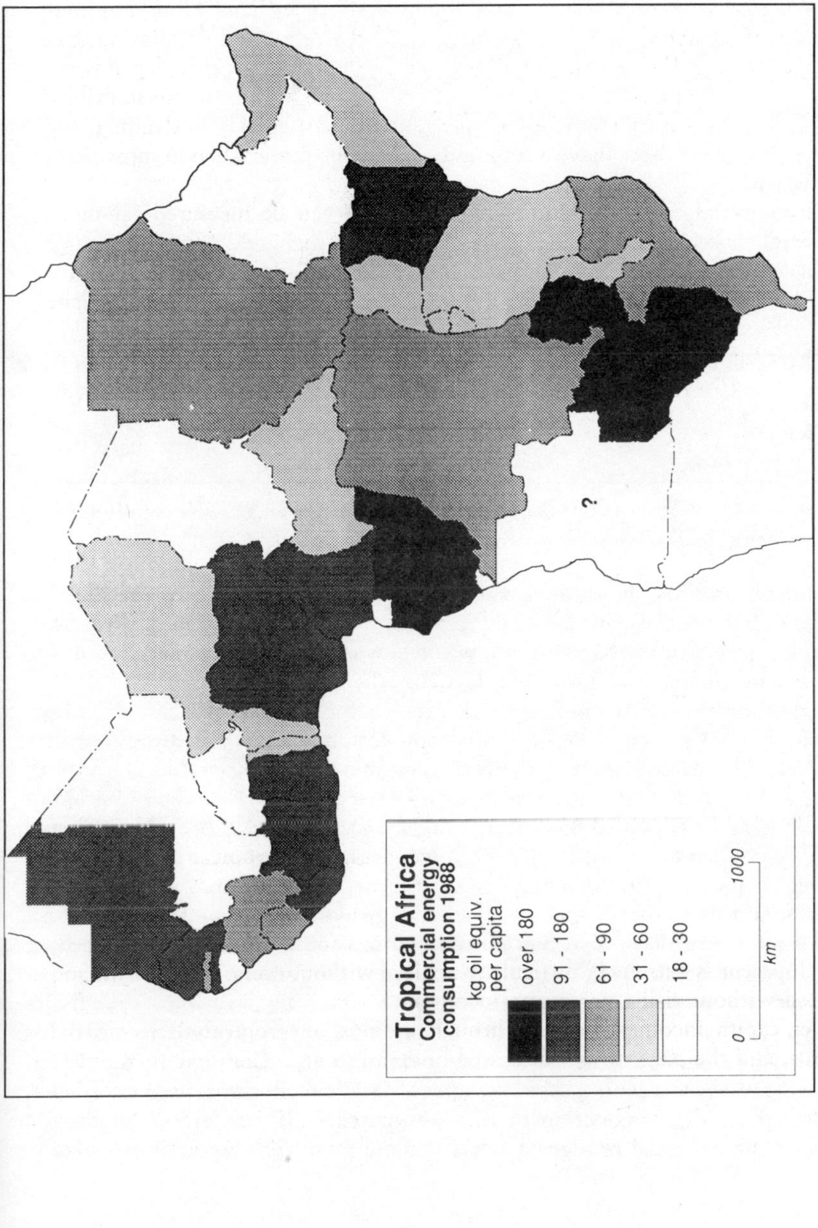

Map 2.2 Commercial energy consumption, 1988

Table 2.2 Income trends in the larger countries, 1965–87

		Average annual % rise or fall in GNP per capita	
	1965–73	*1973–80*	*1980–87*
Nigeria	5	1	–5
Ethiopia	1	0	–2
Zaïre	0	–5	–3
Tanzania	2	–1	–2
Sudan	–2	3	–4
Kenya	5	1	–1
Uganda	1	–6	–2
Mozambique	?	?	–8
Ghana	1	–2	–2
TROPICAL AFRICA	3	0	–3
(South Asia	1	2	3)
(East Asia	5	5	6)
(Latin America	4	3	–1)

Sources: World Bank, *Sub-Saharan Africa: from crisis to sustainable growth* (1989); and World Bank, *World Development Report 1989.*

Somalia and Sudan, while it reached a maximum of 8 per cent annually for the whole decade in Côte d'Ivoire. Not all this income growth was concentrated in the hands of a few: there was a modest improvement in the standard of living of most people across the continent.

During the 1970s annual GNP growth for tropical Africa as a whole slowed to 3 per cent, while annual population growth rose almost to that level. The overall picture therefore became one of economic stagnation, though with more variation from country to country than in the 1960s (Map 2.3). The 1981 World Bank study, *Accelerated Development in Sub-Saharan Africa*, much criticized for its recommendations, provided a full analysis of trends in the 1970s which is very generally accepted. Côte d'Ivoire maintained almost 7 per cent annual growth, and much increased oil revenues brought 7 per cent annual growth to Nigeria also. Cameroon, Kenya and Malawi experienced around 5 per cent annual growth and Sudan showed a marked improvement over the 1960s. The most impressive figure in the whole of Africa was the 13 per cent a year growth recorded for Botswana, mainly due to mining developments. Conversely, the 1970s brought no economic growth whatever in Chad, Burkina Faso or Ghana, brought a slight reduction of total estimated GNP in Zaïre, Uganda and Mozambique, and brought a fall averaging 9 per cent a year in Angola.

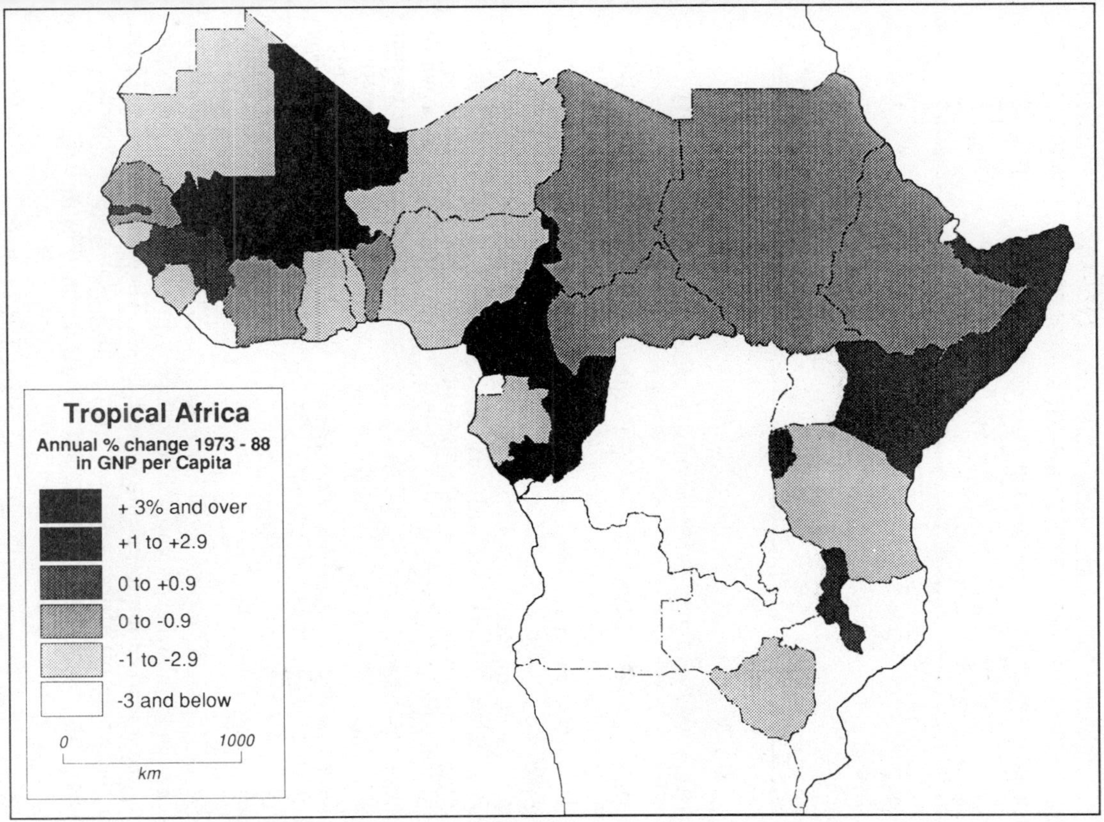

Map 2.3 Annual % change in GNP per capita, 1973–88

Table 2.3 Imports into the larger countries, 1965–87

	Imports in $ million		
	1965	*1980*	*1987*
Nigeria	770	16,642	7,816
Ethiopia	150	721	1,150
Zaïre	321	1,117	1,149
Tanzania	197	1,227	1,150
Sudan	208	1,499	694
Kenya	282	2,590	1,755
Uganda	161	293	477
Mozambique	173	800	486
Ghana	447	1,129	836
TROPICAL AFRICA	4,920	43,570	30,780

Source: World Bank, *Sub-Saharan Africa: from crisis to sustainable growth* (1989)

During the period 1980 to 1987, per capita GNP fell by an average of 3 per cent a year over tropical Africa as a whole (Table 2.2). Real incomes were therefore lower for most people in 1985 than they had been in 1970. The steepest decline was in Mozambique, where terrorist attacks destroyed large parts of the economy and disrupted the lives of millions of people. In Nigeria, falling oil prices contributed to a 2 per cent annual average fall in GNP, or more than 5 per cent per capita; and falling export crop prices even brought a slight downturn in per capita terms in Côte d'Ivoire. Decline continued in Ghana and Zaïre, but there was some recovery in Uganda. This was of course also the period when drought hit other countries, notably Ethiopia, Sudan, and those right across the Sahel. The only really satisfactory economic performance in tropical Africa was in Cameroon, which had 7 per cent annual growth (4 per cent per capita), largely due to expansion of oil production.

In terms of trends, the picture provided by commercial energy consumption is very similar. The annual per capita growth for all of tropical Africa fell from 7 per cent in the 1960s to less than 3 per cent in the 1970s and to almost zero in the early 1980s. Between 1980 and 1987, consumption per head fell quite sharply in countries as diverse as Senegal, Zaïre, Sudan, Kenya and Zambia. Again Cameroon was quite exceptional, with a 3 per cent annual growth.

The volume of imports is also a useful indicator of trends in national economies. According to the World Bank the volume of imports into tropical African countries increased by 6 per cent a year during the 1960s, but by only 3 per cent a year during the 1970s despite a huge increase in Nigeria during that period. In Zaïre and in Zambia, as well as in strife-torn Uganda and Mozambique, annual imports were already falling in the 1970s. During the early 1980s there was a much more widespread fall in the volume of annual imports (Table 2.3). In Nigeria imports were cut between 1980 and 1987 by an annual average of 14 per cent. Sierra Leone experienced a similar cut, while there were annual reductions of 9 per cent in Sudan and 6 per cent in Zambia.

In all these respects the trends in tropical Africa stand in marked contrast to those in South Asia. There, per capita GNP rose by 2 per cent a year in the 1970s and by almost 3 per cent in 1980–7. Per capita energy consumption continued to rise there in the 1980s, and there was even a 4 per cent average annual rise in the real value of imports.

Social indicators

When criteria such as child and infant mortality are used the low-ranking position of African countries is even clearer (Table 2.4), although the *trends* are not quite so discouraging as those in respect of economic activity. According to UNICEF, the mortality rate for under-fives in Europe is about 10 per thousand births, while it is 40 per thousand in China. In tropical Africa the figures range from 110 in Zimbabwe and Kenya to an appalling 300 in Angola, Mozambique and Mali (Map 2.4). The situation is probably no better in Sierra Leone, Guinea, Chad, Ethiopia and Malawi, even though the official figure for each of these countries is slightly lower.

The fact that child mortality rates are around 180 per thousand in both Tanzania and Nigeria suggests that, despite Nigeria's higher per capita income, the poverty of the majority may be just as intense there as in Tanzania. Even high-income Gabon has a very similar rate. Both Côte d'Ivoire and Cameroon, where prosperity might be thought to have spread more widely, still have child mortality rates of about 150 per thousand.

The situation is very similar in terms of life expectancy. This is only a little lower now in China, at 70 years, than in Europe and North America where it is about 75 years. Even in India the estimated figure is now 58 years, matched in tropical Africa only by Zimbabwe and Kenya. The tropical African average, and the figure for Nigeria, is only 51 years, and this falls to only 41 or 42 years in Sierra Leone, Guinea and Ethiopia (Map 10.3). It is hard to understand how the people of rich countries who value their own welfare state can tolerate this situation where life for so many over so much of Africa is so short.

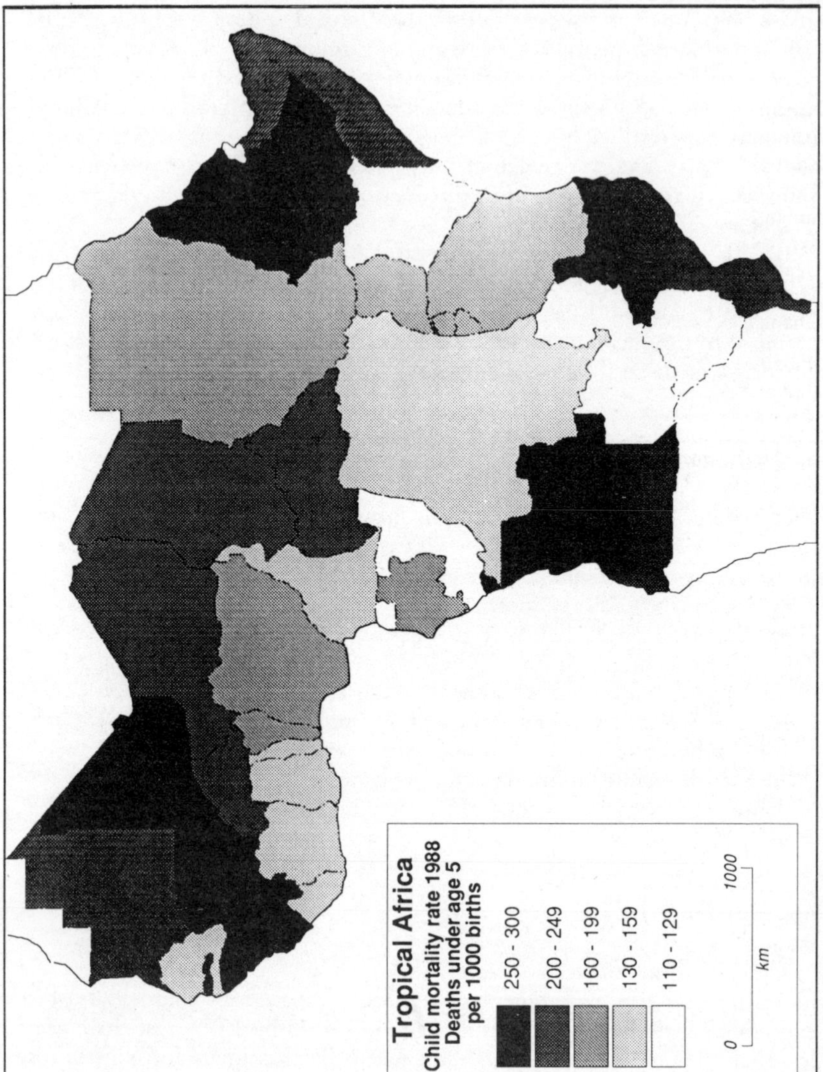

Map 2.4 Child mortality rate, 1988

Table 2.4 Child mortality and life expectancy in the larger countries, 1988

	Population (millions)	*Under-5 deaths per thousand*	*Life expectancy*
Nigeria	110	170	51
Ethiopia	46	260	41
Zaïre	34	140	53
Tanzania	25	180	53
Sudan	24	180	50
Kenya	23	110	59
Uganda	17	170	51
Mozambique	15	300	47
Ghana	14	150	54
(Brazil	145	80	65)
(India	820	150	58)
(China	1,100	40	70)

Source: UNICEF, *The State of the World's Children 1990.*

There is at least some comfort to be found in the fact that child mortality has fallen substantially, and life expectancy has risen, across the whole of tropical Africa over the past thirty years. The current average under-five mortality of 180 per thousand at least represents a great improvement on the UNICEF estimate of 280 per thousand for 1960. There has been a particularly large improvement in Nigeria, which is thought to have then had a rate of about 320 per thousand. The relatively low figures in Zimbabwe and Kenya, and in Zambia, Congo and Senegal, also represent a very substantial change for the better. On the other hand both Mozambique and Ethiopia show only about a 10 per cent improvement over the thirty years.

The current life expectancy of 50 or 51 years compares with only 40 years in 1960. In this case Kenya shows the greatest improvement, from 42 to 59 years, and Ethiopia the least, from 36 to 41 years. It can at least be said for life expectancy that over this thirty-year period the gap between most of tropical Africa and the rich countries has been considerably narrowed.

It must be emphasized, however, that most of the improvement in child mortality and life expectancy took place in the 1960s and 1970s. Life expectancy had already risen from 40 to 47 or 48 by 1979, just three years less than the figure for the late 1980s. The official estimate for Nigeria rose from 40 in 1960 to 49 in 1979, but then only to 51 in 1988.

The picture is very much the same for other social indicators that reflect poverty, such as the school enrolments that will be discussed in a later chapter. In every case African countries are among the world's least well provided, though with much variation from country to country. In every case there has been considerable improvement since 1960, but a slowing or even reversal of that improvement in the 1980s.

Summary

Taking various measures of poverty at national level together, and considering trends over twenty-five to thirty years, tropical Africa shows great diversity, even if attention is confined to the larger countries. Cameroon, Côte d'Ivoire and Zimbabwe are among the more fortunate. Nigeria shared this position for a while, but has recently suffered a sharp fall in income. The same has happened in Zambia over a longer period, and in Ghana over a much longer period. Both Kenya and Tanzania are better placed in terms of social indicators than in terms of income, with Kenya having some advantage over Tanzania in most ways. The people of Uganda have become poorer since the 1960s, but are beginning to recover. Those in Angola have also become poorer, but no recovery is yet in sight. The situation is most desperate for the people of the Sahel countries, Zaïre, Mozambique, Ethiopia and parts of Sudan.

Over tropical Africa as a whole, poverty is far more intense and widespread than in most of Latin America or in China, and now probably even rather more widespread than in India. Perhaps only in Afghanistan, Bangladesh and Kampuchea is poverty as extreme as in the worst placed African countries. Furthermore, across most of Asia and Latin America there are more signs of improvement, indeed of 'development', than in Africa today, and better prospects for the 1990s. This at least seems to be the case from the perspective of the nations or states. The next chapter attempts to consider the situation more from the perspective of individual people.

3
Poor people

We cannot consider poverty in Africa only in terms of national aggregates and averages, however relevant these may be. We must also try to consider how it confronts and is experienced by individuals, families and communities. One author who has recently accomplished this very successfully is John Iliffe in his book on the history of *The African Poor* (1987). Others who provide valuable insights in a West African context are Polly Hill (1977) and Michael Watts (1983) writing on rural communities in northern Nigeria, and Margaret Haswell (1975) writing on The Gambia.

How certain rural communities in Sierre Leone cope with difficult, though not extreme, circumstances is the theme of a valuable micro study by Paul Richards (1986). Coping with poverty, and specifically with drought, is also the focus of a very recent geographical study by Michael Mortimore (1989), again dealing with rural northern Nigeria, and based on fifteen years of research there. Complementary to all these rural West African studies, there is a remarkable portrayal of self-help urban activity among the poor of Nairobi by Andrew Hake (1977).

Equally relevant, perhaps, are numerous ethnographic accounts of African communities, even though they do not generally have an explicit focus on poverty. Many of these demonstrate how people organize their lives when they have very little cash income and very few material possessions. A further source of insight to make up for the deficiencies of this chapter would be a selection of fiction by African writers such as Chinua Achebe, Cyprian Ekwensi, Ngugi wa Thiongo or Meja Mwangi.

Works like these show that poverty in Africa may mean going to bed hungry night after night, 'bed' in this case actually meaning no more than a mat on the floor. In many rural areas poverty means walking a 10 km. round trip to fetch water each day, often water that is even then far from pure. In most cities poverty means living as a family in one small room, and fearing eviction from there when you cannot scrape together the rent.

The distribution of income

All the national averages considered in the last chapter mask variations within countries, both over space and among social strata, and these variations continue through to neighbours within a single village. In every rural community some families are poorer than others, although the differences may not be immediately apparent to the outside observer. Nomadic pastoral communities are no exception, especially when some people have suffered greater drought losses than others. In cities the disparities are even wider, and while in ex-colonial cities rich and poor tend to live in different neighbourhoods, in those of indigenous origin they often live side by side.

However, over large areas of Africa the distribution of both income and wealth is less uneven than in some other parts of the world. In some Latin American and Middle Eastern countries inequalities are such that there are rather few families with around the national average income. In most African countries this is not so. In Tanzania, in Malawi, or in Sierra Leone most families are poor to the extent that they have around the national average per capita income – perhaps between $1,000 and $1,500 a year for a family of six if a realistic value is put on subsistence production. A few are much more affluent, and this leaves some who are even poorer.

In Zaïre, the President has amassed a huge personal fortune, and some of his close associates have also become extremely wealthy. This process continues so that their incomes are also high, and in any case the wealth yields investment income. A further 5 per cent probably also have incomes far above the average. But this leaves well over 90 per cent among whom the range is not very wide: certainly all this vast majority must be considered poor, even if not quite uniformly so. A similar distribution without such a pronounced peak is found in countries such as Mauritania, Niger, Chad and Somalia, poverty being shared by very nearly the entire population.

In Nigeria, in Zimbabwe, in Kenya, and in Sudan, there is a much larger 'middle class' group, including some farmers, some people in business, and some government or private enterprise employees, in between the wealthy few and the poor majority. In Sudan there are also many who are truly destitute, partly as a result of either drought or war. Even in Kenya and Nigeria there are some who would be destitute without the support of their extended families, either as a result of extreme pressure on rural land or due

Table 3.1 Income distribution in selected countries

	Percentage share of all household income				
	Lowest 20%	*Second* 20%	*Third* 20%	*Fourth* 20%	*Highest* 20%
Côte d'Ivoire (1986)	5	8	13	21	53
Ghana (1987)	6	11	16	22	45
Kenya (1976)	3	6	11	19	61
Zambia (1976)	4	7	11	17	61
(India 1983	8	12	16	22	41)
(Brazil 1983	2	6	11	19	62)

Note: Côte d'Ivoire and Ghana are the only tropical African countries for which recent data are available.

Sources: World Bank, *World Development Report 1986* and *1990*

to their failure to find a means of livelihood in the city.

Some attempts have been made to gather data on income distribution comparable to that which exists for other countries around the world, and some are presented in Table 3.1. However, these are based on small sample surveys and are beset even more than national averages by the problems of putting a value on subsistence income, which may represent almost the total income of the poorest 20 per cent of the population. Even in his book concerned explicitly with *Inequality in Africa*, Wayne Nafziger (1988) does not feel able to make much use of this type of information, which is generally the main basis of comparable discussions of inequality in Latin America.

Although there is clearly some diversity among African countries in patterns of income distribution, nowhere do 'the poor' constitute a well-defined minority group on whom we might focus attention – if 'poor' is taken to mean by global standards. By such standards, poverty involves the majority of the population in every country of tropical Africa, and so the majority are our concern in this book. It is, however, worth attempting to identify what sort of people are the poorest of all, as John Iliffe (1987) does in his historical study which is focused on the poorest.

The poorest groups

There is no single category of people who constitute the poorest in material terms. Refugees might be thought to provide such a category, at least at the time of their flight, but while many are absolutely destitute and therefore are given specific attention shortly, some are from the small affluent sectors of African societies and may be able to command a reasonable income in their country of asylum. Instead, a whole range of categories of people might be briefly considered here.

The very poorest include some of those who live in areas remote from towns and transport routes, who are still tied to an almost entirely subsistence economy. Where the land is fertile and pressure upon it is mild such an economy may provide an adequate diet, and even satisfy basic needs for shelter, fuel and so on: but in some of these areas the environment is harsh and any notion of an idyllic, carefree existence would be totally inappropriate. Few people any longer live in such isolation in countries such as Ghana, Nigeria, Tanzania or Zimbabwe: but there are substantial numbers of extremely poor people little touched by the outside world, or by the nation–state, in Ethiopia, in southern Sudan, in the Central African Republic, and in Zaïre.

The poorest also include some in those rural areas that have been most closely tied into the world economy, who have lost access to land and who work for others for extremely low wages. Over tropical Africa as a whole 'the landless poor' are not yet large in numbers in comparison with India or Bangladesh; but their numbers are now rapidly increasing in certain countries, notably Zimbabwe and Kenya. At present those in rural areas who are totally landless generally move either to another rural area or to a city, partly because few opportunities for employment, even on farms, are available locally. But if such possibilities of migration become more limited, as is likely in many areas, the problem of rural landlessness must be expected to increase. Much will depend, of course, on what type of inheritance system emerges in areas where communal land tenure is now being replaced by individual ownership.

Intermediate between the two situations so far considered are the areas where most families have some land, and are involved to some extent in the cash economy, but where the land is now so crowded that each family has only a very small patch. If land is individually owned, it is usually divided on inheritance; if communal tenure still prevails, then ever-smaller plots are allocated to individual households. Rwanda, Burundi and Burkina Faso are three countries where very many people are in this situation. It is also a situation in which rapidly increasing numbers of people find themselves in Anambra and Imo States of Nigeria, in Western Province of Kenya, and in Southern Province of Malawi. Similar conditions were already starting to be experienced in large parts of Eritrea/northern Ethiopia, even before the recent famines, though that is an area where the cash economy has still penetrated only to a very limited extent.

Nomadic pastoral peoples often have very low incomes, even though some individuals or families among them may have much wealth tied up in their herds. There is often much inequality within pastoral societies, and this has been greatly exacerbated by the recent droughts. Not only have some people lost all their animals, but others have been forced to sell theirs at very low prices in order to buy food, and so those more fortunately placed have been able to enlarge their herds further at very low cost. Generally, however, it is only a few who are so well placed, and many entire pastoral communities in the Sahel, in Sudan, in Ethiopia, and in Somalia must be counted among the very poor. Even in Kenya and Uganda, the nomadic or semi-nomadic pastoralists are the groups amongst whom extreme poverty is most widespread. In such countries, governments in which the pastoralist groups are very poorly represented, both in parliaments and in the civil service, have no more idea than their overseas advisers how to tackle the poverty of these people.

There are now also rapidly growing numbers of extremely poor individuals and families in the towns and cities, most of them dependent on very erratic earnings in self-employment. An individual teenager may sleep on the floor of a bar after it closes in the early hours of the morning; a family may live in a shack made from discarded cardboard boxes, at least for a while until the authorities demolish it. Urban poverty is certainly sufficiently widespread, and in some cases sufficiently extreme, to justify a full chapter devoted to it. Tropical Africa does not yet have, however, the vast numbers of pavement dwellers found in Indian cities, who make extreme poverty so visible to those visiting from overseas. Perhaps around a quarter of the poor of tropical Africa live in cities, but probably not more than 10 per cent of the very poorest. They are still very largely living in rural areas, and often largely invisible to those visiting Africa from elsewhere as Robert Chambers (1983, 1985) has stressed in several publications on rural poverty.

Among the poorest groups of people in Africa we should certainly now include many groups who have fled from war or terrorism, or from drought, or from a combination of the two. The term 'refugee' is sometimes restricted to those who have crossed an international border and whose move was the result of political violence. Even within this narrow definition there are now about 4 million refugees in tropical Africa, many of whom are living in temporary camps in conditions of extreme poverty, despite some international assistance, while others are surviving in the rural border areas with the help of the local population. The largest movements have been from Ethiopia into Sudan and vice versa, from Ethiopia into Somalia, from Uganda into Sudan, from Angola into Zaïre, and from Mozambique into Malawi, but there have been movements of desperately poor people across many other borders also. The international refugee situation will be discussed further in Chapter 6. Here we should note that the very poorest also include many who are 'internally displaced', especially in Angola, Mozambique and Sudan. In so far as they do not qualify for international refugee assistance, they may be in a situation of even more dire poverty than many of those who have crossed borders.

The poorest families

No reference was made to gender in identifying the poorest groups in African societies. Neither women nor men constitute a group in the sense in which the word was used there, and both women and men are involved in each of the groups mentioned. Gender is, indeed, left mainly to the next subsection. However, in considering which are the poorest families in most African societies, we should note that many surveys have found female-headed households to be generally poorer than those considered to be male-headed. The poorest households in various rural areas of Kenya, and also in Nairobi, include a disproportionate number of those in which the only adult is a woman. This matter will be discussed further shortly.

The poorest families within any community are often in that position as a result of some specific misfortune, such as prolonged serious illness. This is true anywhere in the world, but the link is closer in countries that have no form of social security provided by the state. Throughout Africa some such security is provided by kinsfolk, but there are always limits to what they can do to help. The severely disabled are also normally cared for by kin, but those with a less severe physical or mental handicap who establish households of their own are likely to have lower than average incomes. Little, if any, research seems to have been undertaken on this dimension of poverty in Africa today. Blindness is one all-to-widespread condition which must contribute to particularly extreme poverty for many families.

Environmental hazards such as drought may devastate large areas, and will be considered in the next chapter; but others such as floods or landslides more often occur on a very local scale, and they may affect some families in a community while others are untouched. The worst locust invasions hit entire districts, but more frequently these and other pests destroy crops on some farms while neighbours a mile away escape. Of more long-term significance for the families concerned are diseases that may wipe out one herd of cattle without affecting those of others in the same community.

Civil war likewise may devastate whole regions, but may be far more random in its impact. Some families may be caught in the cross-fire, suffer injuries and lose their homes and possessions, while others in the same village remain unscathed. Bandits may attack and destroy individual farms, especially when these are dispersed through the countryside rather than clustered in villages. And of course many people throughout tropical Africa often attribute the misfortunes of individual families to evil actions of another type, namely witchcraft.

It is not fashionable to stress the fact that, quite apart from cases of severe handicap, people in any society differ considerably in intelligence and aptitudes, and to suggest that this may contribute to variations in economic success. This seems particularly relevant to the 50 million or more families in tropical Africa who manage their own small farms. The capabilities of many of them may have been grossly underestimated by agricultural 'experts' (Brokensha et al. 1980, Richards 1985), but there are bound to be some who do not find it easy to manage their farms. There will also be some who are very much less energetic than others, which may or may not be due to ill health.

In the cities more than in the rural areas, some cases of extreme poverty are at least partly the result of folly, although it is also not fashionable in academic circles to acknowledge this. Some people, almost invariably men, who can hardly afford food and shelter, spend heavily on alcohol, and cause much suffering to their families thereby. Far more alcohol is consumed in most African cities than in those of most parts of Asia. Thankfully, poverty exacerbated by drug abuse is not such a widespread problem in African cities, though it certainly exists. Similarly, a few people have become destitute through gambling, but no more than anywhere else in the world.

None of these factors are put forward here as substantial explanations of poverty in themselves. They are all merely superimposed on a range of other conditions which cause whole communities to be relatively poor, or which make them highly vulnerable. Within that general situation, however, fortune is inevitably kinder to some individuals or some families than to others, and some people adopt more effective survival strategies than others. Understanding poverty in Africa, as elsewhere, requires that these aspects relevant at the individual level should at least be acknowledged.

Poverty and gender

Since the vast majority of adult Africans are married and living in families, it might seem that gender is not very relevant to poverty. However, some observers feel that we should disaggregate even within families, since income may not be fully shared. If almost all the cash income of the household, either from wages or from crop sales, is controlled by the husband, it is quite possible that the wife is actually living in greater poverty than he is. He may even consume a disproportionate share of the food that is grown and prepared by his wife, leaving her and their children subject to malnutrition.

Such patterns do seem to be all too common in most parts of Africa, though no more so than in Latin America, the Middle East or South Asia. The most distinctive feature of tropical Africa in this connection is the predominant role of women in farming in many areas, so that they may often contribute most to total family income if subsistence is included. In this respect there is often a great difference between the rural areas and the cities, where income-earning opportunities are generally more limited for women than for men.

In some parts of Africa wives and husbands have separate plots of land, and therefore separate farm incomes, but more often they both work on the same plots so that household farm income must be considered as joint income. Likewise, much expenditure must be regarded as being for the benefit of the family as a whole, undermining any attempt to establish just to what extent women in general are 'poorer' than men. Both can be expected to benefit equally from spending on a radio, or on a roof.

A distinction based on gender is more realistic where wives and husbands are separated by male labour migration, which is a long-established pattern in many parts of Africa. Married men move from rural homes in search of employment, both to other rural areas and to the cities, and may remain away for several years. Despite some sharing through remittances, the income and the standard of living of husband and wife may diverge greatly during these periods of absence. If the husband is successful in obtaining employment he may be much better off than his wife: if he is not, then he may be living in more abject poverty than she is. While such separation is very common, especially in southern Africa where it reaches an extreme of 40 per cent of all adult males absent at any one time in Lesotho, it is probably not true to say, as many do, that it is 'ever-increasing'. In a country such as Zambia over the past thirty years, the trend has been for male labour migration to be replaced by movement of whole families.

Male migration contributes substantially to the total number of female-headed households, which have been found to have lower than average incomes in many areas, as noted in the previous section. The matter was raised there because it is not entirely clear how far it is a gender issue, or actually a matter of single-parent households being poorer than average. None of the studies of the subject have compared female-headed households with the few where a man has lost his wife and is bringing up children on his own. Comparison is generally being made with households that some would prefer to regard as joint-headed rather than male-headed.

In spite of the strength of extended family ties, some widows and divorced women live on their own, and they often face extremely difficult economic circumstances in societies that are dominated by men. In matters such as land tenure, patterns differ greatly from one part of Africa to another, and in some areas women have just the same rights as men: but in others they have no rights to land at all. Most commonly they have some rights, but a woman with no husband is unlikely to own or to be allocated as much land as a man. In this respect women may be rather better placed in the cities, where some widows or divorcees gain a modest livelihood from renting out rooms in a building that they own.

A quite different way in which gender is relevant to poverty in Africa is the degree to which development programmes and projects are directed towards men rather than women. This is particularly absurd when the projects relate to agriculture in regions where women are responsible for most of the farm work, or to sectors such as domestic water supply which are primarily the responsibility of women throughout tropical Africa. The by-passing of women in many such projects has contributed to their limited success, and thereby to the poverty not just of women but of whole communities. However, it can no longer be said that women are ignored in academic analysis of development and poverty in Africa. Valuable African material was included in a collection of papers edited by Janet Henshall Momsen and Janet Townsend (1987), while the subsequent two years brought six books in English on women and development issues in Africa, such as that edited by Jean Davison (1988) on *Agriculture, Women and Land: the African Experience*. Such writing is already having some impact on the practice of African governments and international agencies, though any influence on social custom must be a far slower process.

Poverty and age

If we disaggregate the female and male halves of the population in our discussion of the incidence of poverty, then perhaps we should also make a similar distinction between the half who are adults and the half who are children. In most of tropical Africa children really do make up almost half the population, and they have certainly not been the subject of academic attention in the same way as women have in recent years. Again and again the word 'people', even in an African context, seems to refer to adults.

It is really not meaningful to compare adults and children living within the same households in terms of poverty, but attention can be drawn to the ways in which Africa's poverty particularly affects children. Recently UNICEF has begun to do this in a variety of ways, including an annual report on *The State of the World's Children* and a 1985 report devoted specifically to Africa. We might note, for instance, that the incidence of most forms of malnutrition is far higher among children than among adults, and that many diseases, from malaria to measles, cause far more child than adult deaths. A major international programme of immunization and of oral rehydration therapy for diarrhoea has made some progress in many African countries over the past ten years, but there are fears that this may not be sustained. UNICEF has had some influence on the IMF in the late 1980s by demonstrating how the economic adjustment programmes forced on many African countries have had harmful effects on the welfare of children (Cornia, Jolly and Stewart 1987).

One age group among whom the incidence of dire poverty is high are the teenage school-leavers, especially those in the cities. Many of them are unable to find a job, and lack the experience needed for successful self-employment. Many work as apprentices in small-scale enterprises with little or no pay, a long-established tradition in indigenous cities and one that has spread to the new ex-colonial cities also. Some of these teenagers have grown up in the city and still live in the parental home, but others have moved there from a rural home, and while relatives may give them shelter they may do little more to support them. One special category found in northern Nigeria and the Sahel states comprises the boys who join a Koranic teacher, often moving from place to place, and often dependent for survival on alms-giving.

Often less visible to the visitor from outside, but even more vulnerable to extreme poverty, are the elderly. They are a smaller proportion of the population than anywhere else in the world, and young adults take more responsibility for their parents' welfare in tropical Africa then anywhere else: but there are still some old people whose sons or daughters are unable or unwilling to support them. There are others who have had no children of their own, or whose children have all died. With no state security system of any kind for most of these people, they often only just manage to keep alive, with the help of the community within which they live. Even if they are living close to their extended families, the very old must often be recognized as being among the very poorest in terms of their own material possessions and spending power.

As a sad footnote to this section, we might consider the fact that, where poverty in Africa has turned into famine, those who have suffered most have been the very young and the very old. In Ethiopia, in Sudan, in Mozambique, these are the people who have been the most vulnerable.

4
The environmental context

Until very recently social science has largely ignored the natural environment, even in discussions of development and poverty. The analyses of these issues by Walter Rostow and by Gunder Frank, both highly influential and almost diametrically opposed, have this one thing in common. They both pay almost no attention to the environment. Even in discussions focused on tropical Africa it has usually been left to other 'experts' such as botanists, climatologists or soil scientists. In Africa as elsewhere, social and natural science often appear to speak almost entirely different languages: there is certainly very little communication between them.

Geography ought perhaps to be able to bridge the gap, but a few geographers became so carried away with discovering environmental explanations for all human affairs early in this century that there has been a fear ever since of being charged with 'environmental determinism'. So even within this discipline, 'human' and 'physical' geographers tend to work separately. Most writing on Africa by human geographers, my own included, has given little attention to the natural environment.

However, the situation is now changing both globally and with respect to Africa, with the increasing public (and governmental) awareness of environmental issues. Globally, an important step in linking such issues with development and poverty was the publication in 1987 of the Brundtland report, *Our Common Future*, by the World Commission on Environment and Development. Many development agencies, including the World Bank, are at last giving attention to the environmental aspects of their activities. For Africa in particular the 1984 drought had a massive impact on public awareness in the rich world, sustained by books such as Lloyd Timberlake's *Africa in Crisis* (1985). The first broad text on African geography to be written primarily from the perspective of physical geography was produced in 1988 by L. A. Lewis and L. Berry, while 1989 brought a new text by A. T. Grove, also primarily a physical geographer. Increased concern within Africa is exemplified by two Nigerian conference volumes focused on environmental management (Adeniyi and Bello-Imam 1986, Sada and Odemerho 1988).

It might also be suggested that environmental explanations of poverty in Africa were totally out of fashion in the 1950s and 1960s partly because this would have meant pessimism – since the environment is in most ways so difficult to change. The mood then was that 'all things are possible' given a little time and effort. Now there is a danger of things swinging the other way, so that Africa is written off by some people elsewhere in the world as a lost cause, or is at least viewed with undue pessimism. It is only certain localities that might have to be so written off as a result of environmental degradation, though much larger areas can probably only sustain a more or less static population – so that the expected increase must be accommodated elsewhere.

The relevance of many aspects of the natural environment for daily life in tropical Africa is heightened by the fact that three-quarters of the population are rural dwellers, directly dependant on it for their livelihood. It is further heightened by the continuing predominance of subsistence production, making failure of the rains, for example, literally a matter of life and death. Severe drought occurs in Australia too, but there most farmers can obtain a bank overdraft to tide them over a bad year. We are here thinking negatively, but it is equally important to consider the environment positively, in terms of the resources that sustain people. Development efforts require an appreciation of both positive and negative aspects, and also of local people's knowledge of their own environments – as has been eloquently argued by Paul Richards (1985).

The land

Although most wall maps are based on the varying altitude of the land, this is one of the least significant aspects of the environment in tropical Africa. It affects people only indirectly, through temperatures. Slope can be more important, especially in a generally mountainous country such as Ethiopia where it contributes to an immense problem of soil erosion, and where much land can be cultivated only after elaborate terracing. But much of Africa consists of plateau land with relatively gentle slopes. Only in a very few places, such as the Gezira area of Sudan, is the lie of the land ideal for irrigation. The irrigated area in Nigeria has been greatly increased in the

1970s and 1980s, but at very high cost. In this respect the African environment is much less favourable for agriculture than that of South Asia (Adams and Grove 1984). On the other hand there are sufficient large rivers dropping down sharply from plateaux to give Africa 40 per cent of the world's hydro-electricity potential. However, the vast majority of this remains unused, and in sharp contrast to the 1960s, when the Kariba, Volta and Kainji dams were built, no very large new schemes were under way in the late 1980s.

The underlying geology also does not profoundly affect most people's lives, though of course it influences the soils that have formed and can affect local water supplies. A small minority are very profoundly affected, as a result of the highly localized occurrence of valuable minerals. Only very small numbers are directly employed in mining, but the existence of high-grade deposits of copper has had some impact on most Zambians, and oil has had a mixture of good and bad effects on most Nigerians. It might be suggested that lack of mineral resources contributes to the extreme poverty of such countries as Ethiopia, Chad and Mali, but this is not an argument that can be applied to tropical Africa as a whole.

Both geology and slope affect the soil, and this is of immense importance to people whose primary activity is farming. Generalization is difficult because soils often differ markedly over just a few hundred metres, but no-one has ever seriously suggested that Africa has a comparative advantage for agriculture on account of its soils. Fertile soils based on volcanic rock help to make the highlands of Kenya one of the more prosperous parts of the continent, but most African farmers have to contend with relatively infertile soils, leached of much of their mineral content, and often very susceptible to erosion. Most African soils need fertilizers just as much as those elsewhere in the world, but very few people can afford to use them. The best hope in many regions is for more effective integration of crops and livestock, so that manure can be applied more systematically.

Neither its relief nor its geology help to explain Africa's poverty, but its soils do provide part of the explanation. They form a particularly significant part of the environmental context of poverty because there is much evidence that in many areas they are deteriorating. Over vast tracts of land fertility was formerly maintained by the practice of shifting cultivation, the land reverting to fallow for twenty years or more after three or four years of cultivation. As a result of increasing population pressure on the land this practice can be maintained by only a small minority of farmers. Fallows are becoming ever shorter, and in increasingly large areas the land is under crops every year. In some regions fertility decline is compounded by soil erosion, the best known example being the millions of tons of topsoil that wash down every year from the Ethiopian highlands into the Nile.

The climate

The direct relevance of climate to poverty in Africa has become all too clear as a result of the severe droughts of the 1970s and 1980s (Glantz 1987). But rainfall has always been the most critical factor differentiating one part of tropical Africa from another (Map 4.1). It is lack of rainfall that makes the Sahara almost uninhabitable; and it is the spatial pattern of rainfall that largely explains the concentration of the population in a country such as Kenya into one quarter of its territory. The seasonality of the rain is also highly significant. Most of northern Nigeria receives somewhat less rain than the south, but the very different landscapes and lifestyles are due far more to the concentration of the rain in the north into a single wet season. So in Nigeria, as also in Cameroon and in Uganda, there is a much more severe 'hungry season' in the north than in the south.

Variability of the rainfall from year to year is the most critical aspect in relation to poverty and particularly to famine. This tends to be greatest where rainfall totals are least, and nomadic pastoralism is in part a response to this. Erratic rainfall in areas that normally receive just enough for cultivation leads either to concentration on a narrow range of drought-resistant crops or to extremely low yields and resulting hunger in some years. If such hunger is to be avoided there must either be much improved storage and trading systems or a farming system based on the likely minimum rain rather than an average. Rainfall variability, like seasonality, also of course affects other aspects of life, including basic household water supplies.

In addition to annual variations there are also changes over longer periods, and this provides one of the roots of Africa's current crisis. Over large parts of the continent yearly totals were above the previous average throughout the 1950s and 1960s, encouraging the spread of settlement into areas that had previously been considered unattractive. Rainfall has been lower almost everywhere in most years since 1968, so that areas which yielded good crops in the early 1960s have become marginal for cultivation even while pressure to expand the settled area has increased. Year after year average crop yields have remained depressed, and rural dwellers across Africa have had both less food to eat and reduced cash incomes as a result.

Within this phase of lower rainfall there was a further sharp reduction in 1972–3, and again in 1983–4, both in the Sahel and in much of Ethiopia, causing many farmers' crops to fail completely, and changing hunger into famine. In both areas livestock died in large numbers, and those people trying to raise cash by selling animals before they died found only very low prices offered. Meanwhile, prices of grain in the markets rose dramatically. Drought was not the sole cause of disaster in either area or either decade, but it played a major part. In Ethiopia the 1984 rainfall at many recording

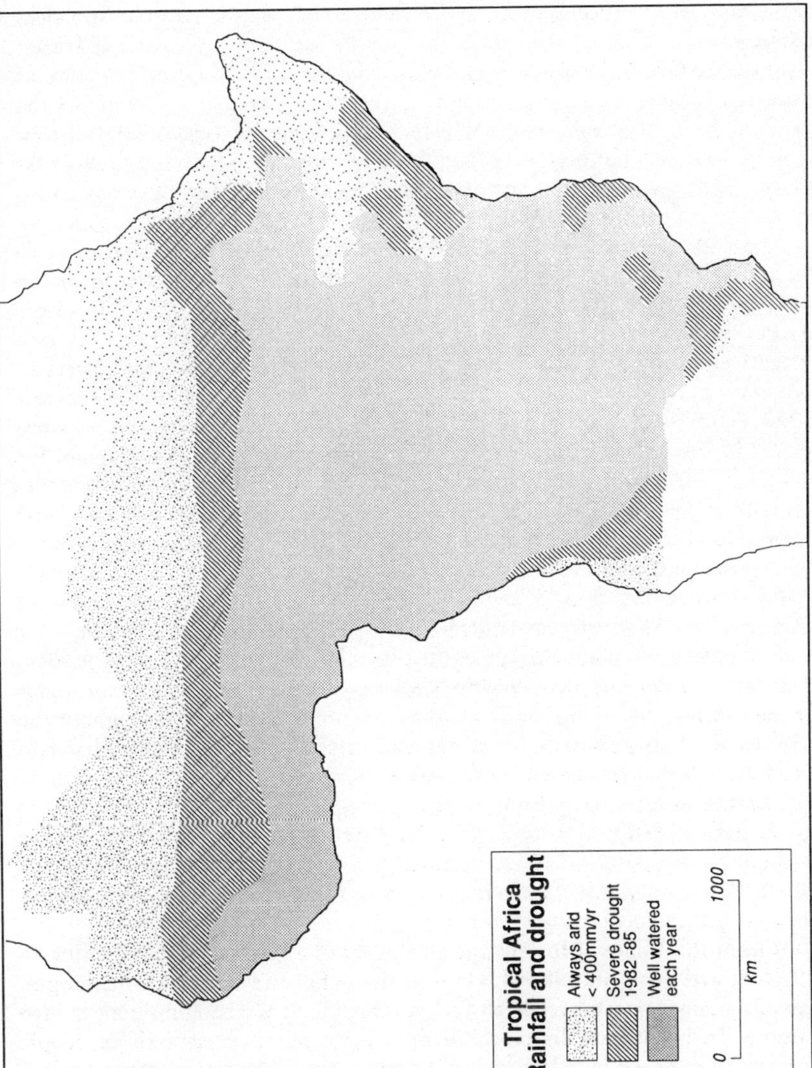

Map 4.1 Rainfall and drought

stations was less than 40 per cent of the long-term average, leading to the lowest-ever flow in the Blue Nile from Ethiopia into Sudan. Drought on that scale cannot do other than intensify the poverty of poor people in a poor country.

Severe drought returned to Eritrea, Tigray and Wollo Provinces of northern Ethiopia in 1987, and again even more intensely to parts of these areas in 1989. The rain also seems to have become extremely erratic in its timing, so that it has been very hard to know when crop planting should take place. At the same time there have been great variations from place to place, even over a few kilometres.

The intense drought of 1983–4 extended from Ethiopia right across Sudan, contributing to crop failure and consequent famine conditions in large parts of that country also. Further to the west, Lake Chad shrank from 25,000 sq.km. to 3,000 sq.km., bringing disaster to a major Nigerian irrigation scheme but providing some new opportunities for cultivation on the former lake bed; while the River Niger was almost dry at Niamey in early 1985. The 1984 rainfall was less than half the 1931–60 average at most places in the Sahel, from Chad and Niger to Senegal and Mauritania: the deficiency in August, normally the wettest month, was particularly widespread and severe. Farmers throughout the region responded and adapted in a wide variety of ways (Mortimore 1989), and starvation was largely avoided, but further impoverishment was the norm.

At other times in the 1980s drought also devastated large tracts of southern Africa, with particularly serious consequences in Mozambique which had been made highly vulnerable by years of war and massive displacements of people. Even in Zambia and Zimbabwe these droughts brought severe hardship, and have made many poor people even poorer: in Mozambique they contributed to very widespread hunger, and to the deaths of large numbers of people, most of them children.

There is no prospect of anything being done to control the rainfall, and even short-term forecasting is proving extremely difficult: but it is being modified inadvertently both by the clearing of vegetation within Africa and by the 'greenhouse effect' which operates at a global scale and is likely to be of increasing significance. The consequences are not inevitably harmful, but they intensify the need for adapting patterns of human activity to changing environmental circumstances. The extent of poverty in Africa in years to come will be profoundly affected by when and where rain falls, and by how people react to this influence upon their lives.

While rainfall is a critical variable across tropical Africa, temperature is to a large degree a constant. In all but the highest mountain areas temperatures are high throughout the year. There has been much speculation about whether this fact has contributed to poverty, in Africa as in other tropical regions, and the matter is still largely unresolved. Can it be just coincidence that most of the poorest countries of the world are in the tropics? Singapore may now be prospering, but is that just a lone exception?

It is very doubtful that high temperatures in themselves lead to poverty through any physiological effects. And some of the consequences for agriculture are beneficial. Plant growth can take place throughout the year, constrained only by the availability of moisture. Unfortunately this is itself reduced by the high temperatures and consequent high rates of evaporation. The tropical conditions are of some indirect significance in so far as a set of innovations encouraging high-productivity agriculture have taken place in temperate environments, and these are not necessarily transferable to the different conditions and different crops of tropical Africa.

Probably the main way in which the heat of the tropics is relevant, and the main reason why there is too close a spatial association between this and poverty to be mere coincidence, is actually to be found in the high incidence of disease. A critical role in the spread of many diseases is played by insects, considered below: but even more basic is the stimulus to the growth of numerous micro-organisms provided by constant high temperatures. It really is hardly surprising that poor people stay poor in communities in which most people are most of the time debilitated by diseases – often by two or three simultaneously.

Flora and fauna

The biological environment is also a highly significant part of the context of poverty in Africa, as exemplified by plagues of locusts which threatened large areas in 1988. Fortunately, this outbreak was largely controlled, but not before some farmers had lost most of their harvest. Less dramatic, but even more widespread, are many other pests which destroy crops both in the fields and in storage. As in the case of fertilizers, there is no less need of insecticides in Africa than in any other part of the world: there is simply no means for most people to pay for them.

Equally relevant as contributors to poverty are insects such as the mosquito and the tsetse fly which transmit disease to people and to livestock. The question of health is explored more fully in Chapter 10, but it is so important throughout tropical Africa that a little more should be said here. Mosquitoes cause poverty through the weakness that results from frequent bouts of malaria, which is considered a normal part of life in large parts of Africa. It has proved possible to eradicate them from small islands such as Mauritius, with extremely beneficial results, but there is no prospect of this across mainland Africa. The effects of the water snails through which schistosomiasis (or bilharzia) is transmitted are equally serious. The incidence is lower, but the matter is of particular concern because efforts to improve people's lives through irrigation schemes have been blighted by the spread of this disease.

The species of tsetse fly that transmit sleeping sickness are more deadly than the mosquito, but they are much less widespread and far fewer people come into contact with them. The species that transmit trypanosomiasis among cattle are much more widely distributed, and they prevent cattle-keeping over vast areas of countries such as Nigeria and Tanzania. Since many people in Africa wish to keep cattle, this has profoundly affected the distribution of population, and so the tsetse fly has attracted much attention. Many almost uninhabited areas could be settled far more readily if the tsetse could be eradicated. However, its importance as a cause of poverty has probably been exaggerated – for instance, when it is suggested that it explains the absence of animal traction and hence of the wheel in traditional African societies. Most people in Africa are affected far more by the mosquito than by the tsetse fly: and far more cattle die each year from the effects of ticks which spread diseases such as east-coast fever. Africa would, of course, benefit from successful tsetse eradication programmes, but many costly programmes have been unsuccessful, and there are often other environmental management priorities.

The much more visible fauna for which parts of Africa are renowned can also be a threat to people, and to livestock, and they do much damage by trampling crops. However, elephants, lions and giraffes – and even crocodiles – are now regarded by most governments that have such wildlife within their borders as national assets, which should be carefully conserved (Anderson and Grove 1987). While large animals are a highly distinctive feature of the African environment, and while they raise crucial issues in terms of whose animals they are and hence whether paying for their preservation is a local, national or global responsibility, their contribution to the relief of poverty is very small. They can bring revenue to Africa from foreign tourists, but as yet this makes a really important contribution to foreign exchange earnings and hence to national welfare only in Kenya. Even there it is not clear whether the total economic benefits greatly outweigh the total costs, either of tourism in general or of wildlife management in particular.

In most African countries a far greater contribution to human well-being is made by rather smaller animals, which provide a welcome supplement to diets in many rural areas. Large numbers are caught, for instance, when annual burning of the land takes place. Even so, most species from field mice to bush pigs must also be regarded as among Africa's environmental hazards in terms of the damage that they do to crops both on the ground and in storage. Perhaps the only elements of the fauna that are entirely an asset rather than a liability are the fish that are caught both offshore and in many lakes and rivers. Efforts to assist rural communities to expand fishing and fish-marketing have brought real benefits to poor people even in inland countries such as Uganda and Chad, and in a country such as Zaïre there is a massive potential for increasing food supplies in this way.

The picture with respect to the flora in some ways matches that for the fauna. The tropical rain forest, which forms part of some outsiders' image of Africa, yields some timber which brings a little export revenue to countries such as Côte d'Ivoire, Gabon and Congo: but far more forest land is simply cleared, mainly by burning, to make way for cultivation as the population rises, with the remaining tree stumps as a persistent obstacle. Very much larger quantities of wood are used locally as building materials; and even larger quantities are cut, from savanna woodlands rather than forest, for fuel. In this way the natural vegetation is a major asset for poor people, but it is a rapidly shrinking asset, and as indicated in Chapter 8, dwindling fuel supplies are becoming a major problem in ever larger parts of Africa. However, if brushwood constitutes an asset, the growth of weeds provides a never-ending problem for most rural dwellers. The constant high temperatures which are of such benefit for crop growth are equally favourable to the growth of weeds. Clearing these takes an enormous amount of effort, mainly from women, all over tropical Africa; and despite these efforts weed growth greatly reduces crop yields, and therefore cuts into both food supplies and incomes all over Africa. This problem, like that of the millions of birds that have to be chased off ripening grain, has been intensified in recent years by the fact that children are increasingly spending their days in (or walking to and from) school.

This last point illustrates the complexity of people–poverty–environment relationships. It is not just a matter of each element in the environment affecting livelihoods. Each element also affects all the others, and all are in turn affected by people in diverse ways. Many further illustrations of this are provided in a recent volume edited by Anders Hjort and Mohammed Salih (1989) which examines the two-way relationships between environment and politics in Africa.

Conclusions

Many aspects of the natural environment profoundly and directly affect poor people in Africa, and especially the rural majority. Fundamentally, it must be viewed positively as it sustains life, but here we have focused on negative aspects since these may help to explain Africa's poverty. Within tropical Africa, and within most individual countries, there is great environmental diversity. There are sharp contrasts even over short distances in a country such as Kenya. But we can at least say that, for many people in many ways, the environment is harsh. It is certainly relevant to the persistence of poverty, and in the form of widespread drought it has contributed to increased suffering in the 1970s and 1980s. But at least Africa is largely spared the hurricanes of the Caribbean and the floods of Bangladesh.

One of the most disturbing features is the extensive evidence of environmental deterioration or degradation. When this involves a shift to a reduced availability of water, the term 'desertification' is sometimes used. Some of the changes, including so far as we know the reduction in rainfall in the 1970s and 1980s, are entirely natural; but others result from human misuse of the environment. Some misuse arises from misguided development policies, but more is a matter of traditional practices that were viable at a low density of population becoming non-viable as density and pressure increases. More understanding of the environment is needed, and this involves mobilizing African rural dwellers' own understanding of it: but traditional management of it must change if it is to support ever more people at a higher standard of living. 'Environmentally sustainable development' can all too often seem like no real 'development' at all.

If poverty is to be reduced, Africa needs improved forms of environmental management, applied much more extensively. More dams are needed, though not necessarily large ones: small structures impounding water at the village level may be just as important. Locusts must be controlled, along with many forms of insect life that plague crops, animals and people. In other cases adaptation to environmental hazards is required, such as the development of more drought-resistant and insect-resistant varieties of crops, and perhaps new breeds of livestock. Only in such ways can the vicious circle be broken whereby not only do environmental problems contribute to poverty, but also poverty forces people to contribute to environmental degradation.

5
The demographic context

Rapid population growth is seen by some people, especially outside Africa, as the chief cause of the continent's persistent or intensifying poverty. It is seen by others, especially within Africa, as largely irrelevant. Neither of these views is accepted here, but the phenomenon is certainly significant enough to merit a chapter to itself, as Morag Bell (1986) demonstrates in her study of *Contemporary Africa*. This is particularly so if we are concerned with *distinctive* features of tropical Africa, for almost all parts of the region have faster rates of growth than anywhere else in the world, with no indication of any slowing down.

A further reason for the chapter is that population growth is surely the most fundamental and most widespread type of change taking place across tropical Africa today – whatever its specific implications for poverty. From the 1950s to the 1960s there was massive and widespread political change basically in one direction – from colonial rule to independence: but since then there has been no clear direction of political change. Through the 1960s and into the 1970s there was economic advance in most parts of the region: but since then there has generally been stagnation. The growth of population, however, continues unabated everywhere, thereby making Africa in 1990 a very different continent from Africa in 1970. Its poverty must be seen in terms of this combination of economic stagnation and demographic dynamism.

The total population of tropical Africa in 1970 was around 260 million. By 1990 it had probably reached 480 million, and United Nations projections for the year 2000 are around 670 million. This means that the population is currently doubling in a mere twenty-one years, with an annual growth rate of just over 3 per cent. This may be compared with annual growth rates during the 1980s of 2·2 per cent in India and 1·2 per cent in China.

Before discussing this rapid growth, something should be said about present absolute numbers. Even before that a comment must be made on the data that we are using, since these are much more unreliable than for any other part of the world. Most African countries have conducted some form of census, but this was often some years ago and invariably many people will have been missed. Conversely, in some countries, notably Nigeria, census returns have been deliberately inflated for local political advantage, and the whole exercise has been declared null and void. No-one knows whether the population of Nigeria in 1990 was 100 million or 140 million. However, it was almost certainly somewhere between these two figures. Broad orders of magnitude generally *are* known, and for our purpose this may really be sufficient. Similarly with regard to growth, the issues are the same whether the actual annual figure is 2·9 per cent or 3·1 per cent.

Population distribution and density

The absolute number of people in tropical Africa as a whole at present in no way constitutes a problem or contributes to poverty. There is no evidence to suggest that people would in general be better off if there were fewer of them. The 500 million represent 10 per cent of the world total, living on about 16 per cent of the world's land. Overall, tropical Africa is still relatively sparsely populated, though no longer as sparsely as is often suggested. It seems to be not often realized that the density of *rural* population is already greater than the world average.

Average densities are, of course, of only limited significance because of the great variations from place to place (Map 5.1). While most of the *land* in Africa certainly has a low density of population, most *people*, and even most rural dwellers, live at a far higher density. Both Burundi and Rwanda have more than 200 people per sq.km., the vast majority rural dwellers, over the country as a whole, and therefore far more in certain districts. Nigeria probably has about 120 per sq.km., but this rises to over 600 in Imo State. Kenya has only 40 per sq.km. on average, but the people are largely concentrated into one-quarter of the country, and some districts which are almost entirely rural, such as Kisii and Kakamega, have more than 400 people per sq.km.

At least 50 million people in Africa are already living in conditions of severe pressure on the land in terms of the present nature of the economy and the technology available to them. In these terms the 'carrying capacity' of the land is already being exceeded: the areas that they occupy can be regarded as

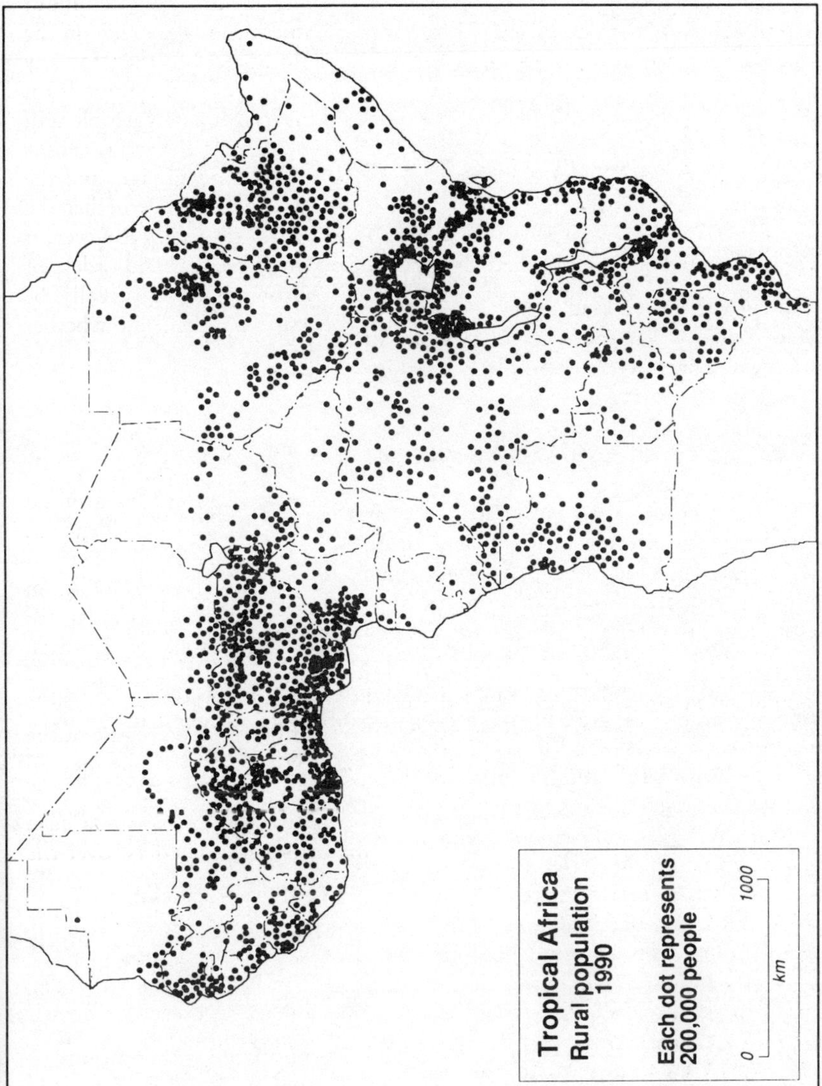

Map 5.1 Rural population distribution

'overpopulated' in the sense that most people would probably have a higher standard of living if they were fewer in number – or if some could move elsewhere. *Any* growth in numbers in these areas presents an added problem unless the local economy and technology changes or unless outmigration can take place. Landlessness is still far less widespread in Africa than in south Asia, but it has begun to appear in some places, often bringing intensified poverty. Environmental degradation is also resulting partly from pressure of numbers on the land in certain parts of many African countries.

The pressure is greatest in some of the very densely settled areas, but it can also be felt in areas with only moderate densities if climate and soil conditions are poor. This applies to large parts of Ethiopia, for example, and to the central area of Burkina Faso. Indeed, some would argue that pressure is now experienced even in some very sparsely settled areas, such as parts of Mauritania, where the nomadic pastoral lifestyle is only sustainable if there are fewer than, say, five people per sq.km.

Urbanization as an aspect of distribution

About a quarter of tropical Africa's people are now living at far higher densities, concentrated in towns and cities (Map 5.2): such urbanization is often regarded as an aspect of 'development' likely to relieve rural poverty, but in some situations it may intensify poverty as well as involving local extreme overcrowding. The proportion of the national population living in cities and towns ranges from less than 10 per cent in Burkina Faso, Burundi and Rwanda to around 40 per cent in Côte d'Ivoire and Congo and 50 per cent in Zambia. In general the level of urbanization is highest in the more prosperous countries and lowest in the poorest, but the correlation is not at all close. Both Chad and Somalia, for instance, are thought to have a higher urban proportion than Kenya.

Along with general population growth, one of the greatest changes taking place across tropical Africa from the 1960s to the 1980s has been the world's highest *rate* of urbanization (O'Connor 1983). The proportion living in cities and towns in 1960 was nearer 10 per cent than 25 per cent, and in several countries it was only 3 or 4 per cent. It was only during the late 1970s or early 1980s that the proportion overtook that in both China and India. This process of change, resulting mainly from rural-urban migration greatly exceeding the reverse flow, has continued through the mid and late 1980s, although it has probably slowed in many countries. Firm evidence on this point is scarce.

The largest city is Lagos, which houses (though far from adequately) 5 to 6 million Nigerians, and it is followed by Kinshasa, the Zaïre capital, with

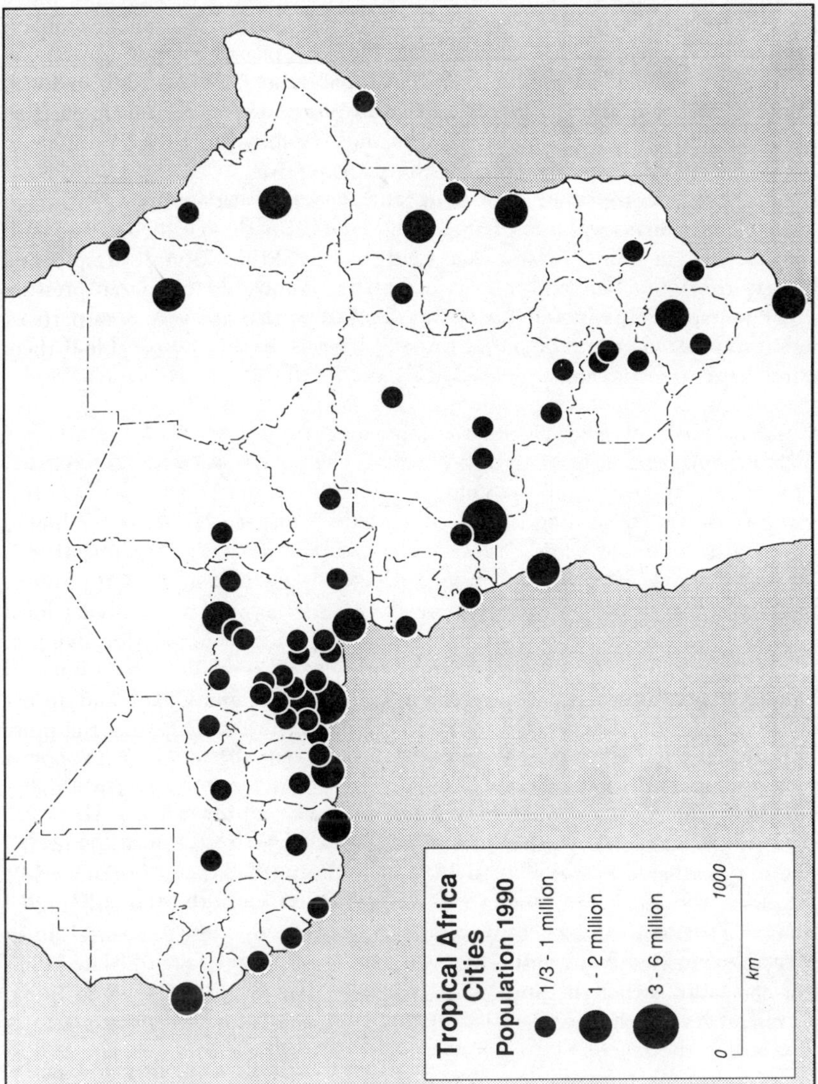

Map 5.2 Cities with over 1/3 million inhabitants

about 4 million. There is therefore no question of tropical African cities being too large in absolute terms, as might be argued for Mexico City, or even Cairo. The capital cities of the larger countries, including Dakar, Abidjan, Accra, Khartoum, Addis Ababa, Nairobi, Dar es Salaam, Maputo, Harare and Luanda, have 1 to 2 million inhabitants, while in the smaller countries half a million is typical. In addition, each country has a set of provincial and district headquarter towns, most established around 100 years ago by the colonial administrations. Nigeria is unusual in having a complex urban system incorporating such indigenous cities as Ibadan and Kano.

Average incomes are much higher in the cities, and even in the smaller towns, than in most rural areas (and this is one reason for the net in-migration); but the gap has been narrowing in most African countries in recent years, and it is possible that the level of urbanization is already too high in relation to the structure of the economy. It is almost certain that the rising level has contributed to Africa's persistent fall in per capita food production. Urban poverty is intensifying, as shown in Chapter 9, but it would be misleading to suggest that, because many city dwellers are very poor, urbanization has caused that poverty. The poverty is common to both rural and urban areas, and often has simply been transferred from one to the other. It is also misleading to draw too sharp a distinction between urban and rural in terms of *people*: rural and urban *places* may be very different, but many people in tropical Africa, and possibly most families, have some involvement in both.

Population growth

The critical population issue in relation to poverty is the rate of growth, in both rural and urban areas, rather than density or distribution – important as those are. The current annual growth rate of 3 per cent for tropical Africa is higher than that for any other part of the world either today or in the past. The data gathered by the United Nations indicate that the lowest rates of growth now occur in the Sahel, the lowest estimates for both Mali and Chad being 2·3 per cent. A few decades ago rates were lower in much of equatorial Africa, but in both Zaïre and Congo they are now around 3 per cent, and the current figure for Cameroon is 3·2 per cent. Much higher rates of growth prevail over most of eastern Africa, rising to 3·7 per cent in Zimbabwe and reaching 4 per cent in Kenya for the decade of the 1980s.

These growth rates result almost entirely from the excess of births over deaths (Table 5.1), for migration both into and out of Africa is now very limited in extent. There is not normally a large new flow even between individual countries. For a while in the 1970s movements from Burkina Faso

Table 5.1 Birth rates and death rates in the larger countries, 1960–88

	Total fertility rate		*Crude birth rate*		*Crude death rate*	
	1960	*1988*	*1960*	*1988*	*1960*	*1988*
Nigeria	6·8	7·0	52	50	24	15
Ethiopia	6·7	6·2	50	44	28	24
Zaïre	6·0	6·1	47	46	22	14
Tanzania	6·8	7·1	51	50	24	14
Sudan	6·7	6·4	47	44	25	16
Kenya	8·0	8·1	53	54	22	12
Uganda	6·9	6·9	50	50	21	15
Mozambique	6·3	6·4	47	45	26	18
Ghana	6·8	6·4	48	44	19	13
(India	5·9	4·3	43	32	21	11)
(China	5·7	2·4	37	21	19	7)
(Brazil	6·2	3·4	43	28	13	8)

Source: UNICEF, *The State of the World's Children 1990*

into Côte d'Ivoire may have reduced the growth rate of the former to little over 2 per cent, and raised that of the latter to 4 per cent annually, but the extent of this migration has now been reduced. For specific years in the 1980s refugee flows have affected growth rates in such cases as Sudan and Ethiopia or Malawi and Mozambique, but they have not been sustained long enough to have a great demographic impact.

The growth takes place despite death rates which have fallen in recent decades but which remain the world's highest. Compared with a world average of 10 per thousand, the death rate for tropical Africa is currently 17 per thousand, with a range from about 12 in Zimbabwe and Kenya to about 24 in Ethiopia, Guinea and Sierra Leone. This incorporates infant mortality rates of 100 to 150 per thousand in most countries, compared with a world average of under 40 and figures of less than 10 in most rich countries. Death rates for all children under five range from 110 per thousand births in Zimbabwe and Kenya to almost 300 in Sierra Leone, Mali, Angola and Mozambique. These appalling figures are, of course, not just part of the demographic context of poverty, but also a manifestation of that poverty, and we shall return to them in Chapter 10.

Rapid population growth in Africa largely reflects birth rates far higher than those prevailing elsewhere in the world. The global average is now about 28 per thousand, including 20 per thousand for China and 32 per thousand for India. The usual estimate for tropical Africa in the late 1980s is

48 per thousand. Birth rates are remarkably uniform across the continent, dropping below 45 in only a very few places, and rising to a maximum of 54 in Kenya.

The same phenomenon can also be expressed in terms of the total fertility rate, or the number of children that each woman is likely to bear in her lifetime. This now averages 2·2 for China and 3·8 for India, but the current estimate for Nigeria is 7 and that for Kenya is 8. For very few countries in tropical Africa is the figure below 6. The latest information from UNICEF suggests that Nigeria has now moved into third place in the world for annual numbers of births, still far below India and China but above both Indonesia and the USSR.

Growth of population on this scale is a new feature of the past thirty years, resulting from the combination of the decline in death rates and the maintenance of roughly constant birth rates. The 1987 crude death rate of 17 per thousand may be compared with estimates of around 27 per thousand for 1960. Combined with a crude birth rate of 48 per thousand for both years, this gives a rise in the rate of natural increase from 2·1 per cent to 3·1 per cent a year. If rapid growth is relevant to poverty, accelerating growth must be even more so – as the later part of this chapter aims to demonstrate.

It is often assumed that birth rates must soon fall, mainly because they have done so elsewhere in the world: such an assumption is quite explicit in many UN and World Bank publications (e.g. World Bank 1986). Yet there is no sign of this as yet in any tropical African country. The 'demographic transition' model, generally regarded as applicable worldwide, may not prove relevant to Africa, at least in the near future (Bell 1986). In most versions of the model the fall in birth rates is supposed to be related to increasing prosperity, and no-one can say if or when that will be a feature of most of Africa. So it is not clear what is expected to cause the anticipated fall in birth rates. They may well remain just as high as now, at least into the next century (Hill 1988).

On the other hand, death rates are probably still dropping as a result of more education and better health care, even if more slowly than in the recent past. The result is an annual growth rate that is still rising slowly in most countries, except where and when mass starvation occurs or war becomes particularly intense. Both of these can have a direct demographic impact on a local scale, but fortunately neither has yet had a measurable long-term impact at a continental scale. Similarly, the scourge of AIDS may soon have a local impact on population growth; but even if the worst scenario is considered this disease, discussed in Chapter 10, could not have a real Africa-wide demographic impact until well into the next century.

Undoubtedly, decision-makers in most parts of tropical Africa must work on the assumption that there will be at least twice as many people around in twent-five years time as there are today. So Africa will once again become a very different place, or set of places. If rural-urban migration continues, the increase will be rather less in some rural districts, although depopulation cannot be anticipated anywhere. Conversely, many African cities may double in population over the next ten years, as they have over the past ten or even eight years.

In order to understand the forces behind these dramatic and continent-wide changes, and before considering their impact on poverty, we must examine some of the causes of persistent high human fertility throughout tropical Africa.

Causes of high fertility

It is clear from surveys in many African countries, such as those reviewed by John and Pat Caldwell (1987), that the high levels of fertility reflect the wish of most women and men to have a large number of children. They do not result primarily from men who do not have to care for the children, and want more, imposing their preferences on reluctant women, as may be the case in some parts of the world where fertility is relatively high. Nor do they result primarily from a lack of knowledge about birth control: some traditional partially-effective methods are widely known, and when more effective methods are brought in they are rarely received with much enthusiasm.

Preferred family size seems to be about seven or eight children among most communities from Senegal to Mozambique, and to be very little lower in the cities than in the countryside. It is much lower than this among some of the tiny number of highly educated women in each country, but primary schooling seems to make very little difference to the number desired – and actually to increase the number of surviving children in each family. Even three or four years of secondary schooling generally has little impact on fertility levels.

Why are more children wanted than elsewhere in the world? Some factors are essentially economic, such as their labour input into farming, tending livestock, fetching water and fuelwood, and so on. Even in the cities many children make a useful contribution to household incomes, and a vital one in cases such as trading on behalf of their mothers who remain in purdah in many Muslim communities. Schooling may reduce the children's labour inputs, but it does not eliminate them, and it should increase the financial support that they can provide later as their parents grow old. With more children, the risk of being left destitute is reduced, and the possibilities of one of them doing really well are increased: this applies even more in the cities than in the rural areas.

Across most of Africa daughters bring bridewealth to their parents at the time of marriage; and there is no equivalent loss in the case of sons since they are normally expected to earn this for themselves. This is the reverse of the dowry system in countries such as India, which represents a flow of wealth down the generations.

Upper- and middle-class urban families have less economic need for many children, but they can even more easily bear the costs involved, especially when they have cheap domestic service. If it becomes inconvenient to care for them, they can usually be sent to grandparents, uncles or aunts for part of their upbringing – often to the delight of these relatives, and often performing useful practical services for them.

Social factors are also important, with a large family bringing enhanced status to both men and women. The childbearing role for women may actually be increased in significance by a move to the city if this largely cuts out their role as food producers. Religion plays a part too, especially in the importance which is attached, in many forms of indigenous African religion, to ancestors and hence to one's own descendants. Even Islam and Christianity in Africa have probably done more to boost fertility than to reduce it. The strength of the extended family means that the pressures exerted by relatives, especially the grandparents, are keenly felt. And in so far as there is some shift to emphasis on the nuclear family, that may initially serve to increase the need to have more of your own children in place of dependence on your brothers, sisters, nieces and nephews.

Producing more children is perceived as increasing the strength of both the family and the wider kinship group, perhaps as a substitute for material wealth. This may extend to an even wider ethnic group. Luo groups in Kenya or Ibo groups in Nigeria will not be keen to limit their numbers unless they can be certain that the Kikuyu or the Hausa are doing likewise. Similar feelings are now emerging at the nation–state level, as they have done in Europe at various times. Even at the continental level, some of the élite point to the fact that before the slave trade Africa's share of world population was larger than it is today (though this will not apply for much longer). For some of my former students who accepted that, at national level, rapid population growth was an economic liability, such considerations were overriding.

Returning to the more personal level, three further points might be added. One is that, in an African society, once you have one or two children you are sure that *they* will need brothers and sisters to help them cope with life's ups and downs. This possibly applies most of all in an urban environment, where sisters and brothers can be of so much help with housing or the search for a job. Again, any breakdown of the extended family system, so that cousins become less effective substitutes, may strengthen this perception.

Attachment to children may also be all the greater because the emotional tie between husband and wife is often less than in some societies. It is surely relevant that marriages are still often arranged by the respective parents, as also in south Asia. In certain African countries, such as Ethiopia, divorce is extremely common. In some African cities, such as Accra, wives and husbands commonly do not live in the same house. It may be in respect of emotional dependence on children even more than economic considerations that the continuing high infant and child mortality is relevant. To have only two or three children seems very risky, and a quite unnecessary risk.

Finally, many adults in Africa find it strange that anyone should ask why they have so many children. As children are seen as the greatest delight in life, whether they are physically with you or not, then surely the more the better. Even if it could be clearly demonstrated that a family of four in a particular situation could have a higher material standard of living than a family of eight, the latter are expected to be happier.

Most of these considerations seem unlikely to change very quickly, and therefore no government birth-control policies are likely to have much impact even where they are promoted with some vigour. Certainly no African government has the power to impose birth control in the manner of the Chinese, but there is no evidence that any would wish to do so even if it could. In many African governments opinion on the merits of any limitation is deeply divided, and in some a majority are opposed to it. Half-hearted family planning programmes put forward by penniless governments in countries that are not experiencing any improvement in their standard of living are most unlikely to have much impact. The concept of family planning is making some headway in many African countries, and is worth pursuing for health reasons alone; but for the vast majority of those reache b by the programmes (as well as for the much larger numbers not reached) the plans will, for the foreseeable future, continue to be for large families.

Consequences of rapid population growth

There is much dispute about the consequences of rapid growth of population, both at the family level and at the national level, as Allan and Anne Findlay (1987) have clearly shown. The view that it hinders development and may intensify poverty has been gaining ground in recent years. This is most evident in China, where vigorous efforts to restrict growth have been implemented, with much success. It is also clear from a comparison of the world population conference organized by the United Nations at Bucharest in 1974 and that which followed at Mexico City in 1984. The statements made by African delegates at the two meetings reflected this attitudinal change, and the majority of African governments now acknowledge that a reduced rate of population growth would be helpful in terms of national economic development. Yet this negative view of rapid growth in numbers is clearly not shared by more than a small minority of people within each country – at least in terms of their own family well-being.

The dangers of rapid population growth are perhaps clearest at the global level, where there must eventually be some limits to growth (Meadows 1972, Mesarovic and Pestel 1975). It is arguable that, in relation to finite global resources, reduced population growth is essential if there is to be any prospect of standards of living in the poorest parts of the world ever rising towards those of the richer countries. If the world population were to increase for long at the African rate of 3 per cent annually, the future for the planet, but especially for the poorer parts of it, would be bleak indeed. The usual African response to this is that the pressure on global resources from even a 1 per cent population growth in North America or a 0·5 per cent annual growth in Europe is greater than that from a 3 per cent growth in Africa.

At the national level, rapid population growth means that huge efforts must be made just to maintain existing levels of service provision, before improvements can even be considered. This applies irrespective of existing numbers and densities, and is a serious problem throughout Africa. In countries with very limited budgets rapid population growth means increasing pressure on the education system, on health care facilities, on water supplies, and so on. In addition, it is proving extremely difficult to provide sufficient employment opportunities for the ever-increasing numbers of school-leavers entering the labour force. In every country a slowing from the present rate of increase would certainly have some beneficial results over the next twenty years by reducing the sheer volume of human need, including the number of mouths to be fed (World Bank 1986).

However, the impact of rapid growth differs in many respects from one country to another, and from one region to another within most countries. In many rural areas there is ample extra land for the ever-greater numbers, and in some it is arguable that increased density of settlement offers advantages. However, more people live in areas where this argument does not apply, and where pressure on the available land is already being felt. In these areas families are having to gain a livelihood from smaller patches of land than formerly, or to extend cultivation on to less suitable land. This may include land that has not been fallowed long enough since it was last used, resulting in reduced yields, or steeply sloping lands, resulting in accelerated soil erosion. Sometimes farm families are now moving into more marginal environments in their search for land, Kenya providing many examples of this.

Where pressure on the land is especially severe some of the next generation of adults will have farms so small that they cannot support a family, or will be unable to obtain any land at all. In the absence of an agricultural revolution that creates employment such landlessness must inevitably intensify poverty. This process has clearly begun in areas such as south-eastern Nigeria, central Kenya and southern Malawi. Some seek a solution by migration to the cities, but rapid natural increase is taking place there too, resulting in increasing competition for the available work opportunities.

It may, of course, still be in the individual's economic interest to have a large family, even if the result of everyone doing so is harmful to the society as a whole. There is no evidence that parents in Africa who have only two or three children are in general better off than those with five or six, even in a narrow material sense. However, it is very likely that the extent of hunger and malnutrition in some households with eight or ten children would have been less if there had been fewer, and that a better standard of health care could have been provided. Once the number exceeds five or six it is also doubtful that security for the parents' old age is much increased. The chance of one being really lucky and making a fortune for the family may be increased, but in this respect the vast majority of parents have to accept disappointment.

One consequence of high fertility, rather than of the excess of births over deaths, is that most women in Africa are either pregnant or caring for a small infant for a very large part of their lives. This inevitably saps their energy and reduces the effort that they can devote to other matters, yet over most of Africa the rural economy depends more on them than on the men. This must have some impact on productivity, as well as greatly lengthening the working day. Even if most rural women in Africa seem to take on this double burden willingly, it none the less constitutes a burden which fewer preganancies would lighten, and probably contributes substantially to material poverty in every African country.

The age structure

One important dimension of rapid population growth is the resulting age structure. In all African countries the ratio of children to total population is far above the world average, and in many it has increased in recent years to the extent that under-eighteens make up more than half the total. Almost no writing on development or poverty in Africa adequately reflects the fact that most Nigerians and most Tanzanians are children. This book is no exception: like most others it deals almost entirely with the adult population, especially since in geneal they are the decision-makers in matters affecting poverty.

The ratio of children to adults is generally seen as economically significant through their dependence on adults for support. In Africa this has intensified recently with the great expansion of primary and secondary education at the expense of part of the children's labour input. A combination of a rising proportion of children and rising school enrolment rates has meant more and more to be supported by those who are working. This is aggravated by the fact that children often do not complete primary school until aged fourteen or fifteen. Of course, all these children (or rather all those who survive) will swell the potential labour force in the future, and will hopefully become generators of wealth: but that does not make the dependency ratio a short-term problem, as is often suggested in Africa, for unless fertility falls they in turn will have to support even more children.

The education which keeps the children out of the labour force itself represents a substantial expense, largely borne by the state in most African countries. Not only do large numbers of teachers have to be paid, but ever more have to be trained; and at the same time ever more school buildings have to be constructed and equipped. Education looms so large in the African scene that it is discussed at greater length in a later chapter – along with health care, which is also needed in larger measure when half the population are children and 20 per cent are under five.

A compensating feature of the African age structure is the small number of old people. In most countries only about 5 per cent of the population are over 65, compared with more than 20 per cent in Europe and North America. However, the difference is much less in respect of the ratio between the elderly and the rest of the *adult* population who must support them. Furthermore, the proportion of all adults who are elderly was beginning to increase in the 1960s and 1970s as health care extended to them. Whether this trend has continued through the 1980s is not yet clear.

Summary

There is no evidence to suggest that rapid population growth is the main cause of poverty in Africa – which was just as widespread when the growth rate was much slower. In so far as the rapid growth results from high fertility it can be seen alternatively as a consequence of poverty. Yet there are clearly circular processes at work, and population growth to varying degrees around Africa does make the alleviation of poverty more difficult. A slowing of the rate of growth would improve the prospects for the material welfare of most African communities, perhaps only slightly for some but substantially for others where pressure on the land and on other resources is severe. The benefit would often be felt through a reduced rate of environmental degradation, as well as through reduced pressure on health and education facilities and a lower dependency ratio.

A slowing of growth almost to zero must inevitably take place eventually, and it is surely preferable for this to be by voluntary limitation of births rather than through a return to much higher death rates. It is, however, difficult to see how this is to come about in the foreseeable future. In many African countries there has been a clear shift of government policy in recent years, but this is unlikely to have much impact on the majority of the people as long as poverty persists. Even if family planning programmes were to be vigorously promoted, there is no reason to expect any substantial fall in birth rates over the next twenty years. Most people do not want this, for they see large numbers of children as a thoroughly good thing, probably the brightest feature of their troubled lives: and none of the individual states are capable of imposing it against people's wishes.

Population growth may indeed be slowed by a rise in the death rate, but all governments and international agencies are trying to avoid this, and they are likely to have more success in this endeavour since it is what ordinary people also want. Unless AIDS spreads to unimaginable proportions, or unless famine returns on a far greater scale than in the 1980s, death rates are more likely to fall slightly than to rise over the next ten or twenty years.

The demographic context on poverty and of any efforts to promote development in tropical Africa therefore comprises a population rising from 500 million today, half of them children, to almost 1,000 million by 2010 – still half of them children and hence with a built-in potential for massive further growth. If fertility is then still as high as now a population reaching 2 billion by 2030, and possibly 4 billion (almost the present world total) by 2050, must be anticipated. Even the highly probable 2010 figure constitutes an immense challenge, and some might say that just ensuring the survival of so many people would represent quite an achievement. To provide a substantially improved standard of living for so many would be little short of miraculous.

6
The political context

Political factors play a large part in perpetuating poverty in tropical Africa. The political structures inherited from the colonial period have proved extremely unhelpful, and there has been much political conflict within African countries over the past thirty years, even if remarkably little armed conflict between one and another. In most countries the state has been greatly preoccupied with its own survival rather than with the welfare of the people, and has had to give much attention to the process of nation-building – with varying degrees of success. Several countries have been plunged into civil war, and some of the world's largest refugee movements of the 1970s and 1980s have occurred within Africa. At the same time today's global political structures do much to keep genuine assistance to Africa from outside to an absolute minimum.

Change and continuity on the political map

People live out their lives in tropical Africa today within a framework of political geography largely superimposed on the continent by the colonial powers one hundred years ago, and reinforced by the granting of independence to most of the colonial territories around 1960. This framework comprises the forty or so countries or nation–states, from Angola to Zimbabwe, to which frequent reference has been made in earlier chapters. Nearly all discussions of African economies, from the orthodoxy of the World Bank (1981, 1989) to the polemic of Fantu Cheru (1989), are presented in terms of these entities, as well as discussions of politics and society such as the very instructive review by Naomi Chazan and others (1988), or Iuean Griffiths' *Atlas of African Affairs* (1984).

There was, of course, a previous totally different political map, albeit one without well-defined boundaries and always in a state of flux. Any atlas of African history demonstrates the rise and fall of empires in many parts of Africa over the centuries, although in other areas local self-government without elaborate political structures prevailed. Within what are now Nigeria and Uganda, for example, highly centralized kingdoms as well as much more loosely structured communities existed in the nineteenth century.

These precolonial structures continue to be relevant to people's lives. In some areas traditional rulers still command respect, even if their official powers were greatly reduced under colonial rule and have since been further eroded. Many people in Nigeria care greatly about the Emir or Oba of their home area, while most Baganda bitterly resented the ousting of their Kabaka by the Ugandan central government in 1966. In so far as the traditional political structure reflected differentiation into ethnic groups or 'tribes', each normally with its own home territory, it must continue to be significant, for identification with these groups remains powerful almost everywhere. In countries such as Brazil or India the term 'tribe' is normally applied only to small groups who make up, even collectively, a minor proportion of the national population: in most African countries it applies to almost everyone.

The importance of such ethnicity in the present context lies mainly in the fact that, conversely, identification with the nation–state is often very weak. There may still be some groups of people within the boundaries of Zaïre who have never heard of Zaïre. There are certainly many for whom the concept has very little meaning. This is no longer true for the majority in a country such as Kenya, but even there among some pastoral groups in the north-east a journey to Nairobi is often regarded as 'going to Kenya'.

None the less, even though many individuals feel no great sense of national identity, and even though some people living close to national boundaries manage to ignore these as they move to and fro, in general it *does* now matter whether one lives in Ghana or in Côte d'Ivoire, in Kenya or in Tanzania, in Malawi or in Mozambique. The massive recent flows of refugees across some African borders bears witness to this. It is often therefore perfectly appropriate to discuss Africa in terms of its component countries, as long as we remember that these are relatively recent and usually very arbitrary divisions, imposed upon Africa and not rooted in African culture.

The colonial legacy

Most of the present-day countries of tropical Africa were in fact created within a very short period in the 1880s, although their boundaries were generally finalized rather later. Most bore no relation whatever to the pre-existing political entities, so that while any notion that history *in*, say, Kenya, began only then would be utterly absurd, it is more reasonable to suggest that the history *of* Kenya began only then. This 'partition of Africa' was largely a matter of agreements made among the colonial powers with no reference to any African opinion. Britain and France dominated the scene, with Belgium, Germany, Italy, Portugal and Spain playing smaller roles until all German territories were taken over by Britain, France and Belgium in 1919.

The only parts of tropical Africa not occupied by the colonial powers were Liberia, which was administered by the descendants of freed American slaves, and Ethiopia, where a long-established empire remained independent apart from a brief Italian occupation in 1936–41. Even in these countries an internal colonial relationship between a ruling privileged minority and a ruled majority might be said to have existed.

The territories of the European colonial powers generally moved to independence within their established boundaries, in some cases peacefully and in others after a period of violence. The process started with Sudan in 1956, Ghana in 1957 and Guinea in 1958. Independence for Nigeria, for most of the former French territories, and for the Belgian Congo (later renamed Zaïre) followed in 1960. Within a few years it had extended to Tanzania, Uganda, Kenya, Malawi and Zambia, but Portugal resisted in Angola, Mozambique and Guinea-Bissau until 1975, while the European settlers resisted in Rhodesia, now Zimbabwe, until 1980.

The extent of continuity in the political–geographical framework from the colonial period into independence has been remarkable. Former Italian and British territories were amalgamated to form Somalia; Cameroon was formed from a large French-ruled territory and a much smaller area administered by Britain; and Tanganyika joined with Zanzibar to form Tanzania. Otherwise, the only significant boundary change was the full incorporation of the former Italian colony of Eritrea into Ethiopia, which is much the most important of these changes in that it has led to decades of bitter armed conflict, thereby exacerbating poverty.

There was a brief war between Somalia and Ethiopia in 1977–8, while Tanzania invaded Uganda to remove Idi Amin in 1979, but in general tropical Africa has been mercifully free of direct military confrontations between neighbouring countries. The many armed conflicts which have dogged Africa since the 1960s have generally been internal struggles, although they have often involved much outside support on both sides, perhaps most strikingly in Angola, where South Africans backed by the United States have battled with Cubans backed by the Soviet Union, with devastating results for local people.

Problems of the colonial legacy

Although the spatial framework left by the colonial powers has largely persisted, it has proved highly unsatisfactory in many ways, and has created great problems for those attempting to administer the independent countries. One very specific difficulty is that Africa has most of the world's landlocked countries. Mali, Burkina Faso, Niger, Chad, the Central African Republic, Burundi, Rwanda, Uganda, Malawi and Zambia are all dependent on other countries' ports for their overseas trade. To the south, Botswana, Lesotho and Swaziland are also totally landlocked, with Lesotho exceptionally vulnerable since it is entirely encapsulated within South Africa.

Some countries have distinctive problems because they are very small in area or population, or both. Others occupy an extremely large area, which is difficult and costly to control. Zaïre is particularly unmanageable in this respect, especially as its population is to a large extent dispersed around the periphery. The same applies to a lesser extent to Tanzania. Mozambique is also a very unwiedly entity, with an appalling lack of communications between Maputo in the south and many of its provinces.

Poor communications are part of a much broader problem which can be designated as a low level of national integration in economic, cultural and political terms. Independent *states* can be created almost overnight, with a parliament and a civil service, and even a local government structure: but this is not true of *nations*, which must evolve over a much longer period. There had been almost no attempt by the colonial powers to foster nationhood, so at the moment of independence there really was no Nigerian or Kenyan nation. (Did the British ever think of a future nation of 'Gold Coastians'?) In so far as there was in each country a tiny integrated 'national' élite who inherited the reins of power, they were usually themselves cut off in many ways from the majority of the population.

Language is an important element in national identity in most parts of the world, and where countries are linguistically divided, as in Belgium or Canada, this is often a cause of political friction. In most African countries many languages are spoken: in both Nigeria and Zaïre there are more than one hundred distinct indigenous languages. In each African country a European language has also been adopted, at least for external contacts, but usually also for government, for large-scale business, and at least for higher education. However, this is often spoken by only a small minority, notwithstanding our frequent use of terms such as 'francophone Africa'. While the adopted language may assist the integration of various parts of the country, it generally also reinforces the barriers between the élite and the mass of the population. Even today, most people in tropical Africa are administered in a language that they themselves do not understand.

Language is just one aspect of the cultural diversity of the people who have been thrown together in the arbitrary 'national' entities left behind by colonial rule. In some ways this may be regarded as cultural richness for these countries, but the resulting political problems have often contributed directly to material poverty.

The greatest progress towards national integration has perhaps been achieved in Tanzania, despite the problem of a population very largely scattered around the periphery of a huge territory, the problem of amalgamating the formerly entirely separate Tanganyika and Zanzibar, and a minimal sense of national identity at independence. Much credit for this must go to both the statesmanship and the personality of former president Julius Nyerere; but it has required much effort from many other people too, some of it inevitably deflected from the pursuit of economic development. One aspect of this effort has been the remarkably successful promotion of Swahili as a truly national language. Many Tanzanians have done their best to disengage from involvement with the state, as Goran Hyden (1980, 1983) has clearly demonstrated, but few have shown any wish to disengage from the nation. The nationwide villagization programme of the 1970s was of dubious economic benefit, as noted later in this chapter, and was widely unpopular, but as a shared experience even this contributed to national identity.

National disintegration and civil war

In several countries the period since independence has been marked by disintegration, especially where particular regions have attempted to secede from the new nation–state, plunging it into civil war. Such wars have caused appalling human suffering, and have also contributed substantially to material poverty. No doubt Chad would still be an extremely poor country after thirty years of peace, but violent conflict through much of this period, in part instigated by Libya, has exacerbated its poverty.

In Sudan the cultural divide between north and south is particularly wide, with many people in the south resenting the dominance of the Arab and Muslim north. The attempt to impose Arabic as the language of national education is one divisive issue: the attempt to impose Islamic Sharia law is another. Armed rebels in the south fought against rule from Khartoum from 1956 to 1972, and the fighting was resumed in 1983, then intensifying horrifically in the late 1980s (Zayd et al. 1988). It has brought the massive Jonglei Canal project on the Nile to a standstill, has prevented the exploitation of oilfields which could greatly assist the national economy, and has directly led to famine in parts of the south, as well as to a massive influx of southerners into Khartoum-Omdurman.

In Nigeria, the former Eastern Region attempted to secede as the Republic of Biafra, resulting in civil war from 1967 to 1970; while in Zaïre it was Shaba Province, formerly Katanga, that tried to secede. In each case mineral wealth gave strength and added incentive to the rebelling region, but also increased the determination of the central government to resist. The Zaïre state was highly dependent on its revenues from Shaba copper, while the Nigerian state was already becoming highly dependent on revenues from the oil found in the east.

Uganda is distinctive in that it inherited from British rule a political structure that gave some autonomy to the very heart of the country, the Buganda kingdom. This led to the almost unique situation of the centre attempting to secede from the larger entity in 1966, the resulting crisis leaving a power vacuum later disastrously filled by Idi Amin. Years of violent conflict since then have shattered what was once one of the African countries with the best economic prospects (Dodge and Raundalen 1987, Hansen and Twaddle 1988).

Both Angola and Mozambique have also been devastated by civil war, although in these cases it has represented a power struggle for control of the whole country rather than a conflict between regions. In both countries forces opposed to the government, and backed by South Africa, controlled large areas throughout the 1980s. In both countries war has brought great suffering to much of the civilian population, both directly and through the intensification of poverty. There is, however, some difference between UNITA in Angola who have fought a military campaign against government forces, and the MNR or RENAMO in Mozambique whose attacks have been not only largely on transport routes, but also on ordinary men, women and children, in health centres and in schools, in their homes and in their fields. This has caused more than 4 million Mozambicans to flee from their home areas, and directly or indirectly caused at least 1 million deaths. However, war has also caused massive mortality and displacements of people in Angola. The United Nations (1989, p. 6) estimates total costs of war between 1980 and 1988 at $30 billion for Angola and $15 billion for Mozambique.

Although Ethiopia largely escaped colonial rule from Europe, the problems of national integration there are as great as anywhere. After World War II, responsibility for the administration of the former Italian colony of Eritrea passed to Ethiopia, but ever since it was fully incorporated in 1962, liberation groups have fought for independence (Cliffe and Davidson 1989). This long war has cost innumerable lives, both directly and through its contribution to recurring famine conditions. Ethiopia is particularly determined to retain control, both because the whole of its coastline is within Eritrea and because there are good prospects of finding oil in the largely empty southern section of Eritrea; but there is a strong case for giving up the costly struggle to hold on to the northern section where most of the people live.

Another factor discouraging the Ethiopian government from considering Eritrean demands is the existence of several other regional opposition movements In the area bordering Eritrea the Tigray People's Liberation Front have for many years been fighting for a measure of autonomy, and they effectively control much of their province. In the south-east of the country many Somali people also resent control from Addis Ababa, and armed conflict continues there too. Even in the south-west there is increasing opposition to the central government among the very numerous Oromo people.

By 1989 civil war was also being fought with increasing ferocity across the border in Somalia. Much of the north of that country was by then controlled by a movement bitterly opposed to the highly authoritarian Siad Barre government. Early in 1990 yet another country began to experience the trauma of war, as rebel forces opposed to the regime of Samuel Doe advanced across Liberia – crippling an economy already in decline as a result of low prices for its main export, iron ore, and as a result of bad government.

African civil wars have contributed to poverty by consuming scarce resources and energies, from trained personnel needed for basic administration to transport capacity and fuel supplies. They have taken labour off the land, have damaged that land, and have taken crops and livestock to feed the military on both sides. They have disrupted trade, often preventing traders from selling in areas of need and therefore discouraging them from making purchases where surpluses are available. Economic and social welfare infrastructure has been destroyed. Long-term development aid cannot be effectively implemented in the areas of conflict, and external aid may be deflected away from the entire country. In these and many other ways war has not only killed millions of people in Africa during the past quarter century through starvation and especially disease, most of them children (Green et al. 1987), but it has also ensured that tens of millions of poor people become even poorer.

At the same time, we must recognize that no country has yet actually disintegrated, and while several of the larger countries have endured civil war, many more countries have been spared this. In countries such as Cameroon and Kenya the process of national integration is far from complete, but regional antagonism has been kept in check. In many others, such as Senegal, Sierra Leone, Côte d'Ivoire, Ghana, Zambia and Malawi, there has been little regional conflict, despite some cultural diversity and often great contrasts in levels of prosperity and poverty between central and peripheral areas. Armed conflict is certainly therefore not the primary cause of continuing poverty across tropical Africa as a whole.

Refugees

One of the most obvious negative impacts of political conflict on the people of some parts of Africa has been the creation of massive flows of international refugees (Map 6.1), partly as a direct result of attempts to impose national integration by force against the wishes of the people (Zolberg et al. 1989). In the late 1980s UNHCR estimated that there were almost 4 million such refugees in Africa, or more than one-third of the world total. In many ways these constitute the poorest of all the people of Africa (Gorman 1987). Most travelled from their homes on foot, and could carry very few belongings with them. Most arrived in the country of asylum with no money at all. Most are now in areas where there are very few employment opportunities for the local population, let alone for a flood of new arrivals.

The largest flow has been from Eritrea and Tigray Provinces of Ethiopia into eastern Sudan, probably involving over a million people. Some have fled as a direct result of the war being waged in both provinces. Others have been famine victims who have feared to go to the Ethiopian government feeding centres. Others again have fled as a result of the combination of physical danger and shortages of food (Bulcha 1988). There has also been a flow of refugees from south-eastern Ethiopia into Somalia. Yet by the end of the 1980s civil war in Somalia as well as in Sudan was inducing many from both these countries to cross borders into Ethiopia.

Sudan has received large numbers of refugees not only from Ethiopia but also from both Chad and Uganda. A valuable study of the total Sudan situation has been provided by John Rogge (1985), while an in-depth study of the Ugandans in southern Sudan has been produced by Barbara Harrell-Bond (1986). In very different ways they both demonstrate the great difficulties of providing material assistance to refugees in areas where most local people are also in dire need.

A more recent refugee flow is that from Mozambique into Malawi, involving 700,000 people by late 1989. Most are fleeing from the violent attacks of RENAMO on the civilian population, but here too famine, itself partly a result of RENAMO activity, has at times been a contributory factor. Almost all the refugees are desperately poor, having been forced to abandon such few possessions as they formerly had, and they are joining a resident Malawian population most of whom are themselves very poor. Then, in

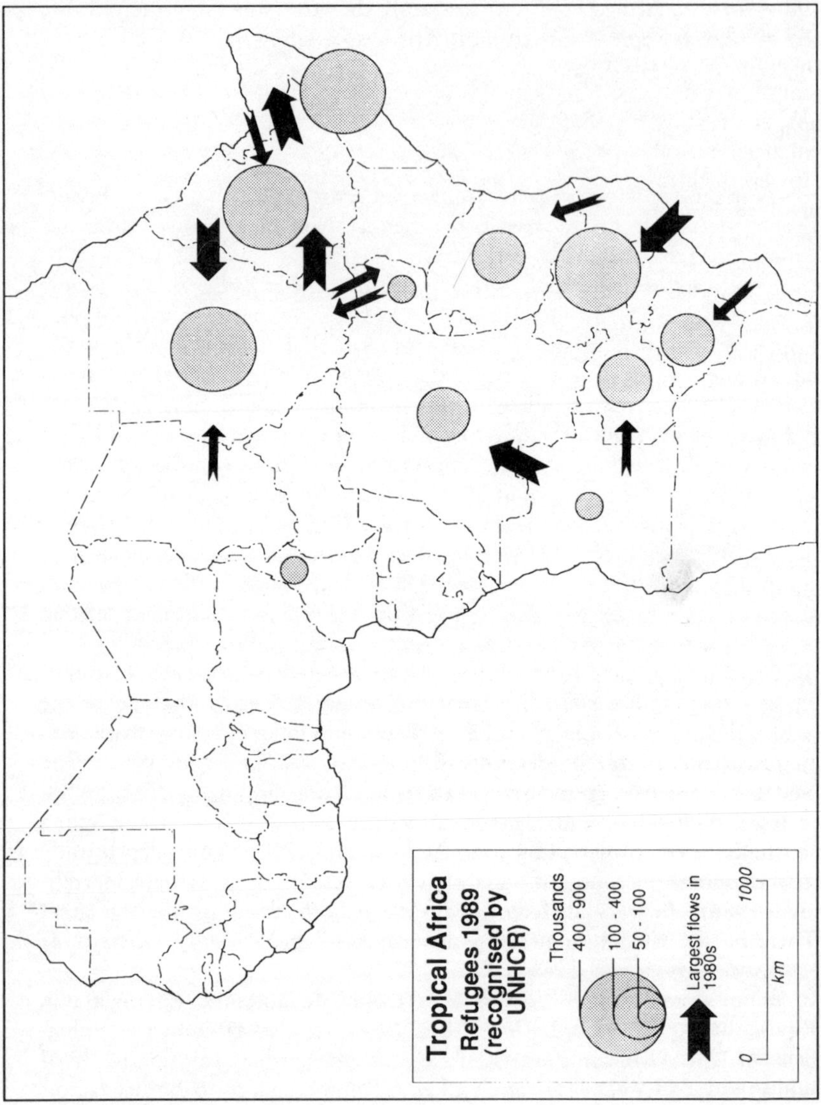

Map 6.1 Refugees, 1989

early 1990 in West Africa, there was an exodus from Liberia of at least 100,000 into Côte d'Ivoire and 100,000 into Guinea.

The general lack of identification with the nation–state may be one factor encouraging refugee movements in Africa, especially where a single ethnic group straddles a political boundary. In this situation the willingness of the host community to accept the new arrivals is generally increased. A common language may be very helpful, and may reduce the psychological stress. However, this in no way reduces the intensity of the material poverty involved in most refugee situations in Africa, or the need for material (perhaps rather than organizational) assistance from overseas. Where land is available, spontaneous self-settlement may be much preferable to large-scale refugee camps, especially as people may then be able to meet their own basic food needs within a few months: but assistance is needed in the form of seeds and tools, water supplies, health care and so on.

The state in tropical Africa

Much has been written on the nature of the state in post-colonial Africa, and particularly on its failings. Probably the most helpful discussions in terms of the significance for poverty are those of Goran Hyden (1983) and Richard Sandbrook (1985). Goran Hyden (p. 195) speaks of the state in African countries as being 'suspended in mid-air above society' and thus of very little direct benefit to most people. Richard Sandbrook presents an even more negative picture, at least for certain countries. 'Only a small minority of African states retains an effective directive capacity . . . The aim of most public officials is simply personal aggrandizement' (pp. 35–6). 'This environment fosters the decay of state institutions . . . Those civil servants who are competent and honest are demoralized by the graft, fraud and theft of public property' (pp. 113–4).

Almost everywhere in tropical Africa the state is weak and fragile, and a major concern of those in power is their own survival. For politicians and for civil servants this takes priority over any concern for economic development. There has been at least an attempted *coup d'état* in almost every country since independence, and several have experienced a series of successful coups. In Benin (formerly Dahomey) there were five between 1963 and 1972. Political instability has certainly been the norm, although Côte d'Ivoire, Senegal, Tanzania and Zambia, as well as Benin since 1972, are among a number of exceptions.

The coups have generally brought the military to power, subsequent coups often reflecting internal rivalries within the military (Bienen 1989), and for most of the period since independence the majority of tropical African countries have been under military rule. Sometimes the distinction between the two is not clear-cut, Mobutu of Zaïre being one of several military leaders who have discarded their uniforms to become civilian heads of state. Ghana and Nigeria are among the countries that have had alternation of civilian and military government – with little to indicate which has been the more satisfactory. Probably the regimes of Jerry Rawlings in Ghana and Ibrahim Babangida in Nigeria in the late 1980s were at least taking poverty more seriously than earlier civilian regimes.

A common characteristic under both civilian and military regimes has been the profound importance of the ideas and personality of the head of state. Nkrumah totally dominated political life in Ghana for a while, as did Kenyatta in Kenya for rather longer. Senghor in Senegal, Houphouet-Boigny in Côte d'Ivoire, Mobutu in Zaïre, Nyerere in Tanzania, Kaunda in Zambia and Banda in Malawi have all been highly influential for long periods. Many sharp differences in policy between Tanzania and Malawi have reflected almost entirely the attitudes of their leaders rather than any fundamental differences among the mass of the population. Richard Sandbrook is probably right to conclude that in the African cultural context there is little alternative to what he terms 'patrimonial' rule.

Robert Jackson and Carl Rosberg (1982) have examined personal rule in Africa in great depth, distinguishing prophets, princes, autocrats and tyrants. It is the tyrants that have been most significant in terms of poverty, which was greatly intensified by the highly destructive personal rule of Amin in Uganda, Bokassa in the Central African Republic (Empire for a while), and Nguema in Equatorial Guinea. All three created dire problems that persisted long after they were overthrown. In Uganda the state almost totally lost its legitimacy in the 1970s, and has had to struggle hard under Museveni in the late 1980s to regain it (Hansen and Twaddle 1988).

Despite its weakness, the state in many countries has set itself a very wide range of tasks, including running much of the large-scale sector of the economy through what are often termed parastatal bodies. This has applied as much in countries ideologically to the right, such as Nigeria, Zaïre and Malawi, as in those inclined more to the left. There is little doubt that in countries such as Tanzania the state has been over-ambitious, given its very limited financial and manpower resources (Hodd 1988). The *ujamaa* villagization programme in Tanzania is a particularly clear example of the state trying to accomplish too much in too short a time, and merits some further discussion. The extent to which it can be branded a failure depends greatly upon which aspect one is emphasizing (Yeager 1989).

The Tanzanian government hoped to persuade almost the entire rural population of 15 million to move voluntarily from highly dispersed homes into new nucleated villages in the early 1970s. It failed to persuade most of them, and so a period of coercion followed. This did bring a remarkable transformation, without the physical violence often associated with such movements of people. Most people grumbled, but then did move. There is no doubt that the programme succeeded in promoting political development, encouraging people to identify with the new nation and permitting far more public participation in politics than would have been possible within the former dispersed settlement pattern. It also assisted the provision of health centres, water supplies, schools, and especially adult literacy programmes, thereby making some contribution to the alleviation of poverty. However, the impact on agricultural production has generally been negative, as people have had to spend far more time walking from their homes to their fields. And far from slowing rural-urban migration, as was hoped, villagization greatly accelerated it by uprooting people from their original homes, and by promising people services in the villages which they could sometimes actually find only by going on to town. Villagization in Tanzania has not caused widespread poverty, but in most respects it has failed to alleviate it.

The expansion of state activity has meant an expansion of expenditure which most of the countries can ill afford. It is sometimes reported that state expenditure in Zaïre in the early 1980s exceeded 50 per cent of the total monetary GNP. The oil boom led Nigeria into a period of great extravagance around this time, typified by some of the spending on construction in the new capital city of Abuja. In both these countries and in many others spending by the state has now been greatly cut. Its role has been reduced in a number of fields, most notably the marketing of crops, now rarely a state monopoly as it was often supposed to be throughout the 1960s and 1970s.

A clear example of unproductive state spending, and one that is sometimes increasing while others contract, is that on military equipment and activity. Military spending in most African countries is not high in per capita terms in comparison with the rest of the world; but in many it does represent a very high, and often increasing, share of the GNP. Although no data are available, the share is probably highest in Ethiopia. Much of its military hardware has been supplied on credit by the Soviet Union, but the Ethiopian state is supposed to pay for it eventually. In every country reductions in military spending would allow far more to be spent on basic needs such as primary health care; but most governments would argue that national security is also a basic need.

Corruption and illegality

Corruption is one aspect of the weakness of the state that contributes directly to poverty. In some African countries a large share of government funds goes into private pockets or into private Swiss bank accounts (Williams 1987). Zaïre provides the most blatant examples of political power being misused to provide riches for the few at the expense of the great majority, as Richard Sandbrook (1985) has clearly demonstrated. President Mobutu himself has become one of the world's wealthiest individuals, and many of those in the government hierarchy follow his example.

Misappropriation of state funds is also extremely widespread in Nigeria and Ghana, and has been regularly exposed with each change of government. It is equally prevalent throughout the state hierarchy in smaller countries such as Sierra Leone. It does, however, seem rather less pervasive in eastern Africa than in West Africa. Both Kenya and Malawi, for example, have a top civil service of some integrity, partly because they are highly paid in relation to the countries' resources; and while Presidents Moi and Banda have both amassed substantial fortunes, they both seem to have done so largely by legal means.

One form of high-level corruption with demonstrable harmful consequences is the payment of large sums to government ministers or parastatal bosses by foreign firms when they are awarded contracts. This means that contracts are often not given to the firm that can provide the best service at the lowest cost. A more serious consequence is that large and expensive schemes are favoured rather than micro-scale forms of development which provide fewer opportunities for a rake-off of this type. A minister is likely to receive a much larger gift for approving a capital-intensive scheme with a large import component than for approving a more labour-intensive project that might benefit far more people.

Lower down the government hierarchy the corruption often involves extra payments being made by the general public, in order to obtain a licence or even a train ticket, or in order to pass through a police road-block. Similar payments may have to be made to obtain 'free' medical treatment, or to get one's child admitted into primary school. It is sometimes suggested that such payments ('dash' in Nigeria) may have a beneficial effect in speeding things up, or 'oiling the wheels'. Usually the whole system is being deliberately slowed so that it can be speeded up for a fee; and whenever 'queue jumping' assists one individual it must cause hardship to all others in the queue.

In absolute terms, the scale of corruption in most African countries is no doubt far lower than in many rich and middle-income countries. But in some African countries at least, the proportion of all commercial transactions that involve some abuse of public office for private gain is probably higher than anywhere else in the world. And while foreign firms are often involved, most do not find it easy to handle this situation, so that corruption is one factor currently reinforcing other aspects of the political climate in discouraging foreign investment in Africa. It certainly does not help Africa's, 'image' in the outside world.

A related problem is nepotism, whereby jobs are given to kinsfolk even when they are far less well qualified than other applicants. This of course applies to some extent in private businesses everywhere, but the strength of the extended family and kinship system in Africa means that it is widespread there even within state structures, and is to many people entirely acceptable. Many would have no respect for a government official who did not assist his relatives in this way, and any resulting inefficiency is therefore tolerated even by those who suffer from it. Even beyond family members, the key consideration in making appointments is often to guarantee someone who can be trusted, rather than to seek someone with proven competence, who is more likely to pose a threat to those currently in power.

The weakness of the state encourages many forms of illegal activity, and some government policies, such as maintaining an unrealistic exchange rate, have provided further encouragement. Frequently, dollars or pounds can be exchanged 'unofficially' for five or even ten times the official rate for African currencies. Similarly, smuggling is rife across many African borders, encouraged by artificial price structures on one side or the other. Such illegal trade usually brings benefit to some poor people, but often involves extra costs for others, including the costs of circuitous journeys to avoid detection. Smuggling is not really the ideal way of marketing crops or providing poor people with basic consumer goods.

In some countries a 'parallel economy' has grown up to such an extent that it rivals the legal economy, especially where the state has lost much of its credibility. During the 1970s '*magendo*' became the only way to obtain many items in Uganda, and became the outlet for the greater part of the coffee crop there at one time. This meant that over half of all commercial transactions were illegal. A similar '*kalabule*' economy has been very widespread at times in Ghana. Digging for diamonds is an important element in the economy of Sierra Leone, but most of the digging and trading is now beyond the control of the state. In the 1980s the parallel economy became very extensive in Tanzania, reflecting the aim of the state to control most commercial activity and its inability to achieve this (Maliyamkono and Bagachwa 1990). It is not true, as is sometimes suggested, that throughout Africa one must engage in illegal activity in order to survive, but it is almost true for Zaïre, as Janet McGaffey (1983) has demonstrated.

Some outsiders are impressed by the ingenuity, and even the efficiency, of the parallel economy in various African countries, but it invariably benefits the rich more than the poor. And, as in the Mafia operations in Italy or the United States, it is often characterized by violence. It may in some cases be of some benefit to the country as a whole, but only because of the deficiencies of the legal and official structures. When the state itself becomes largely corrupt, and indeed evil, as in Amin's Uganda, it may be right to avoid paying taxes and so on: but that is certainly not the general situation across Africa, where illegal activity generally does far more harm than good to poor people.

Ideology

Some people would regard the ideological position adopted by each country, or more correctly by each state, as the most important aspect of the political context for poverty and development. Yet although African states differ greatly in their ideological stances, this often affects people very little in their daily lives. Crawford Young (1982) has shown just how weak is the relationship between ideology and either poverty or development in Africa. The governments of Gabon and Congo are supposed to stand at opposite extremes of the ideological spectrum, but for rural dwellers with a predominantly subsistence economy around their common border this is of very little significance.

During the 1960s the only country with a government committed to Marxism was Guinea, but it was later joined by Benin, Congo, Angola, Mozambique, Guinea-Bissau and Ethiopia. It is Ethiopia that has done most to put the doctrine into practice (Clapham 1987). The 1974 revolution there was followed by nationalization of all large-scale business, very extensive land reform, and the establishment of local decision-making committees in both rural and urban areas. The peasants of southern Ethiopia are no longer subservient to rich landlords, but perhaps they are now more subservient to the state than in the past. There is little evidence that the revolution or the ideological position of the Mengistu regime has greatly influenced the intensity or the distribution of poverty in Ethiopia. Civil war has certainly been a far more significant political factor there, as also in Angola and Mozambique.

Tanzania is distinctive not so much for its ideological position as for the clarity with which this was spelled out in the 1967 Arusha Declaration (Nyerere 1968). Julius Nyerere always insisted that Tanzania should not be regarded as a socialist country, but as one aiming in that direction, giving a high priority to equity issues even at the expense of economic growth. It is much clearer in Tanzania than in a country such as Angola that the ideology of the state has both inhibited the growth of an affluent class and increased the material welfare of the poor majority – albeit far less than was hoped.

Countries with states that have consistently followed a less socialist and more capitalist path include Côte d'Ivoire, Nigeria, Cameroon, Zaïre, Kenya and Malawi. These countries have experienced, with the exception of Zaïre, above-average economic growth, but they also have above-average internal inequality. Not only those at the top, but also those towards the middle of the income range, i.e. very poor people by world standards, have generally fared much better in Kenya than in Tanzania over the past thirty years (Collier and Lal 1984), but for most of those in the lower half there has been little difference between the two countries.

Many other African countries, such as Sierra Leone, Ghana, Mali, Burkina Faso, Rwanda and Uganda, have taken up no clear or consistent ideological position on a left–right axis, and this factor cannot be considered of great importance in relation to their economic performance or the welfare of their peoples. Some heads of state such as Yoweri Museveni of Uganda, and also Robert Mugabe of Zimbabwe, who once inclined strongly towards Marxism, have apparently felt that pragmatism is more appropriate, or safer, in the circumstances of their countries.

Some degree of shift away from state control and planning, and towards private enterprise, has been an almost worldwide phenomenon of the late 1980s, and Africa has been no exception. Under strong pressure from institutions such as the IMF, states from Togo to Tanzania have taken steps in this direction. Privatization of parastatal enterprises has taken place in many countries, and efforts have been made (without much success) to attract foreign private enterprise even to such countries as Mozambique. Nigeria has strongly resisted the direct involvement of the IMF, but it too has taken steps such as the derestriction of crop marketing, formerly in the hands of government marketing boards. Opinion within Africa, as well as outside it, is of course deeply divided on whether this 'swing to the right' will improve the economic fortunes of its people. Hopes that it would bring an immediate improvement have certainly been dashed, and in the short term human suffering has been intensified by widespread cutbacks in government services, as even the World Bank (1989) recognizes. Whether it proves beneficial for more than a few in the long term remains to be seen.

International relations

The political context for poverty in Africa clearly extends far beyond Africa itself, and some see the prime causes of this poverty as lying within Europe and North America and their past and present relationships with Africa. This broader international political context lies largely beyond the scope of this book, but something must be said about it. Independence broke one set of external relationships for most tropical African countries, but in general these countries remain very open to outside influences, and they rely heavily on international transactions to sustain their cash economies. Both foreign aid and external debt are so relevant to poverty in Africa that a later chapter is devoted to each. Here our concern is more specifically political.

Most countries maintain strong political and cultural ties with the former colonial power. All former British territories except Sudan (and the ex-British sections of Somalia and Cameroon) have stayed within the Commonwealth, and most former French colonies are even more closely linked to France. In each case language is a critically important factor, affecting everything from trade patterns to flows of students. Belgium retains much influence in Zaïre, Rwanda and Burundi, as does Portugal in Angola, Mozambique and Guinea-Bissau.

Links to Europe have broadened through the influence of the European Community, and even Ethiopia and Liberia have joined the group of ACP (African-Caribbean-Pacific) associates of the Community. United States influence has increased in what are perceived as potentially important or strategically significant countries, such as Zaïre, Sudan and Somalia, but in general tropical Africa remains of far less interest to the United States than regions such as Latin America, the Middle East and South East Asia. Africa is of even less interest to the Soviet Union, and most African states doubt whether that country has much to offer them. The main exception is Ethiopia, where the Soviet Union has become heavily involved since the 1974 revolution. It has provided military equipment worth several billion dollars, without which Ethiopia would almost certainly have lost control of Eritrea and lost territory to Somalia; but its role in famine relief has been remarkably small. Soviet military equipment is also important to Angola, but there Cuba has played an important role as intermediary.

Over most of tropical Africa rivalry between the superpowers has been of far less significance than ongoing political links with Europe. Towards the south, such rivalry has also been overshadowed by the influence of South Africa. Lesotho is almost totally dependent on the Republic, which surrounds it, especially since almost half the adult male population finds employment there. Botswana and Swaziland are also highly dependent on South Africa in many ways, and closely integrated with it economically. South Africa's role in Mozambique and Angola has been primarily political, through its support for forces opposed to each government – open military support for UNITA in Angola and clandestine support for RENAMO in Mozambique in contravention of the 1984 Nkomati Agreement (Hanlon 1986, United Nations 1989). The direct poverty impact of these conflicts was noted earlier, while there are also much wider implications of South African destabilization policies in Mozambique, including its capture of much of the trade of Zimbabwe and Zambia that would otherwise pass through Maputo or Beira.

Confrontation with South Africa has been a stimulus for efforts at international co-operation among the other countries of southern Africa. A grouping known as the Southern African Development Coordination Conference (SADCC) was formed in 1980, and it has some achievements to its credit in such fields as transport, telecommunications and energy supplies. In general, however, efforts towards political and economic integration across African borders have proved disappointing. The East African Community, linking Kenya, Tanzania and Uganda, collapsed in 1977, and neither the long-standing customs union in equatorial Africa (UDEAC) nor the Economic Community of West African States (ECOWAS) has had much impact on member states. Politically, it is extremely difficult to integrate at the same time as pressing ahead with 'nation-building'; and economically, it has proved impossible to ensure that some members do not benefit at the expense of others.

Potentially, unity among African countries could help to reduce poverty in many ways (Ndegwa 1985), but there is little prospect of this even on a regional level in the near future, as vested interests are too strong. The best hope is for co-operation in relation to specific issues such as disease control or multi-national transport systems. One of the most important of these issues is the management of river basins, but even this can present grave political problems. For instance, the government of Ethiopia has no real interest in consulting with the government of Sudan about its plans for making fuller use of the upper waters of the Blue Nile: yet these plans could have huge implications for the economy of Sudan, and also that of Egypt.

At the continental level, the Organization of African Unity has helped to foster the idea of a common African identity; and it may have helped to minimize political conflicts between member countries. However, very few people would suggest that it has greatly affected the material conditions of life throughout the continent.

Nevertheless, links between African countries are more important than is often supposed. Official trade flows are generally very small, but large amounts of trade go unrecorded. There are also substantial flows of both skilled and unskilled labour, notably in West Africa. People from Burkina Faso provide over 10 per cent of the labour force in Côte d'Ivoire, while Nigeria attracted many workers from neighbouring countries during the oil boom. The interaction across many borders is sufficient to cause those borders to be officially closed and many people to be expelled when it appears to threaten the interests of one of the states. On the other hand, so many of the borders are unmarked that officially closing them rarely has much impact.

The most intense form of interaction is, of course, provided by the flood of refugees pouring across some borders, which was briefly discussed earlier.

Such people are often moving between two countries whose governments have the minimum of contacts with each other, as in the case of Ethiopia and Sudan.

Some movements of people also take place at the intercontinental scale, and these too are profoundly affected by politics. In most African countries there is a need for people from overseas with specific skills: but the perceived political instability is one reason why recruiting agencies in Europe and North America find that Africa is often the least favourite destination for their clients. The result of this is that extra-high inducement salaries must be offered, and even then only third-rate personnel are often sent. It could be argued that one of Africa's current handicaps is its image in the rest of the world.

It is not in fact only outsiders who are reluctant to live and work in Africa. The same applies to some of the most highly-qualified African nationals, so that the 'brain drain' out of Africa is now an increasing problem. A combination of higher salaries, better professional contacts and working conditions, and greater political security has attracted many highly-educated Ghanaians, Ugandans and others to Europe, to North America and into international agencies. In the case of Sudan and Somalia there is also a similar flow to Saudi Arabia and other oil-rich countries of the Middle East. It seems that, in this way as in many others, national identity is too weak to prevent forms of interaction that are damaging to African countries (although beneficial to the individuals concerned), yet it is too strong for any form of compensation to these countries to be considered.

Conclusions

In many ways the division of the globe in general, and the division of Africa in particular, into nation–states is a critically important feature of the political environment, and highly relevant to poverty. It now matters whether you live within Mozambique or within Malawi more than it did fifty years ago even though Portugal then ruled one and Britain the other. It probably matters more now whether you live within Sudan or within Ethiopia, despite the fact that one was then under colonial rule and the other was not. More people can perhaps ignore the state in more ways in Africa than in most parts of the world, but this is not as easy to do as is sometimes assumed, and may cause great hardship. Colonialism left behind in Africa a nation–state system from which it cannot escape, but the job was not well done. Fully-fledged *states* were created, each of them admitted into the inappropriately-named United Nations Organization on independence, but they were fragile structures, and in some cases they have partly collapsed.

Real *nations* could not be created overnight, and the process of nation-building is often a slow and painful one.

The fact that the nation–state system within Africa is still in the process of formation, with efforts being made to build nations on the extremely shaky foundations provided by its states, can make life very difficult indeed for its people. Meanwhile, the fact that the system is so well established globally means that those elsewhere in the world who are in a position to assist in material ways feel only a very limited responsibility to do so; and they also feel that if their involvement were to increase this would not necessarily be welcome. In respect of the nation–state system, Africa does seem at times to have the worst of both worlds. Arguably, the people of Africa would benefit greatly if politics ceased to function so very largely in terms of nation–states, and if instead there were more emphasis on both global and local scales of decision-making.

7
Food and famine

Food is among the most basic of human needs, and producing it is the main economic activity of most women and men in rural Africa, even though they must also provide many other goods and services for themselves and may produce other things for sale. Non-food crops play only a subsidiary role in most farming systems, although they have become very prominent in a few areas. Non-farming activities must also be regarded as subsidiary in economic terms, though still very important, for most rural households.

Food is also a critically important dimension of African poverty, for over much of the continent food crop production, even together with food from livestock and fisheries, falls far short of what is regarded by organizations such as WHO as the minimum necessary for health. Food is brought into some deficit areas from elsewhere, but this rarely fully makes up for the shortfall in local production. Similarly at the national and continental scale imports of food have greatly increased since the 1960s, but this still leaves tropical Africa with far lower per capita food consumption than most parts of the world. Various national estimates are provided in Table 7.1. Supplies would be inadequate even if they were always equitably distributed – which of course they are not, here as anywhere else. Malnutrition is widespread, especially among children: and hunger is a regular part of life for many people, particularly seasonal hunger in the savanna areas which have only a single wet season (Chambers et al. 1981).

These things have probably always been true of at least parts of Africa, but the situation has no doubt also always tended to fluctuate over time. In most areas it has deteriorated sharply in the 1970s and 1980s in comparison with the previous two decades (Commins et al. 1986, Chazan and Shaw 1988). Total food production in tropical Africa has not been falling, as some

Table 7.1 Daily per capita calorie supply in the larger countries, 1965–86

	1965	*1986*
Nigeria	2,190	2,150
Ethiopia	1,820	1,750
Zaïre	2,190	2,160
Tanzania	1,830	2,190
Sudan	1,940	2,210
Kenya	2,290	2,060
Uganda	2,360	2,340
Mozambique	1,980	1,600
Ghana	1,950	1,760
TROPICAL AFRICA	2,060	2,080
(India	2,110	2,240)
(China	1,930	2,630)
(Brazil	2,400	2,660)

Source: World Bank, *World Development Report 1990*

journalistic writings claim, but it has been rising much more slowly than the total population. Per capita production has therefore fallen year by year since the 1960s in many African countries, and there is no reason to suppose that this trend will be reversed in the 1990s. If food consumption has stayed roughly constant, as Table 7.1 suggests, this has depended on increased imports. One factor in this situation is undoubtedly rural-urban migration; and it is impossible to say for the whole of tropical Africa whether food production per head of the *rural* population has or has not been declining. This has probably differed from country to country.

In 1973–4 and again in 1984–5 chronic malnutrition and hunger turned into widespread famines that eventually hit the world's headlines. The 1984–5 famines prompted the writing of Lloyd Timberlake's *Africa in Crisis* in 1985, and several other books then appeared which focused even more sharply upon the famines. This book will not repeat all that was written in these, but the latter part of this chapter must give some attention to famine, even though, mercifully but perhaps only temporarily, it became far less widespread in the late 1980s. First, however, the farming systems by which most people do satisfy most of their basic food needs most of the time will be discussed.

Farming systems

Farming systems in tropical Africa are extremely varied, but in the context of poverty two common features might be stressed. Firstly, most farms are very small by world standards, rarely having more than 5 hectares of cultivated land, and often having only 1 to 3 hectares. Secondly, most are family holdings with no regular hired labour and with few technological inputs beyond a hoe. Even ox ploughs are used by only a small minority of farmers, while tractors are used by an even smaller minority. FAO data suggest that there are only about 100,000 tractors in use on tropical Africa's 50 million or more farms. Similarly, only a small proportion of farmers can afford to use either fertilizers or insecticides, and even then usually only in tiny quantities. Average fertilizer consumption per hectare in most tropical African countries is less than one-tenth that in either North Africa or South Asia.

This does not mean that farming systems are static. Paul Richards (1985) has clearly demonstrated the extent of farm innovation that is taking place in many parts of West Africa, for example. This has been essential in order to cope with population growth, especially where land is becoming scarce; but it has not often raised productivity per unit of effort, or raised incomes, very greatly. Shifting cultivation is still widespread in countries such as Mali or Zambia with abundant poor-quality land; but most rural dwellers in Africa now live at too high a density for this, and have adopted some form of bush fallowing in which land is rested for only a few years between periods of cultivation. In areas such as south-east Nigeria or western Kenya the land must often now be cropped every year, and even twice a year. A few very well-watered areas have long had permanent cultivation with perennial crops such as the banana, but the scope for expansion of these farming systems is very limited. So also is the scope for intensive irrigated farming unless local small-scale impounding of water can become widespread as it is in south Asia. At present less than 1 per cent of the farmland in tropical Africa is irrigated, much of this on the Gezira scheme and its extensions in Sudan.

Both women and men are normally involved in farming, sometimes together, sometimes separately on distinct plots. Initial land clearance is generally a male responsibility, now of falling importance as land is more intensively used; but over much of tropical Africa women have primary responsibility for planting, weeding and harvesting the main food crops. Several books (e.g. Davison 1988) have recently highlighted the great, and sometimes increasing, burden of work borne by most women in rural Africa, who are responsible not only for growing their families' food but also for the supply of water, fuel and much else. Meanwhile, men often concern themselves more with any cash crop that might be grown, or with cattle where these are kept as an adjunct to cultivation. Of course there are many regional variations, such as a smaller role for women in most strongly Islamic areas. Children have traditionally contributed to tasks such as weeding and bird-scaring almost everywhere, but in varying degrees the spread of schooling has reduced their role – perhaps thereby contributing to food supply failures.

Most farming systems are based on producing food for the farm household's own use, but many families produce some surplus over their own needs, at least in good years. Where harvests are highly seasonal, as in the Sahel, much of the crop must be stored on the farm for several months (often with severe losses due to pests); but if cash needs are urgent some may be sold in local markets and replaced by purchases there (at higher prices) later in the year. Where various crops ripen through the year, as in southern Nigeria or southern Uganda, there is a much more steady supply of food for the family, together with a more steady flow of surpluses, notably towards the towns.

In more limited areas food crops are planted with the firm intention of selling a proportion of the harvest. Thus maize forms the main cash crop, as well as the main food supply for the farm families, in western Kenya and in large parts of Zambia and Zimbabwe, as do yams in some central areas of Nigeria. Again the towns now often provide the main market (Guyer 1987). We should also note that in these countries, and in some others such as Sudan, large mechanized farms also make a major contribution to national food supplies, providing (very low) cash incomes for considerable numbers of farm labourers in the process.

There is not a sharp division between cultivators and pastoralists in Africa, as is sometimes suggested. Actually, the great majority of cattle are kept by people whose livelihood depends primarily on cultivation. Other local economies depend on crops and livestock in roughly equal proportions. However, there is a further 3 to 5 per cent of tropical Africa's population who depend on nomadic pastoralism as the main basis of their livelihood. These groups are spread over more than a dozen countries, being of greatest relative importance in Mauritania in the extreme west and Somalia in the extreme east (Monod 1975, Johnson and Anderson 1988). Sometimes diets are based almost entirely on milk and blood: elsewhere some supplementary grain is grown or obtained through trade. This way of life can provide adequate nutrition, but only if the population remains sparse. Where numbers of people, and therefore of animals, increase rapidly, overgrazing can all too easily result. Those such as Richard Hogg (1987) who argue that nomadic pastoralism provides the most rational land use for large tracts of Africa must recognize that if pastoralist families are to include five or six children then half of these will have to seek some other livelihood. It must also be recognized that while it may provide sufficient nutrition, such pastoralism has never yet provided a high level of material well-being in other ways. And at least during the 1980s pastoralists throughout the Sahel and the Horn of Africa, and particularly in Sudan, were among those who suffered the most severe deprivation, whether from drought, from war, or from a combination of the two (Moris 1988).

While nomadic pastoralism prevails, and will continue to prevail, over a larger area of Africa than any other continent, it does involve only a small, and decreasing, proportion of the population. For this reason, the rest of the chapter will be concerned primarily with cultivation and crops.

The major crops

It is remarkable how many discussions of the food crisis in Africa take place without ever specifying the crops concerned. The main food staples grown on small farms throughout most of tropical Africa are three grain crops – maize, millet and sorghum – and the root crop, cassava. According to FAO data, annual production amounts to about 20 million tons of maize and 10 million tons each of millet and sorghum, together with 50 million tons of cassava. It is true that cassava is of much lower nutritional value, but these figures indicate how wrong it is to evaluate the food situation entirely in terms of grain, as is often done. Commentators who say that Africa must now import 20 or 30 per cent of its food are often basing this just on the data for grain.

Millet and sorghum are indigenous to Africa, and must once have provided the staple diet of the great majority of its people. There are several quite different varieties of each, and some are so drought-resistant that they can be grown at the extreme arid margin of cultivation, sometimes by groups who are primarily pastoralists, but yields are generally very low. Only in Sudan is sorghum (there known as dura) widely grown on a commercial basis: elsewhere both sorghum and millet are overwhelmingly grown on a subsistence basis. Maize came from the Americas several centuries ago, and since it is much higher yielding than millet and sorghum, and especially more resistant to losses to birds, it has displaced them in many areas. It is, however, more demanding in terms of both soils and rainfall. Its importance is greatest in such countries as Kenya, Zambia and Zimbabwe, where much is grown for sale, and some on large rather than small farms.

Cassava is also of South or Central American origin (there known as manioc), and although well established in Africa a hundred years ago it was further promoted during the colonial period as a famine reserve crop. It tolerates poor soils, drought and even locust damage, can remain stored in the ground for many months until required, and gives very heavy yields: but in the case of the really resistant varieties much effort is needed to make them edible, and they contribute very little to diets other than carbohydrates. Production estimates are even more a matter of guesswork than for most crops: only a small proportion is sold, and in some years and some places much that is grown is not eaten. The contribution of cassava to African food supplies is therefore very hard to determine, but there is little doubt about its predominant role in some countries, such as Zaïre, and its increasing role in many others as preferred staple foods become more scarce or costly.

Yams are an important traditional root crop, high yielding and with more food value than cassava, but they require both more labour and a more favourable physical environment, and they are largely confined to well-watered parts of West Africa. In equally restricted well-watered parts of eastern Africa, such as southern Uganda, the cooking banana is the main staple. As a perennial, it gives high yields spread through the year, and it requires relatively little labour. Those who can depend on it are fortunate compared to those who must depend on crops tolerant of a harsher environment.

The crops which are of far greater importance in regions such as South Asia, and which are now yielding far more heavily than thirty years ago as a result of 'green revolution' technology, are grown by few people in tropical Africa. Wheat cannot be grown successfully in most parts of the region, and the increasing demand for bread, especially in the cities, has been satisfied mainly by imports of wheat or flour. Attempts at wheat cultivation in Nigeria have proved disastrous (Andrae and Beckmann 1985), and a more successful way of cutting wheat imports there has been found by substituting sorghum flour for wheat flour. Wheat does thrive in parts of Kenya and Zimbabwe, but even there it is grown mainly on large commercial farms. However, we should note that a related, but much lower-yielding, grain known as teff forms the main staple on millions of small farms in highland Ethiopia.

Rice has become a staple crop in the coastal zone of West Africa, from Senegal through Guinea and Sierra Leone to Liberia, and is grown on irrigation schemes elsewhere, often at high cost. Yields are much lower than in most parts of Asia, and while rice has become a first-preference food in many African cities, these can generally be supplied with rice much more cheaply through imports from Thailand than through supplies from the local rural hinterland. Rice perhaps offers more prospects for tropical Africa than wheat, but only if some combination of local and imported technology can increase the returns obtained from the long hours of labour that are involved (Richards 1985).

The list of subsidiary or locally-important crops is very long. All should be considered in any thorough analysis of food supplies in Africa, but only a few can be mentioned here. Pulses are probably the most important, both because they make vital contributions to a balanced diet and because they play an important role in crop rotations – restoring nitrogen to the soil. In much of eastern Africa beans are widely intercropped with maize, while in some drier areas cowpeas or chickpeas form an essential complement to sorghum. Burundi and Rwanda are two countries where pulses are critically important in intensive farming systems supporting dense populations.

In some savanna areas groundnuts became a major cash crop early in this century, but far more are now grown over much of Africa as a staple food crop, either consumed on the farm or sold to supply local vegetable oil mills. Similarly in the forest zone of West Africa, Cameroon and Zaïre the oil palm now contributes far more to local diets than to export revenues.

Food production trends

Food has become a major issue in discussions of contemporary Africa both because of the appalling famines of the 1980s and because it is generally thought that food production is failing to keep pace with population growth, so causing even more widespread hunger and malnutrition.

We cannot actually be certain that per capita food production is falling, for nowhere in tropical Africa is production fully recorded. Nor is the area planted with each crop. National governments submit figures for both area and production to FAO annually, but these are at best estimates and often just wild guesses. Sometimes FAO has to substitute its own estimates, but even these are not always credible. The US Department of Agriculture makes its own estimates, partly from that country's satellite imagery, rather than relying on FAO. As mentioned above, cassava production is particularly uncertain. For 1982 the US figure for Nigeria was 15 million tons, that of FAO was 9 million, while Nigeria's own figure was 7 million.

It is quite possible that the generally optimistic mood of the 1960s led to annual upward revisions far beyond reality, while the reverse may now be true for many countries. The slowing of production growth may therefore be nothing like as severe as the available data suggest. However, there is no doubt that it has slowed to some extent, and highly probable that it has lagged behind population growth (itself not known precisely) during the 1980s. There is also little doubt that the African situation is now exceptional in global terms, and merits particular attention for that reason. We can only assume that the FAO figures used below are valid as broad orders of magnitude, as well as plead that international efforts be made to improve the monitoring of African food production.

In tropical Africa as a whole food production is thought to have risen by

Table 7.2 Per capita food production index, 1975–88

Annual variations (1979–81 = 100)

	Tropical Africa	*Near East*	*Far East*	*Latin America*
1975	110	100	97	95
1976	108	102	96	99
1977	103	98	99	100
1978	102	101	101	100
1979	100	98	98	99
1980	101	100	99	100
1981	99	102	103	102
1982	99	103	101	102
1983	95	100	107	99
1984	92	96	108	100
1985	97	99	109	101
1986	98	101	106	99
1987	94	96	103	99
1988	94	99	109	99

Source: FAO, *Production Yearbook 1988*

about 1·5 per cent annually during the 1970s, representing a 1·3 per cent annual fall in per capita terms. This compares with a 2·5 per cent absolute, and 0·8 per cent per capita, annual rise for the whole world, and with a 2·8 per cent annual absolute rise in south and east Asia. Over the period 1980–6 production in tropical Africa rose a mere 6 per cent, averaging 1 per cent annually though with much variation from year to year. This compares with 16 per cent for this period for the whole world, with 24 per cent for India, and with 34 per cent for China, according to FAO. Per capita production fell steeply in much of tropical Africa in 1983 and 1984, and was still below the 1980 level in 1986 (Table 7.2). A further sharp fall occurred in 1987, and there was no recovery in 1988 or 1989.

Naturally, there has been some variation from one country to another, as indicated in Table 7.3, although in many ways the picture has been remarkably uniform. In Ethiopia, per capita food production fell very sharply in both 1983 and 1984, with disastrous consequences, and it has only partially recovered. In Sudan, 1985 and 1986 brought a stronger recovery, but there was a fall again in 1987. In Kenya, 1984 was an exceptionally bad year, but even there the general trend of the 1980s has been downwards. It

Table 7.3 Per capita food production index for the larger countries, 1982–9

Annual variations (1979–81 = 100)

	1982	*1983*	*1984*	*1985*	*1986*	*1987*	*1988*	*Forecast 1989*
Nigeria	102	97	96	104	108	96	96	95
Ethiopia	102	94	83	88	96	91	88	89
Zaïre	100	99	99	98	99	96	94	92
Tanzania	96	96	94	94	92	91	86	89
Sudan	93	92	83	97	93	78	98	85
Kenya	105	101	83	97	106	97	102	103
Uganda	106	108	88	86	81	84	82	80
Mozambique	96	90	88	87	87	84	84	83
Ghana	92	81	114	104	106	104	108	118

Note: These figures are no more than estimates, since there is no regular recording of food crop production anywhere.

Sources: FAO, *Production Yearbook 1988:* FAO, *Quarterly Bulletin of Statistics*, 3 (1), 1990

has been more steeply downwards in Mozambique. After a fall in the 1970s, per capita production in Nigeria is thought to have been maintained at a fairly constant level in the 1980s, while Ghana actually records an improvement, though from a very low level in the late 1970s. The figures for the Sahel countries in the 1980s show little common pattern, and some of them are really rather implausible.

At the level of specific crops for individual countries, the annual fluctuations can be very much greater. In Sudan the sorghum (dura) harvest averaged 2½ million tons in 1979–81, but it fell to little over 1 million tons in 1984, before recovering to 3½ million tons in 1985 and 1986. Another fall to 1½ million tons occurred in 1987, followed by another full recovery in 1988. The maize crop in 1984 in both Zimbabwe and Kenya was only half its usual size, and in Zimbabwe it was equally bad in 1987.

These large fluctuations in Sudan, Kenya and Zimbabwe may in part reflect the extent of commercialization in these countries, and the extent to which official sales are recorded. Where crops are cultivated almost entirely for subsistence a roughly constant amount is more likely to be planted; and while yields may differ sharply from year to year, when little is ever sold there is less immediate evidence of the variations. People just dig deeper into their grain stores, and then go hungry as these near exhaustion. Only when the situation reaches famine proportions does the shortfall become widely known. In the 1970s government marketing boards were supposed to have a buying monopoly even of food crops in many countries, and this led to some absurd figures on sales of such crops, for in fact large quantities were sold in some years on illegal parallel markets, often across international borders. In the 1980s there has been a general trend towards derestriction, and so less pretence of knowing how much is sold each year.

Causes of lagging food production

There is no consensus on the causes of the slow growth of food production in the 1970s and 1980s – except agreement that it does not reflect any lack of need for more food. Drought in many areas in some years has played a part, as has lower rainfall in the 1950s and 1960s throughout the whole period over much of Africa. Environmental degradation, especially accelerated soil erosion, has contributed to declining yields, as have the shortening of fallows and the movement of people on to more marginal land, both a function of rapid population growth without much technological advance. There have been no technological breakthroughs for most African food crops comparable to the 'green revolution' that has substantially raised wheat and rice yields in Asia (Lipton and Longhurst 1989).

Government policies have often been unhelpful, including the restrictions on marketing mentioned above. Marketing boards have often not been competent to handle food crop surpluses which fluctuate greatly over space and time, and the controlled prices paid by them have often been held down in order to avoid food price increases in the cities. People may often have found illegal alternative markets, but fines, bribes and circuitous journeys all reduce the prices offered to food producers even here. It is too early to say whether opening food crop marketing to legal private enterprises in countries such as Nigeria has had a positive impact on production: it may have helped, but of course there are many other constraints.

African governments are constantly accused of neglecting the food producers in every respect other than marketing. Efforts to assist them through advisory services, credit facilities, or provision of inputs such as fertilisers, have certainly been very feeble in most countries. The governments themselves claim that the problem lies in their own lack of funds: others often point to wrong priorities in the use of such funds as they have. Perhaps more resources devoted to research on food crops would have brought a 'green revolution' for millet, sorghum and cassava, as they have done to a limited extent for maize, but one cannot be sure of that. Certainly there is a strong case for such an effort, as well as for giving more attention to assisting farmers to adopt techniques for raising yields that are already known. One issue that has been grossly neglected is the extent of post-harvest losses due to inadequate storage facilities, on or off farms. In many areas 10 to 20 per cent of the food produced is lost to pests every year. However, problems such as this are not new, and so do not explain the fall in per capita food production or availability.

The massive increase in school enrolments must have played a large part in reducing available labour for food production, leading to lower yields as fewer weeds are removed or more birds are allowed to eat the crops. Furthermore, children too young to make a contribution have constituted an increasing share of the total population over the past twenty years. Even more significant than each of these trends, however, has been the massive migration of young adults from the rural areas to the cities. This migration may have been beneficial to most of them, and may even have been, at least in part, of benefit to the national economies, but it has clearly had a negative impact on food production. Some manage to grow a little food within the cities, and some had no access to land that they could farm within the rural areas; but the great majority would have grown more food if they had remained in their rural areas of origin. It is likely that rural-urban migration, and the consequent rapid increase in the proportion of the total population living in towns and cities, was the most important single reason for falling per capita food production in most African countries in the 1970s and 1980s. In this case any slowing down of such movement, or any increase in reverse movement, could be of great significance.

Even among the rural population, an increasing proportion of adults are now non-farmers, or only very much part-time farmers. The increasing numbers of rural health workers and especially of school teachers provide examples. And even within farming families an increasing amount of time may now be spent on other activities, such as gathering fuel. There is little doubt that in Tanzania the villagization programme not only caused more time to be spent walking to the fields rather than cultivating, but also encouraged more to be spent discussing local politics.

A popular explanation for lagging food production in some quarters (e.g. Twose 1985, Lappe and Collins 1988) is a supposed massive shift of effort not to non-farming activities but to non-food crops. Cash crops are presented as the culprit. There is no doubt some truth in this for certain localities, but across most of tropical Africa the main expansion of cash crop cultivation took place in the 1950s and 1960s (O'Connor 1978), when food crop production still appeared to be almost keeping pace with population growth. During the 1970s and especially the 1980s cash crop production has lagged just as badly as food crop production, as the next chapter will demonstrate. Over tropical Africa as a whole, a shift of attention to cash crops is *not* even a partial explanation for decreasing per capita production

Table 7.4 Leading tropical African importers of cereals, 1984–7

Volume in thousands of tons	*1984*	*1985*	*1986*	*1987*
Nigeria	1,377	1,957	1,369	677
Sudan	518	1,148	651	707
Ethiopia	252	717	974	609
Côte d'Ivoire	536	554	580	675
Senegal	662	496	512	431
Mozambique	430	365	393	406
Zaïre	236	331	361	415
Somalia	330	300	291	344
Angola	374	284	159	280
Kenya	557	279	190	275
TROPICAL AFRICA	8,470	9,620	7,840	7,480

Source: UNDP/World Bank, *African Economic and Financial Data* (1989)

of food crops, though of course a reverse shift from coffee or cotton to maize or millet would be one way of increasing food supplies – at great sacrifice to the incomes both of countries and of individual farmers.

Food imports

Imports provide another, far from ideal, way to increase food supplies, and one consequence of the lag in food production (and one indication that it is real) has been a very rapid growth in African food imports (Raikes 1988). Some food has long been imported into every African country, but in the past this was generally confined to luxuries for the élite and certain preferred foods largely for townspeople. Around 1970 no country in tropical Africa yet imported more than 300,000 tons of cereals annually.

By 1978 cereal imports into Nigeria had reached 2 million tons, and they had trebled since 1970 in several other countries, such as Ghana. In these two countries strict import controls have prevented this growth continuing, and indeed have reversed it; but other countries such as Ethiopia and Mozambique have become major importers of grain, some bought and some received free, so that total imports into tropical Africa have remained high throughout the 1980s (Table 7.4).

However, various misleading statements about the import situation are often made. When cereal imports into Africa are quoted as 25 million tons a year by the mid 1980s this includes 8 million tons for Egypt and 5 million tons for Algeria: in comparison with these countries the imports into most tropical African countries are still very modest. It is also suggested at times that many African countries now import half their food requirements, and that most import at least a quarter, but this idea results from considering cereals alone. In countries such as Zaïre root crops make a much larger contribution to total calorie supply, and these are not imported. The importance of locally-grown root crops and pulses over tropical Africa as a whole is frequently overlooked.

Even carefully-worded suggestions that *cereal* imports into tropical or sub-Saharan Africa may continue to rise by 20 or 25 per cent a year are very implausible. Imports are always into individual countries, and the dramatic increases first in Nigeria and then in Ethiopia are unlikely to be repeated on the same scale elsewhere. Most countries have far smaller populations and are unlikely to experience either an oil boom or a famine on the Ethiopian scale in the near future. In any case, most countries clearly could not pay for imports increasing at this rate, and free donations are unlikely to be provided in ever-increasing quantities. However, unless food production can match population growth more closely than in the recent past, some further increase of imports, mainly in the form of cereals, will be essential.

The greater part of the imports are normally obtained at commercial rates, but the proportion moving in as food aid has increased greatly since the 1970s, especially in response to famine in the Sahel, Sudan, Ethiopia and Mozambique. In 1985/6 900,000 tons of cereals moved into Sudan as food aid, 800,000 tons into Ethiopia, and even 140,000 tons into Mauritania with its far smaller population. The food aid, and especially that moving on an emergency basis, has been largely distributed in rural areas, whereas the commerical imports are destined primarily for the cities and towns. This contrast should not be overdrawn, however, for bread made from commercially imported wheat has penetrated many of the more prosperous rural areas, especially in francophone West Africa, while long-term food aid is now a basic source of supply for cities such as Khartoum and Addis Ababa.

Although cereals now constitute much the largest element in African food imports, many other items are also involved. Nigeria's total food import bill reached $2,400 million in 1981, and cereals accounted for well below half of this. By 1986 the figure had been cut to $1,000 million, of which cereals accounted for $600 million, and sugar, fish and cattle for about $100 million each. Imports of many luxury foods had by then virtually ceased, apart from the large quantities smuggled in through neighbouring countries. Sugar is the largest food import item into some other African countries, even though sugar cane grows well in some part of almost every country, and plantations large enough to satisfy the local demand have been established in many.

Some other parts of the world import food because other forms of activity make them rich enough to do so. Tropical Africa does so mainly because it is too poor to use its own natural resources effectively enough to feed itself. Importing food then makes it even poorer, and ultimately makes individual families poorer too. Unless African countries can either cut the import requirement by producing more food, or produce more of other things to pay for it, poverty will be intensified.

Hunger and malnutrition

Even when imports are included tropical Africa does not have sufficient basic foodstuffs available year by year to meet the needs of 500 million people. The total supply would probably be inadequate even if distribution were completely equitable and efficient. Since there are inevitably inequities, and since the spatial pattern of supply can never exactly match that of demand, the availability of food is at present grossly inadequate. In reality, inequity is far greater than might be deemed inevitable, and the means of linking surplus and deficit areas are desperately lacking in Africa. As a result, the situation in many areas is utterly intolerable. And that is even in the good years, before short-term disasters are taken into account.

Malnutrition, in the sense of a diet lacking in some elements essential for health, is extremely widespread, especially among children (Pacey and Payne 1985). Although it is not easily measured, various surveys have suggested that malnutrition serious enough to cause specific diseases such as kwashiorkor afflicts well over a quarter of all children in tropical Africa. Many make a full recovery from such diseases, but others suffer permanent physical or mental damage. Undernutrition, in the sense of a shortage even of basic staples, and hence of calories, affects even more people at least periodically. In this case adults and children are equally involved. In most of the savanna lands the wet season is the busiest time of year, as land is prepared and crops are planted and weeded; but it is also the 'hungry season' as the new harvest is awaited. Many people cope with this hunger remarkably well (Richards 1986), but it is still a clear manifestation of poverty.

FAO data suggest that average calorie consumption per day over the whole world is around 2,700, and that in the rich countries it is around 3,400. Their estimate for tropical Africa is only about 2,100. It is impossible to say what is really *needed*, especially in view of differing climates, differing proportions of children, and differing lifestyles; but there is some consensus in WHO as well as FAO that this average represents less than 90 per cent of the requirements for a fully active life. And of course, since this is an average, half the population must be consuming less than this.

The FAO estimates do not support the claim that the average level of food consumption, or of nutrition, has been declining in tropical Africa (Table 7.1). But they do suggest that calorie consumption has failed to increase in the 1970s and 1980s, during which time it has advanced from 2,400 to 2,700 for the world as a whole. Increased commercial imports and food aid together seem to have just about compensated for the decline in per capita food production, but no more than this. Without any doubt the absolute number of seriously undernourished people has increased greatly, even in those countries which have not experienced famines.

At individual country level some of the FAO data must be viewed with scepticism. For some years almost the lowest level of calorie consumption has been recorded for Ghana, and almost the highest for Tanzania. More plausible are extremely low levels in Chad, Burkina Faso and Mali, and also in Mozambique, and a level high enough to approach the world average in Côte d'Ivoire.

With regard to malnutrition, no comprehensive set of data on a country-by-country basis yet exists. The surveys that have been undertaken reveal no clear geographical patterns. Malnutrition seems to be equally widespread and severe in western and in eastern Africa, in the Sahel and in equatorial rain forest areas. It is quite impossible to say how many children die as a result of it in any area, for deaths are usually due to a combination of malnutrition and some specific disease to which it may have made the child more susceptible: but the seriousness of the problem almost everywhere is beyond doubt.

Famine

Although both hunger and malnutrition were already very widespread in Africa in the 1960s, famine was limited to only very small areas, notably some remote parts of Ethiopia and war-torn districts in Zaïre and Nigeria. However, the early 1970s brought devastating famine to much more of Ethiopia and to large parts of the West African Sahel. An even more critical and widespread famine situation followed in the early 1980s, affecting several countries profoundly (Map 7.1) and more than twenty in some degree, and prompting a massive, if somewhat belated, international response.

Much has already been written on these disasters. Thus the Ethiopian famine of 1973–4 is well documented by Jack Shepherd (1975) and by Mesfin Wolde Mariam (1985); and that of 1983–5 by Graham Hancock

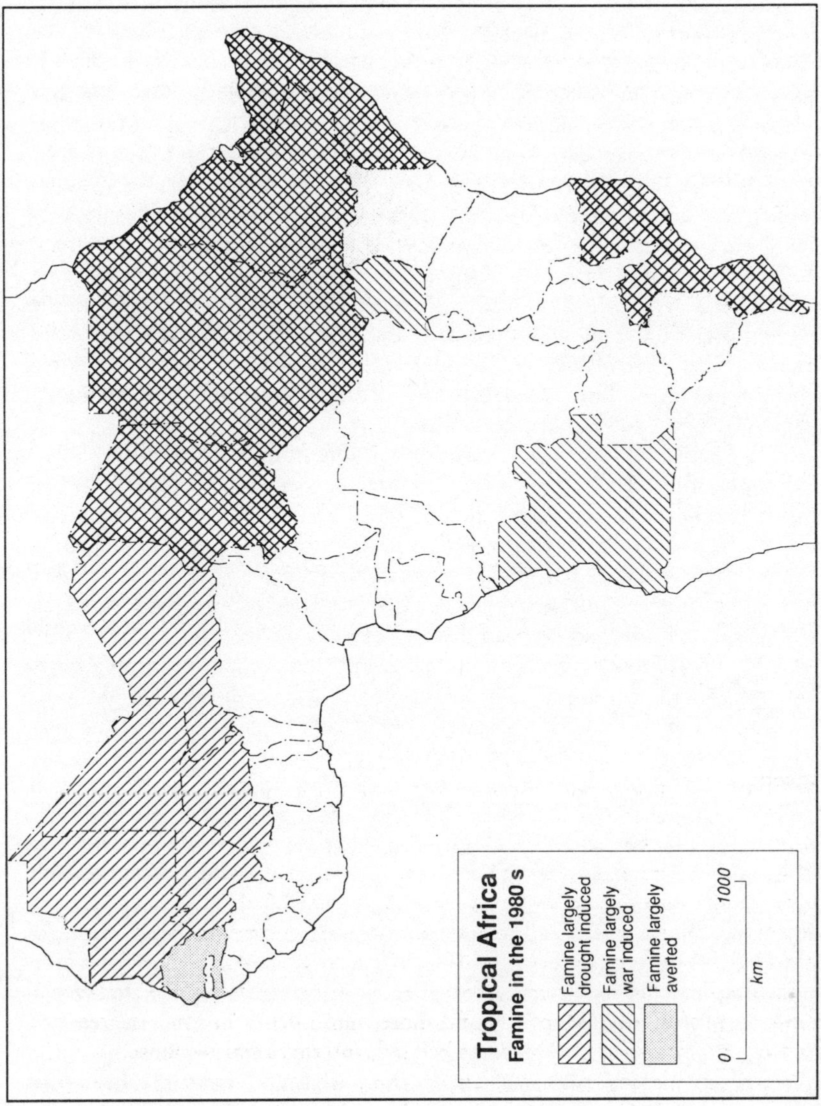

Map 7.1 Countries suffering famine in the 1980s

(1985), Peter Gill (1986), and Hugh and Catherine Goyder (1988). The head of the United Nations relief operation, Kurt Jansson (1987), has provided his account, as has Dawit Wolde Giorgis (1989), who headed Ethiopia's own relief organization. Nothing new can be added here.

One point to be stressed is that famine is not typical of tropical Africa, and was not even in 1984–5. It was then continent-wide in the sense that areas in western, eastern and southern Africa were all afflicted, but far larger areas did not experience it, including those occupied by the great majority of the population. The international media publicity was very necessary, but it produced an unfortunate image of Africa around the world.

A second important point is that famine is certainly not new to Africa. The fullest records exist for Ethiopia, where it has recurred over the centuries. Elsewhere the distribution, frequency and severity of famine in the past is more a matter of speculation, as are the causes of it, but famines did occur as John Iliffe (1987) has demonstrated. However, in absolute terms, more people must have been directly affected, and far more indirectly affected, in the 1980s than ever before.

Really severe food shortages began to build up in many areas during 1983 as drought intensified across much of Africa, and even in that year 150 million people were said to be 'at risk' when FAO appealed for emergency food aid from overseas. For the great majority of these people the impending disaster was averted by national and international action, or did not in fact materialize: but by mid 1984 at least 30 million people were suffering extreme deprivation and were in urgent need of help. By the end of 1984, when Michael Buerk's and Mohammed Amin's report from Ethiopia burst upon the world through the BBC, the crisis was reaching its peak. It is thought that more than 10 million people in various parts of Africa had by then left their homes in search of food. Between one and two million people, mostly small children, died during 1984 at least partly from starvation. Such deaths continued into 1985 when the relief efforts eventually became fully operational and better harvests were reaped in many areas. By 1986 the Africa-wide crisis was over as far as the rest of the world was concerned, although of course the silent crisis of hunger continued.

Although more than twenty countries experienced severe food shortage, famine was largely averted in some of these, such as Kenya, and affected only small parts of some others, such as Nigeria. Its greatest impact in 1984–5 was in Ethiopia, followed by Sudan both chronologically and in terms of severity. There was much suffering, and some starvation, throughout the Sahel too, from Mauritania through Mali, Burkina Faso and Niger into Chad, as also in Somalia. It was less intense at that time in southern Africa, but there it has persisted longer, especially in Mozambique.

Famine in Ethiopia

In Ethiopia the national Relief and Rehabilitation Commission was already sounding the alarm early in 1983, although its appeals were not backed up by the military government as strongly as they might have been; and by early 1984 it considered that the country needed 900,000 tons of grain to be brought in during that year to avoid mass starvation. UN bodies backed this evaluation only to the extent of 125,000 tons, but mainly because it was thought that the ports could handle no more than this. A far greater actual need was acknowledged by many outside observers, but only the October 1984 BBC television film showing what was actually happening by then brought a major international response. By then probably half a million deaths had already occurred, and many more were to follow.

The worst conditions were in Wollo Province, north of Addis Ababa, and further north in Tigray, but there was also much starvation in Harerghe Province in the east and over much of Eritrea in the far north. All of these areas have rugged terrain and extremely poor communications, and this often meant sharp differences in conditions over quite short distances. Even when one locality had surplus food this often could not be transported to deficit areas even 50 km distant, or else moving it incurred such costs that those in need could not afford to buy it.

Lack of food and inaccessibility together forced millions to abandon their homes, many trekking towards relief camps and feeding centres strung along the few motorable roads. These factors, together with ongoing civil war, led a further half million from Eritrea and Tigray to walk 20, 50 or even 100 km. to the Sudan border. This refugee flow is clearly caused by a combination of famine and politics when it includes many people who are starving but who dare not go to government feeding centres for fear of being drafted into the army to fight against their own people. As refugees they took the problem of famine with them into Sudan, since most arrived there destitute.

The years 1986 and 1987 brought a great improvement in the food situation in most parts of Ethiopia, but 1988 brought a further threatened crisis. By this time both the government and foreign agencies were better able to handle the situation in the government-controlled areas, and widespread famine seems to have been averted. However, civil war had by then taken further areas outside government control and thus made them dependent on extremely difficult supply routes through Sudan. Despite the efforts of Eritrea's and Tigray's own relief agencies, some people continued to die of starvation in these areas.

Famine in Sudan, the Sahel and Mozambique

Sudan received less publicity than Ethiopia because, although just as many were at one stage at risk there, far fewer people actually died of starvation (Abdel-Ati 1988, De Waal 1989). Famine conditions developed later than in Ethiopia, for there were larger past surpluses on which to draw; many of the people involved are traditionally more mobile than those in Ethiopia and went in search of food or work before starvation point was reached; and the United States took on the main responsibility for a massive relief operation.

Nevertheless, directly or indirectly, lack of food killed tens of thousands of people in the Red Sea Hills, in Kordofan, and especially in Darfur towards the Chad border. Distances are vast, roads often non-existent, and merchants often corrupt, so that in many remote villages no grain was available at affordable prices to make up for local crop failures. Many people moved in search of food, and where they congregated infectious diseases spread rapidly. Furthermore, the Sudan government, and President Numeiry in particular, refused for many months to admit to the crisis, so that the relief effort came too late for many people.

Sudan too has been plagued by civil war. This contributed to famine in Kordofan and Darfur only indirectly, by weakening the government and diverting its attention towards the war zone in the south. However, it has been the primary cause of more limited incidences of famine within the south, which have continued to occur through the late 1980s. At times these have involved the Sudan People's Liberation Army laying siege to government-held towns and preventing food reaching them either from the surrounding rural areas or from afar.

In the Sahel zone of West Africa harvests were very poor in 1982, 1983 and 1984, while grazing greatly deteriorated over this period. These conditions posed a threat to food supplies for most people in Mauritania, and for many in Mali, Burkina Faso, Niger and Chad. At least one million were seriously affected in each of these countries, many having to abandon their homes and some dying of starvation. Mass starvation was avoided only by the shipment of more than a quarter of a million tons of grain from overseas to each country. Even in spite of this, more than 100,000 may have died in Chad, yet another country beset by civil war. Niger, by comparison, benefited from a calmer political scene and a large commercial inflow of food from Nigeria, paid for mainly by sending cattle south in exchange. Famine did not return to the Sahel in the late 1980s, as many feared it might, but the whole area is clearly highly vulnerable, and far from adequately supplied with food.

Much of southern Africa had a succession of five poor harvests, and even Zimbabwe, normally a grain exporter, had to import massively in 1984.

Generally, however, deficit areas within this region were somehow supplied with their basic needs; and the state's handling of the situation in Botswana has won particular praise (Borton and Clay 1988). The main exception is Mozambique, another country where violent conflict rages. Already by mid 1985 over 3 million Mozambicans were very short of food, and the situation subsequently deteriorated. There are no reliable estimates of starvation deaths, but by late 1989 over 4 million people had abandoned their homes, of whom 700,000 had fled into Malawi. The fighting may in most cases have been the main reason for flight, but farming had been so disrupted over vast areas that most of those on the move were also suffering dire hunger. This was all too evident among the majority of those arriving in Malawi. Angola is yet another country riven by civil war which has experienced widespread famine, although the extent of it is even less well known outside the country (perhaps even inside it) than in the case of Mozambique.

Causes of famine

Much debate has taken place about the causes of these African famines, and some statements have been made that hardly justify the term 'debate'. Some writing has referred to famine and drought as if they were almost synonymous: other people have suggested that famine has almost nothing to do with drought, and is entirely the result of human action. Some writing blames the spread of export crops despite the fact that most famine areas have no major export crop and most areas of export crop production lie far from the famine-stricken areas.

The worst African famine situations have as their immediate cause a deadly combination of drought and civil war. As was shown in Chapter 4, rainfall in the early 1980s, and especially in 1983 and 1984, was in many areas far below the long-term average, and harvests were extremely poor in 1984 largely for this reason. Many of the areas experiencing famine were those where the drought was most intense. At the same time, as was shown in Chapter 6, civil war has profoundly affected all aspects of life in several countries during the 1980s. Sudan, Ethiopia, Chad and Mozambique are all among these countries in which war has taken labour away from food production, has gravely disrupted trade, and has diverted government attention away from food problems. Civil war alone has been enough to cause famine in some cases, but this and drought together have brought devastation on a vastly larger scale.

These specific conditions have been superimposed upon the more general conditions of environmental degradation, weakness in the agricultural economy, failings in the inherited nation–state system, and exceptionally rapid population growth, all discussed in various parts of this book. Each of these can be considered as a partial cause of famine, or at least of people's vulnerability to famine when more specific environmental or political events occur. So also can the wider international context, where the economic and political structures permit the rich to consume a grossly disproportionate share of the world's food resources, albeit in the form of grain-fed meat rather than grain itself. Yet at the opposite extreme in terms of scale, personal and family circumstances make some people far more vulnerable than others, and become additional causes of individual deaths from starvation.

Amartya Sen (1981) has gained renown for his thesis that famines are often not caused by food availability decline, but are better understood through what he terms 'entitlements' to food. In some ways this is arguing that poverty itself is the basic cause of famine, and certainly the main explanation for its incidence. He stresses that within any community it is the poor rather than the rich who starve to death. While there is much truth in this, in Africa as elsewhere, it must also be noted that various parts of Africa *have* experienced a food availability decline, often at a local scale superimposed on a national scale superimposed on a continental scale. *Both* a lack of food *and* a lack of access to it are relevant in this case.

Response to famine and food shortage

Famine often brings a dramatic response at all levels. Individual African families may first sell their livestock, then sell all their other possessions, and finally abandon their homes. National governments may declare a state of emergency and mobilize relief efforts. Both Kenya and Botswana undertook such efforts with much success in the mid 1980s, and there has been a tendency for outsiders to undervalue the national relief efforts in both Sudan and Ethiopia (Borton and Clay 1988). Ultimately, as in these two cases, a large-scale international effort may be launched. Vivid accounts of these have been provided by Peter Gill (1986), Kurt Jansson (1987) and Colin Fraser (1988).

There has been much less evident response to the long-term deficiencies in African food production, yet this is also desperately needed. It is these deficiencies that make people vulnerable to famine when drought or war strikes, and they also contribute directly to illness and premature death on a massive scale through malnutrition. Some of the possible government responses are reviewed in volumes such as that by John Mellor and others (1987). Only a few can be mentioned here as examples.

Government 'feed the nation' campaigns in Nigeria and Ghana in the

1970s are thought to have had little impact, but food crop production has been increased in some parts of Nigeria in the 1980s through the encouragement of large- and medium-scale highly commercialized farming. In Sudan sorghum production was greatly increased in 1985, partly through a shift from other crops such as cotton and groundnuts on the tenant farms in the government-controlled irrigation schemes, but by reducing crop exports this has exacerbated the country's debt problem. In several countries there have been moves to increase incentives for small farmers to produce a surplus over family needs by raising the prices offered by marketing boards, or by permitting private merchants to buy at higher prices in a more competitive situation.

Three ways in which the state might do more to help small farmers to increase food production are through research on improved crop varieties, provision of credit, and provision of improved storage facilities at the local level. Improved storage also has a direct role in famine prevention, as does the establishment of early warning systems, monitoring both climatic fluctuations and farmers' reactions to these (Curtis et al. 1988). In view of the very limited resources of all African governments, all such measures require international financial support, and also need to build on farmers' own initiatives and innovations.

Other relevant responses are even more wide ranging, but also even more demanding on resources. These include doing whatever little can be done in the short term to improve environmental management, to encourage some reduction in the rate of population growth, and to improve transport facilities especially at the local level. They include improving rural dwellers' access to fuel and water supplies, so that energy can be diverted from these concerns to food production. They also include actions to reduce the rate of rural-urban migration, and to encourage reverse movement, although past efforts in this field have been singularly unsuccessful. The most urgent need of all, both to improve the overall agricultural situation and specifically to prevent famine, is of course political stability and an end to violent conflict. But how is that to be achieved?

8
The wider rural economy

The economic activities of most rural households in Africa involve much more than just food production. Indeed, they involve much more than just agriculture, and it is in many ways misleading to label African rural dwellers as 'farmers' as if this were their full-time occupation. This applies equally to women and to men, and probably applies more comprehensively than in most parts of Asia and Latin America, where there is often more specialization of labour, even in rural areas.

The livelihoods of the majority of families include fetching their own water from a well or stream, gathering their own fuelwood, and also building their own houses. Many people make some of their own utensils and furniture, and some engage in craft production for sale, especially during a slack season in the farming calendar. Many 'farmers' have to be part-time traders and transporters, selling their own produce in local markets, or carrying the coffee or cotton that they have grown to the nearest buying point, perhaps with the aid of a bicycle. Most have to be part-time nurses and teachers within their own families to a greater extent than in other parts of the world; and some perform the type of religious and administrative roles in the local community that are the task of full-time specialists in many other societies.

In various parts of rural tropical Africa there are some households whose income comes mainly from labouring on the farms of others, as Ken Swindell (1985) has demonstrated, though this is less widespread than in most of Asia and Latin America. There are more households in which occasional wage labour, on farms, on local roadworks, or whatever, makes some contribution (Livingstone 1986). In any village there are now also likely to be a few people who are primarily shopkeepers, and a few who are full-time employees of the state. And an important further element in many rural economies throughout tropical Africa is now provided by remittances from those who have migrated to the towns and cities.

Despite this great diversity of activities, farming is the main source of cash income, as well as of the household food supply, in most African rural areas. As indicated in the last chapter, there is often a marketable surplus of basic food crops such as maize: but in many places crops such as cotton or coffee have also long been grown entirely as a source of cash, and these cash crops should now be discussed.

Cash crops

In many parts of Africa cultivation of cash crops on small farms was encouraged, or even forced, during the colonial period, primarily for export overseas. Often this export-orientation continues, although local industries now absorb part of the supply of crops such as cotton. This makes both nation–states and individual families highly dependent on world market prices, which have been highly unfavourable during the 1980s.

Cash crop cultivation has been condemned by some writers as a primary cause of famine, but it is doubtful whether this is true of many areas. In countries such as Ethiopia and Chad the main cash crop regions have not been famine regions, while most famine areas have few cash crops. People need some form of cash income, and producing a surplus of basic food crops may not be the best way of obtaining this. On small farms in southern Ethiopia or central Kenya, coffee yields far more income per hectare than any food crop, even when world prices are depressed. In the Sahel cotton survives certain seasonal drought patterns better than most food crops, and so farmers may be well advised to diversify into cotton for security. In parts of the Sahel the shift to groundnuts grown for export probably went too far, but to argue from this that cash crops are the cause of Africa's food deficit is quite unjustified.

A stress on excessive cash crop cultivation was particularly inappropriate in the 1980s, since all available data suggest that in general these crops had an even poorer production record than food crops in the 1970s. Tropical Africa's total volume of agricultural exports in 1981 was only 80 per cent of that in 1971, and only 60 per cent in per capita terms. During the 1980s there was some modest expansion, but not sufficient to keep pace with population growth. This poor performance has played a large part in the general economic crisis besetting so much of Africa; and World Bank reports have stressed, perhaps overstressed, revival of export crop production as the key to renewed economic advance.

Coffee, grown mainly but not entirely on small family farms, is much the most valuable agricultural export from tropical Africa. Coffee-growing areas are among the most prosperous of all rural areas in both western and eastern Africa. The crop has clearly brought benefit to the people of southern Côte d'Ivoire and southern Uganda. It brings a standard of living well above the Tanzanian average to the people living on the slopes of Kilimanjaro, and it is the leading export of Kenya. For several million people, coffee-growing provides an escape from extreme poverty, but it is only possible in areas with a high rainfall and no long dry season.

Africa's coffee production and export volume have remained almost static between 1970 and 1988, at around 1·2 million tons a year; and Africa's share of world production has fallen slightly. The geography of coffee production has also been very static, with Côte d'Ivoire in the lead, and with Ethiopia and Uganda maintaining their positions just behind, despite all their political traumas. There has been some expansion in Kenya and in Cameroon, offset by a partial collapse as a result of civil war in Angola.

Cocoa is second in value among Africa's export crops, earning $2,200 million in 1986 compared with $3,200 million for coffee. Its distribution is more restricted, but it has been similarly beneficial to the producing areas, and to the growers. Again, production has remained almost static, being very close to 1 million tons in 1966, 1976 and 1986. World production rose meanwhile from 1·3 million to 2 million tons, so that Africa's share fell from three-quarters to only half the total. African production rose somewhat in 1987 and 1988.

In the case of cocoa, the geography of production has been far from static. In 1968 Ghana produced 420,000 tons, Nigeria 230,000, Côte d'Ivoire 140,000 and Cameroon 90,000. By 1988 the figure for Ghana had fallen to 240,000 and that for Nigeria to 120,000. Meanwhile there had been dramatic growth to 720,000 tons in Côte d'Ivoire, and a modest rise to 130,000 tons in Cameroon. Failure to replace old and diseased trees in Ghana contrasted with a massive replanting programme in Côte d'Ivoire, and this goes far to explain the contrasting general economic trends in the two countries in the 1970s. A thriving cocoa sector helped to maintain higher incomes in many other sectors of the economy in Côte d'Ivoire than in most African countries. However, by the late 1980s the boom there had passed its peak, while there was some revival of cocoa production and exports in Ghana.

Cotton ranks third among the agricultural exports of tropical Africa, but although it is grown by more people than either coffee or cocoa, its value is much lower – $600 million in 1986. It thrives in relatively dry climates, and can be grown in some parts of almost every country. However, it often must compete with food crops for both land and labour during the annual growing season, so each farmer plants only a little. It really provides a pitifully small income, but in areas where perennials will not grow it is often better than any alternative.

Production in 1988, at 900,000 tons of lint, was no higher than in 1978, and only a little higher than in 1968. Sudan is the leading producer, and there two periods of expansion since the mid 1960s have each been followed by contraction, as either yields have fallen or a shift to food crops has been considered necessary on the Gezira and other irrigation schemes partly managed by the state. Production has sagged in Tanzania, and has slumped in Uganda, Mozambique and Nigeria; but meanwhile it expanded rapidly in the 1970s in Zimbabwe, in Mali, and in the north of Côte d'Ivoire, and then in Benin in the 1980s.

Groundnuts became the chief export crop in Senegal and in northern Nigeria early in this century. The crop has not virtually disappeared, as crude export figures might suggest, for it now supplies local oil mills; and it remains the chief source of cash income for many farm families. But over the past twenty years production has fallen by one-third in Senegal and by half in Nigeria. Groundnuts continue to provide the main export, as well as the main source of cash income in The Gambia, but production has remained static there for twenty years, despite population growth. The crop became important in Sudan in the late 1960s, as a form of diversification from cotton, but there too production fell sharply in the 1980s through a combination of reduced yields and reduced plantings to make way for sorghum.

In 1960 palm oil was still one of the five main agricultural exports from tropical Africa, which then accounted for three-quarters of world production. By 1986 Africa accounted for less than 20 per cent of the total, and exports had almost ceased except for some new large-scale plantations in Côte d'Ivoire. Local sales still bring some income to small-scale farmers in both Zaïre and Nigeria, but by the mid 1980s Nigeria was importing over 150,000 tons a year from Malaysia.

For several small-farm cash crops grown in more limited parts of Africa, such as pyrethrum and cashew nuts in Kenya and Tanzania, recent years have brought declining production. Tobacco also has not expanded as rapidly as was at one time hoped, perhaps fortunately in world health terms.

The greatest success story over the past thirty years has been provided by tea, once considered as only a plantation crop, but now grown in Africa mainly on small farms. Total production has risen from only 50,000 tons around 1960, and 120,000 tons around 1970, to 270,000 tons in 1988. But this success is largely confined to one country, for Kenya now accounts for more than half the total African production. Planting very small patches of land with tea has brought a much improved income to many families in parts of highland Kenya, but this is something that cannot be replicated over many other parts of Africa.

Poverty in rural Africa has intensified in the 1980s partly because per capita export crop production, as well as food crop production, has fallen, and partly because world prices have fallen. Coffee prices have fallen persistently over the past twenty years apart from a boom in the late 1970s and a brief rally in 1986. In the case of groundnuts, the fall has been even more persistent. For tea there was a sharp price rise in 1984, but the trend since then has been downwards. Similarly, sagging cocoa prices have led Côte d'Ivoire to abandon plans for expanding production there to a million tons a year, and have hindered Ghana's efforts at revival. These falling prices reflect a low demand for many of these commodities, and this casts doubt upon the World Bank view that increased crop exports can form the basis of economic recovery in most African countries. They would be competing against one another in very restricted markets, while facing ever-increasing competition from other countries such as Brazil and Malaysia.

Low world market prices provide a large part of the explanation for stagnant or falling cash crop production, but in some countries the policies of crop marketing boards have also contributed (Bates 1981). In Ghana over 70 per cent of the price received by the Cocoa Marketing Board was at one stage passed on to the growers, but by 1979 this had fallen to 30 per cent. Many such bodies have been accused of both gross inefficiency and corruption, and in several countries, including Nigeria, crop marketing was handed over to private enterprise in the 1980s. The situation is not identical everywhere, of course, and relatively efficient organizations have given better services, and a larger share of the export price, to coffee and cocoa growers in Côte d'Ivoire, and especially to tea growers in Kenya.

A more fundamental constraint on expansion of cash crop production is shortage of land in the environmentally favourable areas. As population rises, more and more land is required for food crops. In this situation, increased production of cash crops must depend on raising the yield from each hectare of both food and cash crops.

Large-scale agriculture

A tiny fraction of all the land in tropical Africa, but a higher proportion in certain countries such as Kenya and especially Zimbabwe, is under some form of large-scale cultivation, wholly commercialized and providing wage employment for poor people. There are widely differing views about whether these large farms and plantations are contributing to African poverty or helping to relieve it.

These enterprises often occupy high-quality land, are sometimes foreign-owned, and always pay very low wages to most of their workers, and they are much criticized on all these counts. It does not follow, of course, that the people of Africa would be better off if none of these enterprises existed. They do contribute to the continent's food supply and export earnings, and their workers might not be able to obtain higher incomes in any other way.

A distinction should be made between the large mixed farms of the Kenya highlands, Zambia and Zimbabwe, originally established by individual European settlers, and plantations, scattered over many more countries, that were generally established by foreign companies. The former aimed to reproduce the farming economy of parts of Britain, while the latter were designed for the monoculture of tropical crops.

Many of the large mixed farms, especially in Kenya, have already been subdivided for settlement schemes to meet the needs of families who have access to very little land. This process will have to continue as pressures build up further, as Diana Hunt (1984) has well argued for Kenya, and it can lead to more intensive use of the land and hence higher crop yields. Other large farms have been bought outright by the local élite, or by co-operative groups, sometimes bringing no great change to the farming system. Where farms of over 1,000 hectares are each owned by one family, in a country in which the majority have holdings of less than 5 hectares, this clearly is a foundation for gross inequality. There is therefore likely to be increasing pressure for land reform, with a maximum permitted size of holding, not only in Kenya but also in Zimbabwe and even in Zambia.

The plantations present a very diverse picture. Those producing tea in Kenya provided the basis for the highly successful smallholder tea development mentioned above. Those producing sisal in Tanzania, on very much poorer land, have largely been abandoned as competition from synthetics has brought down world prices for this fibre. Some large plantations are still owned by private companies based in Europe, but many have been established since independence by governments, as in Côte d'Ivoire. In contrast to the large individually-owned farms, the question of inequality does not arise, but it remains very uncertain whether expansion of plantation agriculture would be an efficient way of using land and reducing poverty in Africa.

The largest number of new plantations established in the past thirty years have been intended to satisfy the local demand for sugar, and these have made a small but useful contribution to development in almost half the countries of tropical Africa. In many cases it has been an effective form of import substitution. However, the largest of all the new sugar schemes, at

Kenana in Sudan, has proved far more costly than anticipated. This scheme was intended to be expanded sufficiently to provide a large surplus for export to the Middle East. As world sugar prices have fallen while the cost of equipment has risen, it is clear that Sudan has added to its debt burden in order to produce a commodity that could be obtained more cheaply from overseas.

Livestock rearing

Livestock provide an important source of food, and were therefore mentioned in the last chapter, but they are not kept in Africa entirely for that purpose. Some groups use cattle for ploughing or camels as beasts of burden, for example. In many societies cattle are the form in which wealth or capital is customarily held; and brideprice still commonly involves a transfer of cattle. These are economic motives for keeping livestock just as surely as milk or meat production, but they are often regarded by outsiders as 'unproductive' uses of the animals. Certainly cattle do sometimes assume great social, as well as economic, significance for their owners, as among the Dinka of southern Sudan.

The existence of some essentially pastoralist groups was noted in the last chapter, especially because some of these have suffered severe famine in recent years. In Mauritania and in Somalia pastoralists may constitute a majority of the rural population, but over tropical Africa as a whole they form only a small minority, and do not even own most of the livestock. Far larger numbers of cattle, goats and sheep are kept by people who are primarily cultivators. However, they are often not at all closely integrated into the farming system. Most communities do not use their cattle for ploughing, and only a few apply manure systematically to their fields. In some areas where manuring has been customary it is now decreasing, as ever more cow dung is used as fuel. Highland Ethiopia is one area where this is happening, with disastrous results for soil fertility. Since most cultivators cannot afford fertilizers, the case for making more effective use of manure in many parts of Africa is very strong. At the same time more use might be made of cattle to meet such basic needs as local transport: the ox cart is rare in tropical Africa.

There are large tracts of Africa where cattle cannot be kept because of the presence of the tsetse fly, which transmits the fatal disease trypanosomiasis. However, it is not obvious that most people living in such areas are poorer than those living elsewhere. Great efforts have been made to clear large areas of tsetse fly; but it is possible that greater benefits would result from increasing the economic return from cattle where they are already present in large numbers, rather than from extending the areas over which they can be kept. The need for tsetse control is greatest where the fly threatens to spread into areas occupied by people who now keep cattle and wish to continue doing so.

In purely economic terms it is also possible that much benefit would result from some diversion of attention from cattle to sheep, goats, pigs and poultry, both as food items for farm families and as sources of cash income. Goats are already extremely widespread in tropical Africa, but have received far less attention from governments than cattle: pigs are at present found only in a few areas. In various parts of Africa there are taboos on the eating of eggs, but these are now tending to break down as their nutritional value is recognized. Poultry farming is becoming a popular part-time activity of some wealthy people, notably on the fringes of many Nigerian cities: but a few chickens are also kept by many poor rural dwellers, and up-grading these could be one very appropriate response to increasing pressures on land in many areas.

The dilemma presented by the poverty of the predominantly pastoral people of course remains. Some African environments will support no form of livelihood other than low-density nomadic livestock rearing. This is increasingly recognized, but neither governments nor international agencies know how poverty can be significantly reduced in such situations.

Fisheries

Fisheries might also have been considered in the chapter on food, for fish is an extremely valuable source of protein, and a very useful complement to predominantly starchy diets. They are discussed here instead mainly because fish are very largely caught to provide a source of cash income rather than as a source of food for those catching them. Fishing and trading in fish provide a livelihood for at least a million people living beside Africa's coasts, lakes and rivers.

There is some large-scale fishing off both the Atlantic and Indian Ocean coasts, but this takes place from the major ports and so does not form part of the rural economy. Some employment is provided by this activity, but far more people are occupied in small-scale fishing from canoes in inshore waters, in coastal lagoons, in lakes and in rivers. From the lakes of East Africa smoked fish are moved by self-employed traders to markets throughout the region. Many of them cover remarkable distances by bicycle. Fishing is an activity that has expanded at least in line with population growth, and there is scope in some areas for even more rapid expansion, especially if more canoes can be fitted with outboard motors. There are, of course, other areas where overfishing has already begun to deplete the stocks of fish, so policy on fisheries must differ from place to place.

Fuelwood

Depletion of resources is being experienced much more widely across Africa in respect of fuelwood, in ways that profoundly affect the poor (Leach and Mearns 1988, Munslow 1988). Some areas of rain forest remain almost untouched in Zaïre, Congo and Gabon, and there is some large-scale timber extraction in these countries and in the coastal zone of West Africa: but far larger areas are covered with drier forest or with savanna woodland, and some of these are being used ever more intensively as sources of building poles and fuelwood.

Gathering of fuelwood takes place on a subsistence basis to a far larger extent than fishing. It is one of the regular activities of most rural households, often involving a long walk with a very heavy load. It seems to be a task for women and children, rather than men, almost everywhere. Increasing pressure of population on the land is lengthening the distances over which fuel has to be carried, while rising school attendance has meant that children are less often available for the task. Where supplies are really scarce, fewer cooked meals are prepared and impure well water is less often boiled before use. In areas such as highland Ethiopia, fires can less often be lit to keep out the cold.

Even some rural families must now buy fuelwood in local markets, while towns and cities have to be supplied with wood or charcoal over distances of up to 100 km. In this case, wood cutting and charcoal making provide a useful source of income for rural families. The process is, of course, not sustainable unless extensive replanting is undertaken, and Paul Harrison (1987) reports encouraging developments in this field from several parts of Africa. He also stresses the potential for fuel-saving through improved types of cooking stove which can be produced very cheaply by local enterprises.

Twenty years ago it was widely assumed that either electricity or kerosene would gradually take the place of fuelwood in all towns and many rural areas: but sharp rises in oil prices have made kerosene far more expensive, while few rural dwellers in Africa can afford to make any use of electricity even if a supply is within reach.

Other rural activities

As was noted earlier, many people in rural Africa build their own houses and make most of their own furniture and utensils, as well as growing their own food. But in many communities there are some specialists in such activities, who gain some cash income from them even if not on a full-time basis. The building of houses and even storage barns is becoming more commercialized, while many villages have one or two small furniture-making enterprises.

Some traditional crafts of rural Africa, such as pottery and basket-weaving, and various forms of metal-working, suffered greatly from the spread of imported manufactured goods early in this century. Many survived, however, and have expanded along with population numbers, especially in the more remote areas or where quality was sufficient to make them competitive with factory products. Income from such crafts is especially important in much of the West African Sahel, where the long dry season means that little work can be done in the fields for some months each year. Improved communications have allowed many craft goods made in Sokoto and Borno States of Nigeria to find markets far away in the south of the country.

Trade tends to be concentrated in towns and cities, but periodic rural markets are a feature of many parts of Africa, and small shops are found in every village. Trading is a part-time activity for many people, mainly men in some areas and mainly women in others, but for some people buying local produce and selling goods from the cities or from overseas provide the main source of income. The fortunes of these traders is clearly very dependent on the condition of the rural economy in general, which means that few have prospered in the 1980s. Sadly, one exception is provided by those merchants in countries such as Sudan who were able to take advantage of famine conditions to sell hoarded grain at exorbitant prices. Another is provided by those who have made a good living out of smuggling coffee, gold, diamonds and many imported goods across the thousands of kilometres of unmarked national boundaries. The largest profits have gone to masterminds based in the cities, but many rural dwellers have participated in a small way.

Another element in the rural economy is employment by the state in activities ranging from primary schools to the police. Until the 1980s such employment was increasing rapidly, especially in countries such as Tanzania whose political system involved a large role for the state, with a particular emphasis on the rural areas. But now there have been huge cutbacks almost everywhere. In Zaïre, for example, many teachers have lost their jobs, in some cases after many months of working without being paid. As well as being disastrous for the individuals, these cutbacks have repercussions throughout the local economy.

However, it should be stressed that employees working for wages are far outnumbered almost everywhere by people who work on their own account, and primarily as farmers. The 1978 census of Tanzania, for example, recorded 234,000 rural dwellers in permanent employment, 148,000 in temporary employment, and 6·4 million working on their own account or in family enterprise. Similarly, it recorded 6·3 million men and women engaged in farming or fishing, compared with only 460,000 primarily engaged in non-agricultural work. Census data for rural dwellers in Ghana indicate a similar picture.

Remittances

One further ingredient in many rural economies is provided by the remittances sent home by those who have migrated to the cities. Most such migrants feel some obligation to support the members of their families who have remained in the rural areas, and surveys in several cities have indicated that the majority do make remittances on a regular basis. In many rural families sending one or two sons or daughters to find work in the city forms part of a survival strategy. They may have sacrificed to pay school fees as a long-term investment, and some financial return on that investment is expected. In this way rural-based families can each secure a small share of the comparative riches that the cities are thought to offer.

This pattern is by no means unique to Africa, but it does seem to be more widespread in many parts of Africa than anywhere else in the world, involving more than half of all families in some localities, such as some within western Kenya or northern Ghana. In most parts of both South East Asia and Latin America far more rural-urban migrants appear to lose contact with their home areas within a few years.

Very little is known about the amounts of money or goods that are sent or taken to the rural areas, but surveys in Nairobi suggest that more than 10 per cent of all urban earnings may be involved there. In so far as city populations are growing rapidly, it might be expected that remittances in aggregate would be increasing, but a counterbalancing factor is that migrants are accounting for a gradually decreasing share of these city populations. Remittances are certainly not sent to the same extent by the second generation who were born in the city, even when they have parents who have returned to a rural area. Furthermore, the size of the flows will no doubt have been reduced in the 1980s by the fall in real wages in most cities.

In the rural areas of both Malawi and Mozambique the flow of remittances from migrants working in South Africa has been much reduced, although it continues to be of great importance in Botswana and absolutely crucial in Lesotho. In West Africa many rural communities in the Sahel depend to some extent on funds sent across national boundaries, notably from workers in Côte d'Ivoire to their homes in Burkina Faso. There are even some intercontinental flows, such as from migrant workers in France to their home communities in Senegal and Mali, or from Saudi Arabia to Sudan and Somalia. The remittances are minute in relation to the Saudi or the French economy, but they can be of vital importance to the economy of a Sudanese or a Sahelian village.

It would be helpful to know more about the uses to which the remittances are put. Some funds go into house-building, in part for the long-term benefit of the sender. Some are used for the family's day-to-day purchases, for medical expenses or for school fees. The few surveys that have been done do not indicate that a large proportion of the funds remitted is invested in agriculture or in other economic activities. Investment in equipment or fertilizers, or in something such as on-farm storage facilities, would often be very worthwhile, but most rural families have other even more pressing and immediate needs.

Without any doubt, the uses made of remittances will differ greatly from place to place and from one family to another. An enquiry in one locality might reveal some households spending part of what they see as 'extra' money on beer and cigarettes, while others are dependent on this money to buy staple food in the hungry season while waiting for the next harvest. However, these remittances do always play some small part in relieving rural poverty.

Conclusions

Are most rural dwellers in tropical Africa today better or worse off than they, or their parents, were twenty years ago? In parts of Côte d'Ivoire, Cameroon, Kenya and Zimbabwe, many are considerably better off. In parts of Ethiopia, Uganda and Mozambique, most are worse off in almost every way. Often the situation is less clear-cut. In much of Tanzania people have less cash to spend now, but do have better access to water supplies, health care and schools, the mass villagization campaign of the 1970s having contributed to both sets of changes.

Everywhere some individuals have become destitute, while a few have enriched themselves. In general, disparities have probably increased, most notably in pastoral and semi-pastoral societies where some families have enlarged their flocks and herds with animals bought at very low prices from those forced by famine into distress sales. But for the great majority the past twenty years have brought very little change in material well-being. Families are generally larger, as infant and child mortality has been reduced, and far more children are now attending school; but most rural households are producing and consuming much the same today as they were in the late 1960s.

In every country, but perhaps most obviously in Nigeria in the 1970s, some rural dwellers have increased their incomes by moving to the cities. At the peak of the oil boom in Nigeria such a move paid dividends far more often than not, although some of the gains will now have been lost. What of those left behind? Out-migration has clearly relieved pressure on the land in some areas, but in others the loss of young and energetic labour has weakened the local economy, though remittances provide some compensation for the families involved. The urban economy itself is the subject of the next chapter.

9
Urban poverty

There is still far more rural poverty than urban poverty in tropical Africa, since 70 to 75 per cent of the population lives in a rural environment and average incomes are higher in the cities. But urban poverty is increasing at a faster rate, since the population of the cities is rising by 5 to 7 per cent a year, compared with an average of 2 per cent in the rural areas, and since in many cities incomes are falling in real terms. Furthermore, people are more aware of poverty in the cities as affluence is visible close by. Even those who might regard themselves as prosperous in most rural areas will tend to consider that they are poor in a city where other people have incomes ten times higher.

The cities and towns (Map 5.2) are very diverse in origin (O'Connor 1983). Some of the indigenous cities represented spatial concentrations of wealth in precolonial societies, but at all times most people living within their walls were poor; and at the start of this century they were all cities of the poor by global standards. Some of the colonial cities then being established became even more extreme concentrations of affluence, but the rich expatriates were always outnumbered by local people, most of whom were very poor. Since independence the distinctions between these different types of city, and also between the different sections of 'dual' cities such as Kano or Khartoum-Omdurman, have tended to become blurred, and some very similar processes are now taking place almost everywhere.

The much faster population growth in the cities is largely due to massive rural-urban migration. This may have slowed somewhat in the 1980s, and return urban-rural migration may have increased, but the rate of net movement from the countryside to the cities over the thirty years between 1960 and 1990 was certainly higher than in any other part of the world. Basically, therefore, a relatively prosperous small urban population has been joined by poorer former rural dwellers moving in for a share of what the cities can offer. Many of the migrants are coming to join relatives already in towns, and in this case they may literally take a share of the city dwellers' income (and housing). This process clearly lowers per capita income, and usually per capita provision of services and so on, in the cities, even though it is not the very poorest from the rural areas who have migrated.

In some places the migrants have in fact included the very poorest, where famine has driven destitute rural dwellers to the cities in search of food – or of the means to acquire it. This happened in the mid 1980s throughout the Sahel, from Mauritania in the extreme west to Sudan in the east. The population of Nouakchott, the new capital of Mauritania, doubled within a year as destitute pastoralists flooded in. Thousands trekked to Khartoum-Omdurman from western Sudan, while some of the refugees from Ethiopia swelled the populations of towns in eastern Sudan.

Of course, many migrants manage to find work in the cities, and succeed in their goal of becoming less poor than they were in the rural areas. But this process usually takes time, so that meanwhile poverty has been brought into the city; and many secure only an income well below the previous urban average. Competition for jobs, and for opportunities as self-employed workers, has lowered average earnings in almost every African city. Rarely has the minimum wage rate kept place with inflation, while more and more people fail to rise above the minimum rate – if indeed it is enforced.

Gender is a significant element in this situation in cities such as Nairobi, Dar es Salaam and Lusaka, where the proportion of female migrants has been rising. In some cases a wife, perhaps with children, has been coming in to share one urban income. More often the women also seek incomes in the city, but either on a part-time basis or with lower than average male earnings even for very full-time activity. It is arguable that female migration has tended to intensify poverty wherever women, who were very fully occupied doing the bulk of the work on farms, move into cities which offer poorer opportunities to them than to men.

The emphasis so far has been on incomes, but poverty is also affected by expenditures. A given cash income that might be considered adequate in a rural area where people are growing their own food and maintaining their own houses, might be grossly inadequate in a city where accommodation has to be rented and food has to be bought. More and more city families now grow some of their own food wherever they can find a scrap of land, but this has to be supplemented in the market, where prices are normally higher than in rural markets. Fuel is another expense for most city-dwellers whereas it is often available free in the countryside, while water supplies may also require a cash payment. Transport from home to work is a further daily expense for many people, though some walk remarkably long distances. All these are essential expenditures: in addition there are far more opportunities for spending on non-essentials in urban than in rural areas, and people may become poor as a result of this. Even a family with a reasonable income may live in poverty if one member spends a large proportion of it on drink, for instance.

Urban poverty in Africa in the past has been very effectively documented and discussed by John Iliffe (1987). This chapter will consider, rather more superficially, the situation today. Some greater detail for one country may be found in a recent symposium volume on Nigeria (Makinwa and Ozo 1987).

Gaining a livelihood in the city

The economy of most African cities is based primarily on administration and trade, and only secondarily on manufacturing. The urban poor, therefore, are more often clerks or hawkers than factory workers. However, from the perspective of the urban dweller seeking a livelihood, the distinction between *sectors* of the urban economy in these terms is less significant than differentiation based on *scale* of organization. Reference is often made in the literature to 'formal' and 'informal' sectors (ILO 1972, Sandbrook 1982), but since the so-called informal sector may have its own formality, the simpler terms 'large-scale' and 'small-scale' may be preferable. And it is helpful to think also in terms of an intermediate sector rather than to be satisfied with a crude dichotomy.

The large-scale sector might be taken to include all forms of government activity, including education, health care and military, along with private firms, foreign and local, employing more than a given number of people, say ten or twenty. For someone seeking a job either as a clerk or as a cleaner, working for a large-scale employer is what matters, rather than whether it is public or private, a hospital or a factory. The small-scale sector might be taken to include all forms of self-employment, and perhaps enterprises with only one or two employees or apprentices. Whether the self-employment is shoe-making or just shoe-shining, it is a very different type of livelihood from work in a large organization.

In such fields as health care and finance the distinction between large- and small-scale enterprises is very clear. There is very little interaction between modern hospitals and traditional healers; and a bank is very different from the young man offering local currency for dollars at double the official rate. In such fields as retail trade there have always been small shops occupying an intermediate position between the international trading firms and the self-employed market traders. One field in which an intermediate sector has become very evident in recent years is road transport, as individuals have invested in two or three minibuses to compete with inadequate municipal bus services.

During the colonial period the small-scale sector was almost non-existent in cities such as Harare (then Salisbury) and very small even in Nairobi, whereas it formed the whole basis of the urban economy in Ibadan and various other Nigerian cities. This contrast has now been much reduced as large-scale activity has expanded in Ibadan and other indigenous cities while a small-scale sector has rapidly grown in the cities of colonial origin: but some important variations from place to place still remain. One specific contrast relates to the earning opportunities for women. The very extensive small-scale trade of the cities of southern Nigeria, Ghana and Côte d'Ivoire is largely dominated by women, whereas their role is far smaller in market trade in Tanzania, Zambia and Zimbabwe.

Certain assumptions commonly made about the small-scale sector in African cities should perhaps be challenged. One is that it can almost be equated with the poor, incomes being consistently lower than in the large-scale sector. In fact there is a large and increasing overlap between the two, though as some small businesses thrive they do tend to move into the intermediate sector. Another is that it is the sector of last resort, for those who cannot find work in the large-scale sector. In fact many choose it in preference, and some who have worked in large enterprises decide to use skills and experience that they have gained to set up on their own. A third assumption is that the small-scale sector is characterized by ease of entry. In fact it is very hard to break into some such activities, including some forms of crime, unless you are from the right group or have the right contacts. Waiting at the factory gate with a hundred others may be far easier.

The assumption that most small-scale activity was either illegal or antisocial has long been challenged, but this has led some to ignore the fact that in every city some people *are* gaining their livelihood through criminal activities. An abundance of burglars and pickpockets is in part a direct result of poverty, though no doubt most could have found alternative occupations. It is sometimes suggested that such crime helps to redistribute wealth from rich to poor, but all too often those who suffer loss are those who had least – those who could not afford a padlock for their door, or who did not have a door. While most thieves appear to be male, illicit brewing of alcoholic drinks is a female-dominated activity in many cities. Often this is combined with prostitution, but poverty drives many more women to turn to this as a source of income. Almost incredibly, it continues to be widespread even in cities such as Nairobi and Lusaka where tests have shown 90 per cent of prostitutes to be HIV-positive and almost certain to die of AIDS.

The small-scale sector might also be taken to include domestic service. Disparities between rich and poor in most African cities are such that at least

10 per cent of households can afford to employ one or two domestic servants. This means that 5 to 10 per cent of the working population are gaining a livelihood in this way, fairly evenly divided between men and women. Domestic wage employment is most extensive in cities with large expatriate populations, for the local élite often depend on the unpaid services of members of their extended families; but as board and lodging is provided, this may still constitute a means of livelihood for poor people.

The notion of a privileged few in regular wage employment and a vast mass of poor people in 'the informal sector' or 'petty commodity production' must be discarded. It is a picture of what perhaps might have been if powerful trade unions had been established, or if African countries had remained dominated by a few large foreign companies. In fact in most cities the majority of households have at least one member employed in a large-sale or intermediate-scale enterprise, and many of these are in no way privileged (Sandbrook 1982). Incomes for most employees are extremely low by international standards, and so also is job security. National and city governments took on more and more staff in the 1960s and 1970s, but they have often had to lay some off in the 1980s. Wage rates have fallen far behind inflation, and at times there is no money in the state coffers to pay the wages. The nationalization of foreign firms may have reduced the outflow of profits overseas, but it has rarely led to a real increase in wages for the workers. Where factories are operating far below capacity the result has been somewhat fewer employees and reduced pay for the majority who remain on the payroll.

The picture has, of course, not been uniform across all tropical Africa. In Uganda, for example, the large-scale sector partially collapsed in the 1970s under the Amin regime. Even the intermediate sector was badly hit, since much of that had been run by the Asians whom Amin expelled. The illegal *magendo* economy which arose instead is not easily categorized, since it ranges from individuals fending for themselves to highly organized large-scale coffee smuggling. It has enabled a few people to get rich very quickly, but it has also led many middle-income former employees, and some who have remained in government employment, to become poor.

In Nigeria the story has been very different. The creation of a federal structure of first twelve, and then nineteen, states led to a great expansion of public employment, paid for by oil revenues. Increased oil prices brought a further boom to the economy in both the early and late 1970s, when both public and private wage employment increased further. Wages were higher than in neighbouring countries, drawing in many labour migrants. All this stimulated much small-scale enterprise also in most Nigerian cities. While some got hurt in the rough and tumble of Lagos, Port Harcourt and Kano, many people moved out of extreme poverty and on to a rapidly rising income. However, the fall in oil prices in the 1980s, which has provided some relief to most African countries, has brought a major setback for Nigeria. The resulting massive cutbacks in public expenditure have had an immediate and substantial impact on large-scale wage employment, and reduced the incomes of many urban households.

The labour force in every city in the world includes some people who are underemployed and some who are totally unemployed, but in poor countries with no form of social security the extent of unemployment is limited by the fact that households with no form of income could not survive. Those who are totally unemployed in African cities are mainly school-leavers who are supported by their families while they seek work, and these families are not usually the poorest. Some who might be designated unemployed are wives who are actually much occupied with domestic tasks, but who would like to supplement the family income or to have a separate income of their own. In many cases these domestic tasks include cultivation of some of the family's food supply. If the main breadwinner of a household loses a job, then he or she will normally find some other source of income, however unsatisfactory, or perhaps return to a rural home.

The unsatisfactory source of income may well constitute underemployment in the sense that it is not making very productive use of people's time. Some people in African cities work extremely hard for long hours, and yet have very low incomes: clearly they are being exploited, either by another individual or by the system in which they find themselves. Such people can in no way be seen as underemployed. But others work either much less hard or for much shorter hours – sometimes from choice, sometimes not. One example is provided by those who find only intermittent work as casual labour, particularly on building sites. Another is provided by the petty traders who may sit for many hours with their goods, but who attract only ten or a dozen customers each day.

There is widespread poverty in African cities – partly because people are not sufficiently rewarded for the work that they do, so that a primary school teacher, for example, earns less than one-tenth of what she or he would earn for essentially the same work (with far better conditions) in Britain – and partly because there is not sufficient productive work for them to do. The needs are there, both for goods and for services, both within the cities and in the rural areas that these should be serving, but the means to pay people to provide the goods and services are not.

The impact of recession, debt and structural adjustment

In many ways the harsh economic conditions of the 1980s have been felt even more acutely in the cities than in the rural areas. Zambia is exceptional in tropical Africa both in having a population that is almost 50 per cent urban, and in having several urban centres with economies based primarily on mining. A huge fall in copper prices has had a disastrous impact on these towns, and also less directly on Lusaka, the capital city. Zambia borrowed funds from overseas in the hope of repaying when copper prices rose again, and is now among the most heavily indebted African countries; but debt, discussed in Chapter 12, has affected almost every country, as have the austerity and structural adjustment programmes adopted in efforts to overcome the problem.

Manufacturing is a subsidiary element in the economy of most African cities, and this has been affected, indeed devastated, even more than agriculture by the recession, and especially by the need to cut imports. Shortages of fuel, raw materials and spare parts have caused factories throughout the continent to operate far below capacity, and production of many manufactured goods was lower in 1989 than in 1980. Devaluations which have brought some assistance to export agriculture have increased the costs of industries catering almost entirely to local markets but heavily reliant on imports. High interest rates have ruled out the type of borrowing from overseas which provided capital for industrial expansion in the 1960s; and multinational corporations have in general been disinvesting in Africa in the 1980s.

Cuts in government spending have also often affected the cities more than the rural areas, partly because such spending has been heavily concentrated there. City hospitals reliant on the government health budget naturally feel the impact more directly than traditional healers in remote rural areas. The breakdown of electricity supplies is of more concern to urban residents and enterprises than to most in rural areas: and it is only in the cities that the collapse of refuse disposal services is a burning issue. Similarly, it is in the cities that mass protests at government cutbacks, and at the IMF's insistence on these, have occurred, notably in response to the withdrawal of subsidies on basic foods in Sudan and in Zambia.

The consequences of urban poverty

The most visible consequence of poverty is perhaps the housing that occupies the greater part of most cities, and that is considered in the next section. Less visible, but equally serious, are the implications for other elements in the standard of living. Various expenditure surveys show that poor urban dwellers spend most of their income on food, yet in spite of this diets are deficient in both quality and quantity. While famines have not struck cities in the way they have struck some rural areas, and while cases of starvation are rare, many people are frequently hungry, and malnutrition is widespread especially among children.

In contrast to most rural areas, a piped supply of clean water is available in most urban neighbourhoods; but many people cannot afford a connection to their homes, and some communities on city fringes are dependent on polluted wells and streams. Electricity is also available, but most cannot afford to use it for anything other than lighting, and many not even for that. The proportion of households with cars varies considerably, from over 5 per cent in Harare and some Nigerian cities, to well under 2 per cent in Dar es Salaam and Addis Ababa; but this still leaves the vast majority almost everywhere using public transport or a bicycle if they can afford it or walking if they cannot. At rush hours, buses and minibuses must be tightly packed if they are to operate cheaply enough for most people to use them.

In each of these respects conditions were improving in most African cities in the 1960s and early 1970s, but have been rapidly deteriorating since then (Stren and White 1989). Not only the absolute number but also the proportion going to bed hungry has been increasing. As the cities have expanded, the proportion without access to a pure water supply has increased. And ever more people are having to walk ever longer distances to work.

Housing for the urban poor

In rural Africa most people live in a house, however rudimentary it may be. In urban Africa most people do not. Nor do many live in blocks of flats. The majority of urban households live in just one room in a single-storey building, with other households occupying the adjacent rooms. All the households normally share the use of some place for cooking and some type of toilet facility, usually a pit latrine. These buildings are generally owned by private individuals, who may themselves occupy one or two of the rooms. Most of these owners have only one such property, and many are just as poor as their tenants: in most cases they have simply been in the city much longer, or were even born there. A class of rich landlords has not yet emerged in most African cities.

The situation whereby at least three-quarters of households rent their accommodation prevails in nearly all the cities of tropical Africa (Amis and Lloyd 1990). The main exceptions are some of the old indigenous cities of Nigeria, where a much larger proportion of the population are urban-born and live in long-established family compounds. The high proportion renting in most cities is due partly to the fact that they simply could not afford to buy or to build a dwelling, and have no access to any facility for obtaining a mortgage loan. But it is also related to the fact that most are of rural origin, do not strongly identify with the city, and intend to return to their home areas at some stage. Indeed, many are saving in order to build a house in their rural home, and some have one half built there already.

The amount of rent that people must pay for their room varies considerably from city to city, and between one neighbourhood and another. Almost everywhere rents are higher nearer the city centre than on the fringes, where crude shacks have sometimes been erected by farmers keen to supplement their crop income but not expecting huge returns. Rents rose sharply in Nigerian cities during the oil boom, but in Ghana they have been tightly controlled and rarely account for more than 20 per cent of household expenditure. This control has discouraged new building, leading to ever greater overcrowding.

Occasionally the one room is occupied by only a single individual, though even when people are in town on their own they more often share with someone else to save on rent. Much more often the room is occupied by a family of four, five or six people. Most couples in African cities aim to have at least six children, and often it is only after they have had two that they consider taking up two rooms. Before they have children, and even afterwards, they are very likely to have a brother, sister, niece or nephew living with them. Indeed, by no means all the poor are either owners or renters, for in every city there are always many recent arrivals who are lodging with relatives or even quite distant kinsfolk, until they can find a place of their own.

This practice of sharing accommodation, however crowded it may be, helps to explain the lack of large numbers in most African cities with no roof over their heads. There is no equivalent to the tens of thousands of pavement dwellers in Calcutta and Bombay, though in many cities there are a few thousand living in makeshift shelters on patches of waste ground – people with no kin in the city or whose kinsfolk have thrown them out. The main exception to this generalization is the refugee situation, when large numbers suddenly flee to the cities from drought or from war. When they are internal refugees no international body is responsible for providing shelter for them, and often they have to fend for themselves. In the late 1980s, for example, there were large tracts on the edge of Khartoum occupied by people who had fled from the fighting in southern Sudan – tracts which were inundated by floods in August 1988.

Except in such circumstances, 'squatter settlement' in the usual sense of the term is not very common in Africa today. In countries such as Nigeria,

Ghana and Côte d'Ivoire it has never been extensive, as a combination of kinsfolk and the private legal housing market have coped with even the rapid influx of the 1960s and 1970s. In the colonial cities of eastern Africa more people arrived at that time without finding relatives, and the private housing market was more poorly developed, so much squatting did take place in cities such as Nairobi and Lusaka. Now suitable land is harder to find there, and more alternatives are available for those needing shelter in the city. Squatting in the sense of occupying a patch of land illegally and building one's own dwelling on it continued to be a widespread practice in both Kinshasa and Dar es Salaam through the 1970s; but even there it is now more common either to build partly for renting out or to be one of the renters, and as land is taken up further from the city centre the process becomes semi-legal in that local chiefs have often given their approval (for a fee).

This brings us to the question of the role of the state in the housing of the urban poor. In many West African cities its role has always been very slight, government housing being confined to some of high quality for colonial officials and their local successors, and quarters for groups such as the police. The main exception is Abidjan, in Côte d'Ivoire, where the booming economy in the 1970s permitted the state to construct more than 50,000 rental housing units during that decade. In East African cities much more was done by the state during the colonial period, partly in order to exercise greater control. In Harare (then Salisbury), the urban poor were almost all supposed to be male adults and to live in government hostels. In Nairobi several city council housing estates were built, and this practice continued for a while after independence though the supply soon began to fall well short of the demand. The state also played a negative role there by demolishing squatter housing that some of the poor built for themselves in the 1960s (Hake 1977), often brutally and with no alternative provided.

Today, even in Nairobi, there is little bulldozing of spontaneous settlement, but also little government construction of housing for the poor. Instead, the Kenya state has aimed to assist a larger number of people by upgrading some of the more substantial former squatter settlements, and by a major site-and-service programme. This approach, also adopted in Dar es Salaam, Lusaka, Dakar and many other cities, involves the state demarcating plots, providing access roads, water pipes and sometimes sewerage, and in some cases building a shower and toilet on each plot. The plots are then allocated to people who will build a dwelling around this core, usually with some credit facility for the materials. Basically the state is doing what must be done on a large scale, leaving individuals to do what they are able to do for themselves.

The site-and-service approach has been criticized as failing to reach the really poor, and it is true that most plots are allocated to lower-middle-income people, who can build three or four room units. However, it is providing housing for many people who are far from affluent, while it is now generally also providing some housing for poor people in the form of the rooms which most of the official occupiers rent out in order to pay back their loans. These schemes alone cannot solve Africa's urban housing problem, but they should not be written off as a failure.

It is increasingly recognized that the state can do very little to assist with shelter for the poor in most African cities. It cannot afford to house them adequately, and is unwilling to build housing at standards so low that people can afford it. In many cases rents would have to be so low that they would not cover the cost of collecting them. Even if the resources were available, there should be no question of subsidized urban housing when there is no possibility of this for rural dwellers. Some self-financing site-and-service schemes continue to be established, some squatter upgrading continues to take place; but the main role of the state is now seen to be designating suitable areas for people to house themselves or to build rental housing, and hopefully providing some services such as piped water to those areas (Stren and White 1989).

The role of the state thus lies more in planning than in housing, but even planning is extremely difficult when it has to be planning for poverty. The international planning profession has little experience of planning neighbourhoods where rapidly increasing numbers of people with extremely low income can organize their own housing. There is no doubt whatever that the housing conditions for most poor people in African cities will continue to be appalling for the foreseeable future, and that the new housing for the extra millions will be no better than the old. Yet can planners really work on that assumption? Perhaps the one thing that makes the urban housing situation at present just tolerable is that most people can identify with, and perhaps eventually escape to, another 'home' in the countryside. Unfortunately, this may cease to be true as an ever-larger proportion of city-dwellers are urban born rather than migrants of rural origin.

City and countryside

Urban poverty has had a separate chapter, but as indicated at several points the rural–urban divide is far from sharp. The distinction between rural and urban *places* may be as clear as elsewhere in the world, but that between rural and urban *people* is far less clear than in regions such as Latin America or the Middle East. Many poor people spend part of their lives in the countryside and part in the city. Most urban dwellers were born in a rural area, and many hope to live there again, at least in retirement. Some spend part of each year in the city and part on the farm. Men in rural northern Nigeria may go to find work in Kano during the dry season; women in Nairobi may go to help on the family farm during the wet season.

In a country such as Zambia, perhaps a majority of poor families (and some richer ones) have a foot in each camp. Poverty leads families based in the rural areas to send one or two members to the city to appropriate a share of its perceived wealth. Poverty also leads families based in the cities to maintain a stake in their rural area of origin in case their means of support in the city should be lost. In Kenya the incentive to maintain such a stake in the country is particularly strong, both because there is some very productive land and because such land is increasingly scarce. Poverty, and the lack of any form of social security, is a major reason for those who cease work in Accra or Lagos or Kinshasa to retreat 'home' for their remaining years.

These urban–rural links cast some doubt on some aspects of the 'urban bias' thesis put forward by Michael Lipton (1977) in his cleverly-titled book *Why Poor People Stay Poor*. It is hard to accept for Africa the claim that there is a fundamental cleavage and conflict between 'the urban classes' and 'the rural classes'. If urban bias in these terms were as extreme and extensive as Lipton suggests, there would in fact be almost no such thing as urban poverty. The key element that must be added is spatial and social mobility.

Most African urban dwellers, including top decision-makers, retain deep roots in the countryside, and are fully aware of its needs. They are not wholly urban *people*, but they have themselves perceived urban *places* to offer the best opportunities, and have *chosen* to live in them. It is hardly surprising, therefore, if they consider them the best places for various forms of state and private investment which then concentrate opportunities there even further. Undoubtedly 'urban bias' in this form is intense throughout tropical Africa, contributing to a wide rural–urban gap in average income and welfare: but this gap in turn provides the main incentive for further massive rural-urban migration. And as Vali Jamal and John Weeks (1988) have shown, continuing in–migration, natural increase in the cities, and the recent decline in investment there, have all been such that the gap has narrowed in the 1980s in most African countries. Urban poverty therefore certainly does exist in Africa, on a massive and increasing scale: and while 'urban bias' is also still very widespread, it is most certainly only one factor among many causing poor people to stay poor in the rural areas of Africa.

10
Education and health

Education and health are both among the most basic human needs, and can be regarded as vital aspects of material well-being in the same way as food or housing. For every individual family in tropical Africa there are spending choices between these services and all types of goods, even though in some countries both primary education and basic health care are supposed to be free. Even where fees are not charged, families often cannot afford payments for books and uniforms, or for drugs, or the bribes that headteachers or medical staff may demand. Sending older children to school of course is costly in terms of the loss of their labour or their income.

Similar spending choices must be made by all governments, as well as by aid agencies and by the religious bodies still active in these fields in Africa. Ever since independence most African governments have chosen to spend very heavily on education, while spending very much less on health care. In 1987 education accounted for 24 per cent of all central government expenditure in Ghana, and for 23 per cent in Kenya. The equivalent figures for health were 8 per cent and 7 per cent. Even so, no government can afford to build as many schools or employ as many teachers as are needed. And in health care very difficult choices have to be made regarding just how the very limited budget is spent.

Levels of education that remain unsatisfactory despite much improvement over the past thirty years, and levels of health care that have improved less and must be considered grossly inadequate, are thus both dimensions of African poverty, whether we are thinking of the national scale or of families and individuals. Provision of both services varies considerably from place to place, and both tend to be concentrated in cities and towns; but even so both are aspects of urban as well as rural poverty.

Levels of education and literacy

Most discussions of education in Africa, and all the data submitted to UNESCO or published by bodies such as the World Bank, relate entirely to the system of formal schooling brought in from Europe by Christian missions and colonial governments. We must remember that this system was always superimposed on indigenous forms of education, which still play an important part in shaping people's lives (Bray et al. 1988). These mainly take the form of learning within the family, as in all societies around the world, but often the wider local community is also involved.

An intermediate form of education, which long predated that brought in from Europe, is a feature of many Islamic areas. From Senegal to Sudan and Somalia, many children still attend Koranic schools, and for some this is their only experience of school. The main purpose of the teaching is normally memorization of the Koran, but much else may also be learnt, including literacy in Arabic in some cases. In many areas it now seems to be mainly children from poorer families who attend these schools, and the experience does not seem to help most of them to escape their material poverty, however much it strengthens their Islamic faith.

However important indigenous and Koranic education may be for many children, the situation now throughout Africa is that when people speaking English or French use the word 'education' they are normally referring to the system of primary schools, secondary schools and tertiary-level institutions brought in from Europe. It is this system that has been expanding rapidly since independence, and that forms the basis of the national education programme everywhere. In some countries all schools are administered by the state; in others Christian missions still play a major role, as in Zaïre, Rwanda and Burundi; in yet others the state system has been supplemented by local initiatives such as the many Harambee schools in Kenya.

Data for enrolment rates in primary education pose a problem because of the variable ages at which children participate. Rates may even appear to exceed 100 per cent, where large numbers of over-age children are still in primary schools. However, the broad picture across Africa is fairly clear (Table 10.1 and Map 10.1). Thirty years ago primary enrolment rates in many African countries were among the lowest in the world, but they have now greatly improved, generally overtaking the rates for South Asia. Over tropical Africa as a whole, it is thought that about 70 per cent of children aged 7 to 12 now attend primary school, compared with only 30 to 40 per cent in the early 1960s. In this respect, 'development' has certainly been taking place in every country during this period, though its extent has differed greatly from one country to another, and also from one district to another within some countries.

Table 10.1 Primary school enrolment rates in the larger countries, 1960–87

	Male		*Female*	
	1960 %	*1987* %	*1960* %	*1987* %
Nigeria	46	85	27	70
Ethiopia	11	46	3	28
Zaïre	88 (?)	84	32	68
Tanzania	33	67	18	66
Sudan	35	59	14	41
Kenya	64	98	30	93
Uganda	60	76	32	63
Mozambique	60	76	36	59
Ghana	52	78	25	63

Note: Figures can exceed 100% because of over-age children attending primary school.

Sources: UNICEF, *The State of the World's Children 1990:* World Bank, *World Development Report 1990*

In Zimbabwe, Zambia, Kenya, Cameroon and large parts of Nigeria something approaching universal primary education has been achieved. Togo is not far behind, and on the basis of the official figures, which some regard as highly suspect, nor is Zaïre despite its very low ranking in terms of per capita income. By contrast, primary enrolment rates are still only 25 to 40 per cent in Guinea, Mali, Burkina Faso, Niger, Chad, Ethiopia and Somalia. Most of these are among the lowest-income countries; but other factors are also relevant, such as the fact that most are strongly Islamic countries where there was much, and is still some, resistance to western education especially when provided through Christian missions. This has particularly affected schooling for girls.

These contrasts were already well established thirty years ago, and it is possible to argue either that disparities have been growing ever wider or that there has been some 'catching up' by the poorest countries. Primary enrolment rates in Kenya have doubled since 1960, from 47 to 94 per cent: in Ethiopia the rise has been smaller in absolute terms, from 7 to 35 per cent, yet this represents a five-fold increase. The situation is perhaps better assessed by disaggregating within this period, and concluding that countries such as Kenya and Zambia forged ahead in the 1960s and early 1970s, but then slowed inevitably as they approached 100 per cent enrolment so that countries such as Ethiopia and Burkina Faso began to 'catch up' on any reckoning by the late 1970s and early 1980s. The poorest record for the

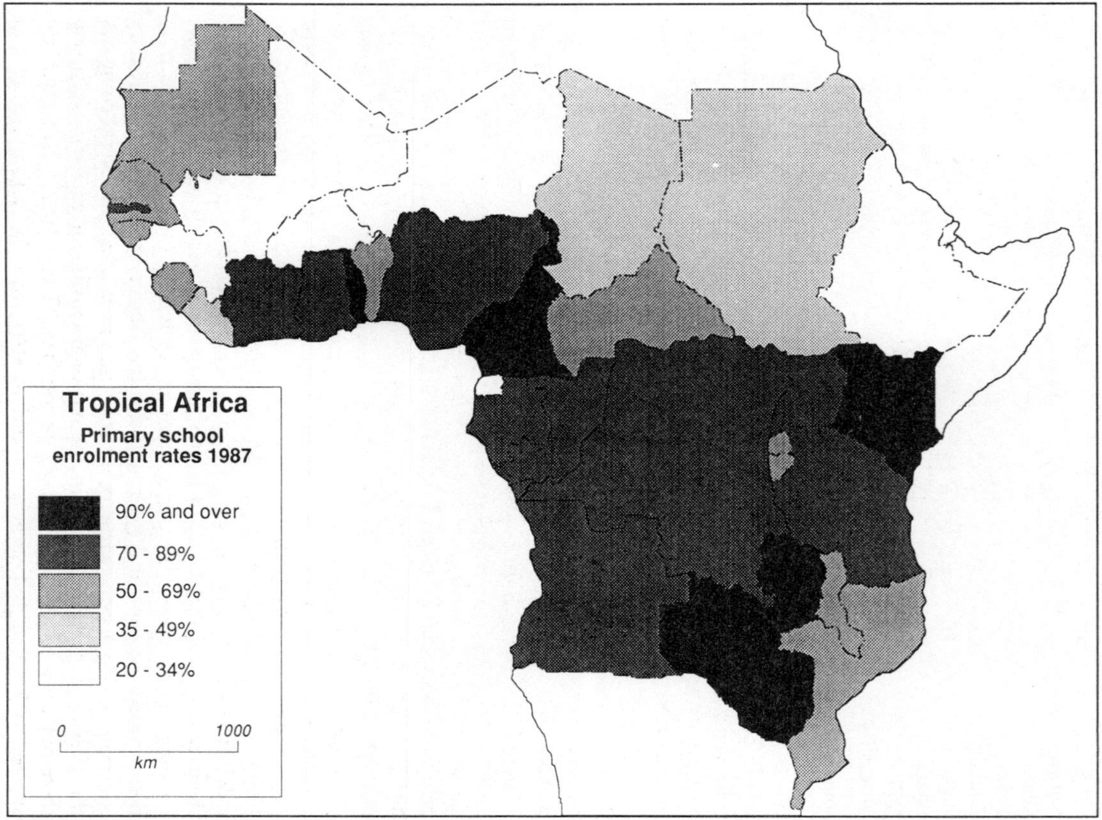

Map 10.1 Primary school enrolment rates, 1987

Table 10.2 Primary school enrolment in selected countries, 1980–7 (*millions*)

	1980	*1984*	*1985*	*1986*	*1987*
Nigeria	13·8	13·0	12·9		
Kenya	3·9	4·4	4·7	4·8	5·0
Tanzania	3·4	3·5	3·2	3·2	3·2
Zimbabwe	1·2	2·1	2·2	2·3	
Sudan	1·5	1·6	1·7	1·8	
Ghana	1·4	1·5	1·5	1·6	1·6

Note: Primary education covers more years in some countries than in others.

Source: UNESCO, *Statistical Yearbook 1989*

whole period is that of Somalia, with a rise only from 13 to 20 per cent, followed by Mali, with a rise from 10 to 21 per cent. The best is probably Tanzania's, with an enrolment rate rising from 25 to almost 70 per cent. The nationwide 'villagization' programme may have adversely affected agriculture, but it has certainly assisted the spread of education.

The national figures often mask great regional variations. In Sudan the national enrolment rate is around 50 per cent, but this rises to over 80 per cent in parts of the north, including the rural Gezira as well as the capital city, while it falls to a mere 10 per cent in southern Darfur and Bahr el Gazal in the far south-west. In Nigeria virtual 100 per cent enrolments throughout the south contrast with rates below 60 per cent in some northern States, and below 40 per cent in some Districts within these. Even in Kenya, where nearly all children have some schooling in most Districts, only a quarter of primary-age children are in schools in the nomadic pastoral areas of the north-east.

Under-provided regions that might have begun to catch up have been particularly hard hit by the onset of economic stagnation or decline in the 1980s. Over tropical Africa as a whole, primary school places seem to have more or less kept pace with population growth even during this decade, but the pace of expansion has slackened almost everywhere (World Bank 1988). Existing schools have been taking in more pupils, but fewer new schools have been opened than in the 1970s, and this has meant little spread of primary education into the poor and remote areas that have none. In several countries the 1980s did bring a decline in the national enrolment rate, and in a few there has even been a fall in absolute numbers (Table 10.2). This certainly applies to Nigeria and Tanzania, and to strife-torn Somalia, Angola and Mozambique.

We should note that the spatial variations in enrolment, at both national and regional level, are very much greater for girls than for boys. Since the rate for girls never exceeds that for boys this means that national rates are often much lower for girls. In Zimbabwe, Tanzania and Kenya they attend in almost equal numbers; but in Mali, Niger and Chad there are almost twice as many boys as girls in school. Across most of the Sahel a clear majority of girls never attend school, and less than 10 per cent complete a full primary education. Poor parents throughout this zone are prepared to make sacrifices to send their sons to school, but often not their daughters, largely due to the influence of Islam.

Secondary education has expanded even faster than primary education in most African countries since independence, but from extremely low levels. Even now enrolment rates are generally far below those of China, India and Indonesia, but this gap has certainly been narrowing. Again, there are great differences between one African country and another. Both in Zimbabwe and in Ghana about 40 per cent of children aged 13 to 16 attend secondary school. In Nigeria, Sudan and Kenya the figure is between 15 and 25 per cent. Ethiopia and some Sahel states have done relatively more at secondary than at primary level, with an official figure of 12 per cent enrolment in Ethiopia in 1987. By contrast, only 4 per cent of this age group are in secondary school in Tanzania, where the priority has been placed on a little education for everyone, and the proportion is equally low in Rwanda, Burundi and Malawi.

There are sharp contrasts not only in enrolment rates but also in the extent of change in recent years. The high rate in Ghana had already been reached by 1980, since when the situation has remained static, whereas the rate in Zimbabwe rose only from 6 per cent in 1965 to 8 per cent in 1980 but then shot up to 46 per cent by 1986. Rapid expansion in Zaïre continued into the early 1980s; but in Togo the rate appears to have fallen from 34 per cent in 1980 to only 24 per cent in 1986; and there has been a fall from 12 to 9 per cent in Guinea. Even in Côte d'Ivoire, despite its relative prosperity, there has been a rise only from 18 to 19 per cent over this period. Where enrolment rates have fallen, this has often been partly the result of imposition of fees where none were previously charged.

Data for regional variations in secondary school provision are of less value than those for primary schools, since there is much more inter-regional movement to secondary schools. Some are boarding schools, while many city day schools have pupils who have come from far away and lodge with relatives. However, there is little doubt that the numbers from such poor regions as southern Sudan or even northern Ghana who attend secondary school, either in their home region or elsewhere, remains extremely small.

The discrimination against girls is even more widespread and extreme than at primary level. According to UNICEF, there are twice as many boys as girls in secondary school in more than half the countries of tropical Africa. Nigeria is quite typical, with 40 per cent enrolment for boys but only 14 per cent for girls. More extreme are Guinea-Bissau, with 18 per cent and 4 per cent, and Chad, with 10 per cent and 2 per cent. In Chad it is almost impossible for a girl from any but the richest families to receive a secondary education.

For tertiary-level education, the story is much the same, on a micro-scale in terms of numbers though not in terms of expenditures. Most African countries have at least one university, but most cannot afford to maintain them, at least not to international standards, without thereby using up a grossly disproportionate share of the total national education budget (World Bank 1988). In Nigeria oil revenues were used to finance a massive expansion of the university system: now that these revenues have fallen, it is clear that this is beyond the country's means, and some of the new institutions are universities in name only.

At this point there should be a discussion of special educational provision for the physically and mentally handicapped, especially since more children in Africa suffer such disabilities than in most parts of the world. There is an appalling incidence of blindness in some areas, notably along similium-fly-infested valleys in West Africa; while it is widely recognized that severe malnutrition in infancy can lead to permanent brain damage. How many children may have been so affected by the famines of the 1980s can only be a matter for speculation.

Partly as a result of poverty, the need for what is termed in Britain 'special education' is far greater in Africa. Yet in a country such as Britain the costs per pupil are far higher than in most schools, and in most African countries these extra costs rule out any possibility of catering for this need (Ross 1988). There are a few institutions doing remarkable work, but they represent a few drops in the ocean, and it is an ocean which is probably now expanding even beyond the general rate of population growth.

The level of adult literacy is another important feature of societies which reflects on education and is closely associated with the degree of poverty, though we should note that this is something not easily measured. It is thought that three-quarters of the adult population of Zimbabwe are literate, compared with just under half in Nigeria and only one-quarter in Sudan (Table 10.3). Estimates of only around 15 per cent are usually made for Burkina Faso and Niger. In every country there has been a great improvement since 1960, the increase from 25 to 45 per cent in Nigeria being typical. Again, however, the estimates have not been rising as rapidly through the 1980s as through the 1970s.

Tanzania is a very special case, for much of the effort that might have been put into expanding secondary and tertiary education there has instead been

Table 10.3 Adult literacy rates in the larger countries, 1970–85

	Percentage literate			
	Male		*Female*	
	1970	*1985*	*1970*	*1985*
Nigeria	35	54	14	31
Ethiopia	8	?	?	?
Zaïre	61	79	22	45
Tanzania	48	93	18	88
Sudan	28	33	6	15
Kenya	44	70	19	49
Uganda	52	70	30	45
Mozambique	29	55	14	22
Ghana	43	64	18	43

Source: UNESCO, *Statistical Yearbook 1989*

put into a massive adult literacy programme. The result is a literacy rate of 90 per cent, with very little variation from one region to another, or between women and men. Almost everywhere else many more women than men are illiterate (Map 10.2). In Kenya, for instance, the current estimates are 70 per cent for men and 50 per cent for women; in Ghana they are 65 and 45 per cent respectively; and in Sudan they are 33 per cent and a mere 14 per cent.

The expansion of the school system has resulted in far higher literacy rates for those in their twenties than among older people, as well as a rise in rates for the total adult population. However, the general growth of population is such that the absolute number of adults in tropical Africa who cannot read or write is probably still rising year by year. Here is a clear example of a vicious circle, in which illiteracy and poverty feed on each other.

Some implications of educational expansion

In terms of school enrolments, education has constituted much the most successful aspect of development in post-colonial Africa. Governments have given it a high priority, for it is politically popular and threatens no powerful vested interests; and both the building of schools and the training of teachers have proved much easier to accomplish than, say, increasing productivity in agriculture or setting up profitable factories.

However, any assessment of success should consider more than just numbers of children in school. For example, it is widely accepted that quantity has often been achieved at the expense of quality – though the latter

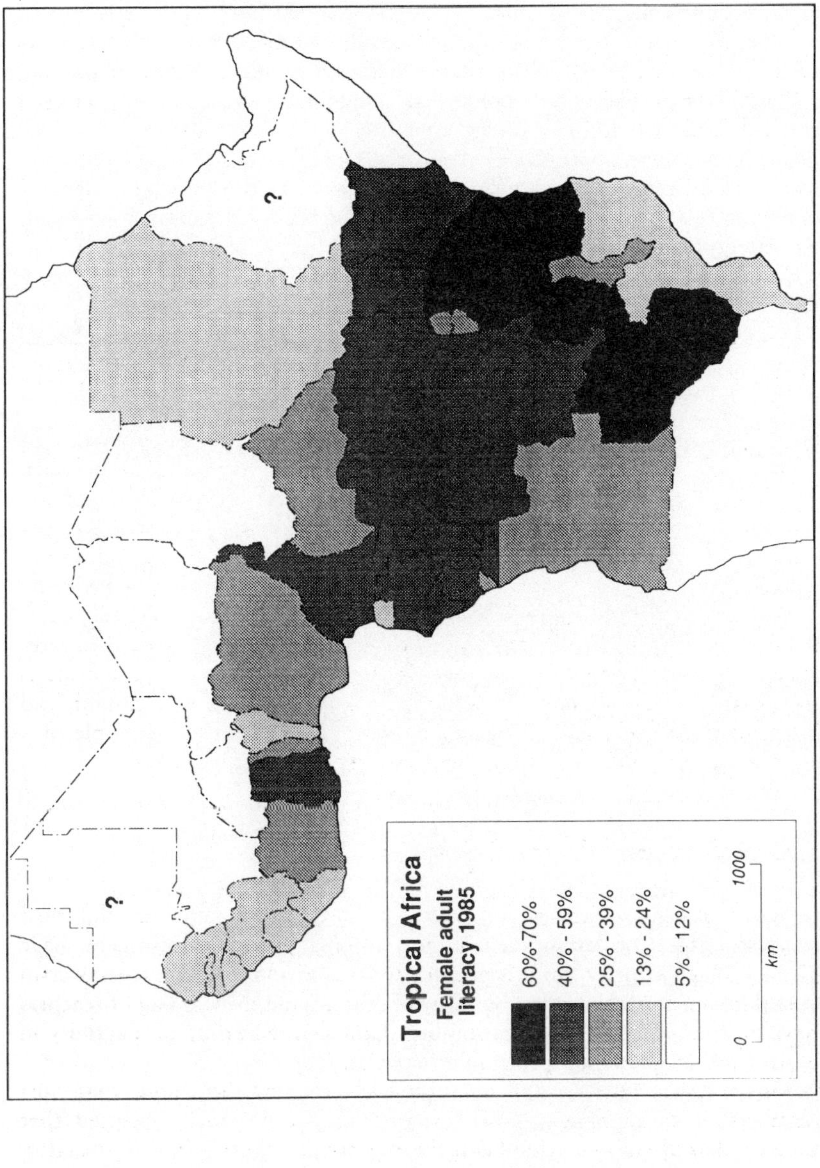

Map 10.2 Female adult literacy, 1985

is far more difficult to measure. There are many poorly-qualified teachers, and many so poorly and even irregularly paid that they must take time to earn a supplementary income. There are many very poorly-equipped classrooms, even in secondary schools, and during the 1980s funds for items such as paper and books became increasingly scarce in country after country.

Questions are also raised about what is taught. The colonial legacy in the curriculum is still too evident in some areas (Court and Kinyanjui 1986). Possibly what was appropriate when only a small minority attended school needs modification when nearly all do so. Deteriorating employment opportunities for school-leavers may not have been sufficiently considered. Yet attempts to change the curriculum in the direction of greater relevance to a predominantly rural self-employed population generally meet strong resistance from parents, and indeed from the children themselves.

For each individual family, education can contribute much to the relief of poverty. Children who have been to school normally have better economic prospects than those who have not, being better able to compete in the job market. But more education for all may just increase the level of qualifications required to obtain a given income, unless it clearly results in some form of higher productivity. The extreme case of benefit to the individual but not to local society is provided by the 'brain drain', through which the most successful pupils from rural schools go off to the city and even off to work overseas. Fortunately for the rural communities, it is very common in Africa for remittances to provide some compensation for such losses of trained people, bringing some benefit to their families and to their local home areas.

Despite these queries, there is no doubt that the expansion of education has brought economic gains to African countries by increasing people's productivity and imparting skills that are much needed. Without it, the continent's present economic predicament would surely be much worse. The main policy dilemma is whether each item of expenditure on education could yield more benefit if deployed elsewhere. Universities are particularly vulnerable when this approach is adopted, since they are so expensive to maintain.

It must be acknowledged that up till now the spread of western education in Africa has tended to increase inequalities in society. It has helped to produce a tiny élite with incomes several hundred times those of the poorest, and a rather larger group who might be termed 'middle-class' but who are still far more affluent than the majority. It has contributed to increasing regional disparities within each country, as for example between south and north in Nigeria, Ghana and Côte d'Ivoire. It has also accentuated inequality in many countries between men and women, higher enrolment rates for boys giving them more opportunities than girls in later life, and increasing their already large share of power in society. Within nations, as internationally, education has provided some people with increased opportunities to exploit others as well as to benefit others. All over Africa, secondary schools for a few, and universities for even fewer, have tended to create pockets of privilege, and even the extended family system has been unable to disperse these very widely.

Once a given level of education is available to a majority, its extension to the remainder should be a move towards equality: and that is now the situation with regard to primary education in many African countries. This lies behind the Tanzanian emphasis on universal primary education rather than more secondary school places. At primary level, regional disparities have even been reduced in Nigeria, where equity has not been a high government priority. Similarly, in much of Africa inequality between boys and girls has at last begun to be reduced in primary education.

In the African context, education also has an impact on welfare in such indirect ways as its role in nation-building, but it can work both ways. In Tanzania it has surely played a positive role, helping to build a sense of national identity that has contributed to political stability. Yet in Nigeria one of the roots of the civil war lay in the educational superiority of most Ibo people over most other Nigerians, and especially most northerners. In Sudan, gross educational disparities are one cause of conflict between south and north, yet efforts to extend Arabic-language education from the north into the south only serve to increase hostility.

When these considerations are added to such basic matters as more primary schooling meaning that crops are less well weeded, and that many women must divert some effort from cultivation to fetching water and fuel, it is clear why the expansion of education may be seen as a somewhat mixed blessing for Africa.

Disease and health care

Particular parts of Africa have been devastated by famine, and larger areas have had to endure years of civil war, but the unhappiest feature of tropical Africa as a whole is perhaps the appallingly high incidence of disease. This was briefly discussed in Chapter 4 as one of the most significant features of the African environment, and as a major contributor to poverty.

Some data for life expectancy and for child deaths were provided in Table 2.4 in Chapter 2. Not only in Ethiopia but also in Guinea and Sierra Leone, life expectancy at birth was still thought to be only 41 or 42 years in 1988 (Map 10.3), compared with 70 years in several Asian countries, including China. In each of these three African countries, and also in various others from Mali to Malawi, more than 14 out of every 100 babies die within their first year, and more than 25 fail to survive to the age of five. Since these are national averages, the situation must be even worse in certain regions of each country.

Even in countries with much higher average per capita incomes, such as Cameroon and Côte d'Ivoire, the ravages of disease are almost as intense. Both have a life expectancy of only 51 to 53 years, and an infant mortality rate of 93 to 95 per thousand. Almost everywhere premature death is even more characteristic of the rural areas than the cities, where health care is more readily available, but the impoverishment of the cities discussed in the last chapter (together with the emergence of AIDS) has brought rising death rates in some in the 1980s.

Disease is, of course, not only a matter of early death, but also a pervasive problem closely related to poverty for many of those who live a long life. Most people in Africa are ill for much of their lives, often suffering from several diseases simultaneously. There are areas where the majority have to live with the effects of bilharzia, and areas where most people live with only partly suppressed malaria. Ill-health was stressed as a critical factor in Margaret Haswell's study of The Gambia entitled *The Nature of Poverty* (1975), for there as elsewhere a vicious circle is in operation, in which sickness and lack of income reinforce each other. Unless this circle can be broken, many development efforts are bound to be largely in vain.

In health care, even more than in education, indigenous practice carried forward from precolonial times remains important, although data on it are almost entirely lacking. The data submitted to international organizations relate entirely to the system brought in from Europe during the colonial period, even though some people still have no access to this and many have only very limited access to it. Various forms of indigenous medicine are clearly of value to people throughout tropical Africa, in towns of colonial origin as well as in rural areas as Charles Good (1987) has documented for Kenya, though both its nature and its effectiveness differs greatly from place to place. Yet the prevailing poverty means that the resources available to traditional healers are everywhere very limited.

There is very little interaction between the indigenous and introduced health care systems – far less, for example, than in China or India. In areas where both are available, people must take their choice as to which they will use; or they may try first one and then the other, sometimes with very unfortunate results. Even if unlimited finance were at the disposal of the western health care system in Africa, much could be gained from integration with the best of indigenous practice. And since this is far from the case, the argument for combining the best of both systems is even stronger (Last and Chavunduka 1986).

Indigenous healing alone can certainly not be regarded as adequate

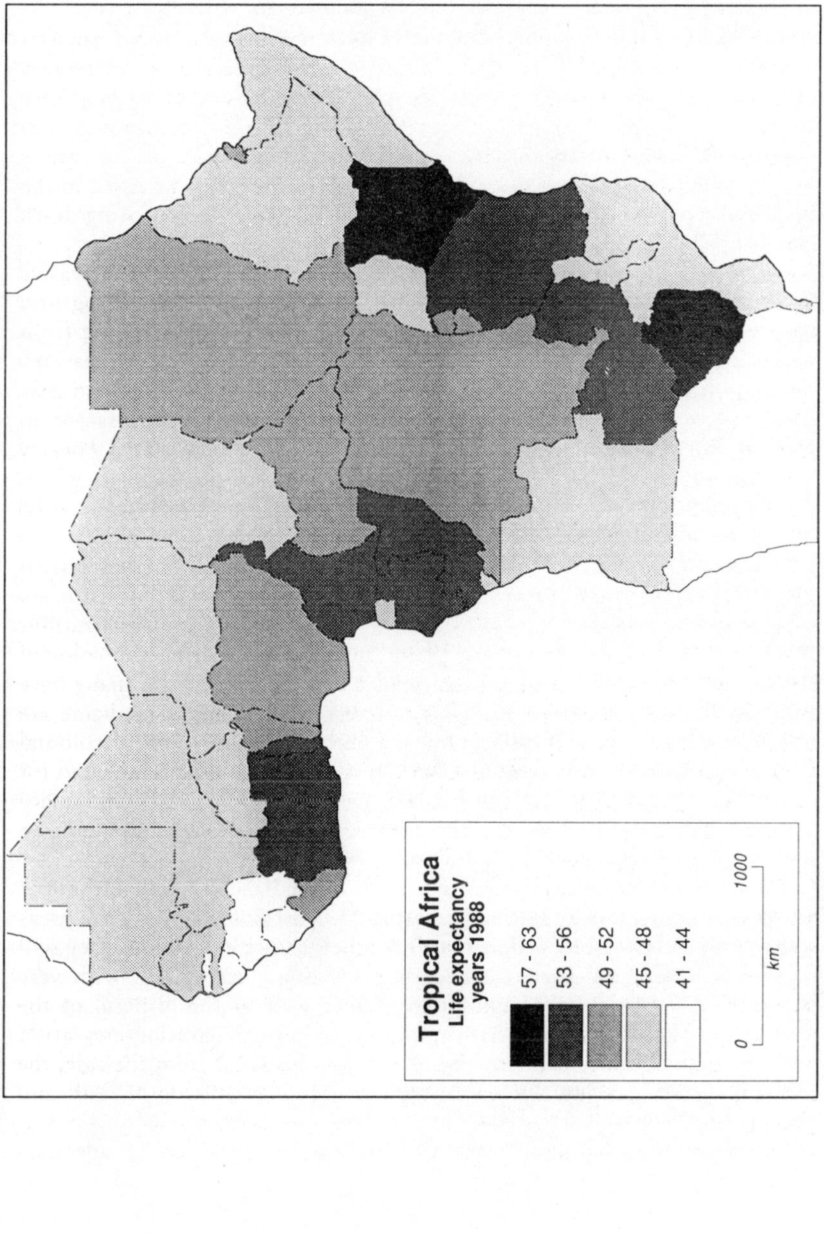

Map 10.3 Life expectancy, 1988

anywhere, since disease is so widespread and since mortality rates are so high. Western medicine is urgently needed, and it has already brought some health improvements in every country. Yet in comparison with the rest of the world, the trained personnel and the physical facilities available are very scarce.

The growth of western health care

In 1960 there was only one medically-qualified doctor per 50,000 people in tropical Africa, compared with one per 12,000 for all poor countries, and one per 1,000 in the rich countries. In Ethiopia, Rwanda, Burundi, Chad and Burkina Faso there was only one per 80–100,000 which means that most people had no chance of ever seeing a doctor.

By 1980 the situation had substantially improved, in spite of rapid population growth, so that there was one doctor for about 20,000 people. This then compared with one per 5,000 for all poor countries, and one per 600 for rich countries, so that the global disparities had remained more or less constant.

The extent of the improvement over this period differed considerably from one African country to another (Table 10.4). In Nigeria, oil revenues permitted an advance from one per 60,000 to one per 10,000; and dramatic increases in the availability of doctors also occurred in Cameroon, Zaïre and Sudan. In many other countries, from Senegal to Kenya, there was a more modest improvement of around 50 per cent. In Tanzania, however, the increase in doctors only just kept pace with population growth, to give one per 18,000 in both years, with higher priority being given to increasing numbers of lower-level health workers. There was also no improvement in Ethiopia. Meanwhile in Uganda there was a deterioration from one per 15,000 to one per 25,000, as both foreign and local doctors left the country during the political traumas of the 1970s (Dodge and Wiebe 1985), and an even greater exodus ocurred from Angola and Mozambique.

The limited data available for the 1980s suggest that, as in the case of education, some improvement has continued for tropical Africa in general, but at a much reduced rate. By 1987 there was probably one doctor for about 17,000 or 18,000 people. There seems to have been a large-scale recruitment of doctors in Malawi, and some further improvement of the ratio in Nigeria in the early 1980s; but at that time many doctors were leaving Ghana, where the ratio apparently fell from one per 7,000 people in 1980 to one per 15,000 in 1985. Meanwhile, the ratio continued to improve steadily in regions such as South Asia, where by 1985 even Bangladesh had one doctor per 7,000 while India reached one per 2,500.

Table 10.4 Population per doctor in the larger countries, 1965–84

	1965	*1984*
Nigeria	29,500	8,000
Ethiopia	70,200	79,000
Zaïre	35,100	?
Tanzania	21,700	26,200
Sudan	23,500	10,100
Kenya	13,300	10,000
Uganda	11,100	21,900
Mozambique	18,000	38,000
Ghana	13,700	14,900
(India	4,900	2,500)
(China	1,600	1,000)
(Brazil	2,500	1,100)

Source: World Bank, *World Development Report 1990*

It is arguable that for most of the very poor, who may never have access to more than a rural health centre or dispensary, numbers of people with some nursing skills are more significant than numbers of doctors. The data here are beset by problems of definition, but those published by the World Bank suggest a better relative position for Africa than in the case of doctors, though with less improvement since the 1960s. In 1960 tropical Africa had one 'nursing person' for about every 6,000 people: by the late 1980s there was roughly one for every 3,000. In this case, the figures for India are little better, and those for Bangladesh decidedly worse.

Again, Nigeria has been able to achieve a massive improvement, from one per 7,000 to one per 1,000, but not to continue the improvement into the late 1980s. In this case Ghana's great advances in the 1960s have been succeeded by stagnation rather than decline, so it remains relatively well served, as is also Tanzania though the qualifications of many of the health staff are very basic. Meanwhile, both Mozambique and Ethiopia still have only one nursing person per 6,000, as in the early 1960s. In both countries many people are still totally dependent on traditional healers or on self-help medicine.

Health care might seem one of the more unproblematic aspects of development, for better health is an improvement appreciated by everyone. Yet the spread of western medicine may not be to the benefit of all. Where it occurs more rapidly than population growth it may present a threat to the livelihood of traditional healers, and within the western system there are sharply conflicting views on priorities. Ben Wisner (1988) is one who is highly critical of much that has been done.

It has even been said that the medical profession constitutes an obstacle to the health of the majority, since they so often insist that money and effort must be concentrated on providing the highest standard of care for a few. Some of the resources spent on increasing the number of high-salaried doctors working with sophisticated equipment in Kinshasa or Nairobi might well have been diverted to a programme of primary health care in the remoter rural areas of Zaïre and Kenya. Tanzania has to some extent done this (Gish 1975), at the same time as improving most people's access to health care through the villagization process. Some have spoken highly of health-care systems that cater for the majority rather than the few in the areas of Eritrea outside Ethiopian control.

Many people would argue that the usual emphasis on curative medicine at all levels is misplaced, and that far more attention should be given to preventing sickness. Improved sanitation could make a large contribution, but in most parts of Africa this is at present deteriorating as population rises, especially in the overcrowded cities and in urban fringe areas that may have no sanitation arrangements other than shrinking patches of bush. In every African country something is done by government to explain and publicize ways to reduce the incidence of disease, but in most countries such publicity could be given higher priority.

Much disease could be eliminated if people had access to adequate supplies of clean water, and the lack of this is one of the clearest manifestations of poverty in Africa (Cairncross 1988, Lindskog and Lundqvist 1989). UNICEF data suggest that over three-quarters of the total population has clean water on tap in North African countries such as Egypt and Algeria, and that over half do so in India. Even in Nigeria only one-third do so, while figures for other tropical African countries are as low as 12 per cent in Mali, 10 per cent in Zaïre and 6 per cent in Ethiopia. This is yet another aspect of life in which there was some improvement in the 1960s and 1970s, but generally none in the 1980s.

The most impressive achievements in disease prevention over recent years have been the immunization programme undertaken in the majority of African countries, sometimes reaching more than half the children of a given age. These programmes, supported by WHO and UNICEF, have probably already saved the lives of millions of children. Immunization against measles, diphtheria, whooping cough, tuberculosis, tetanus and polio is not highly expensive, and has proved practicable even among poor people in poor countries. The present geography of immunization in tropical Africa is in fact not closely related to that of poverty. By 1988 over 70 per cent of children were being immunized by DPT vaccine not only in Zimbabwe and

Kenya but also in Tanzania and Malawi. The countries where less than 20 per cent were covered included Guinea and Angola as well as impoverished Niger, Mali, Chad and Ethiopia, and the coverage was only 33 per cent in Ghana and Côte d'Ivoire. Given determination, immunization is something that can be maintained and extended despite the cuts that are being made in health budgets throughout Africa.

Another low-cost programme supported by WHO and UNICEF is oral rehydration therapy whereby children suffering from diarrhoea are given a simple solution of salt and sugar. This has had such an impact in reducing infant and child mortality that, in combination with immunization and the encouragement of breast-feeding rather than unhygienic substitutes, it has been presented by UNICEF as a 'child survival revolution'. Howeer, the revolution is by no means complete yet, for this therapy has not spread as rapidly in Africa as in Latin America and Asia, and diarrhoea still kills over one million African children every year.

One totally successful WHO campaign in Africa has been the eradication of smallpox. Other campaigns have been less successful, notably the efforts to reduce the incidence of malaria. The mosquito has proved very resistant, and mortality from malaria is increasing in many areas. Little progress has been achieved against onchocerciasis, or river blindness, which affects many millions of people in West Africa. Also in West Africa there was a resurgence of yellow fever in the late 1980s.

Leprosy is another disease that is widespread in Africa and resistant to all attempts to eliminate it. This disease seems to be particularly associated with poverty, for its victims are often severely disabled, and are sometimes rejected by the local community and even their immediate families. It is notable that a whole chapter is devoted to leprosy in John Iliffe's book on *The African Poor* (1987).

AIDS

AIDS is not a widespread African disease – yet. However, the health scene in parts of Africa was dramatically altered in the 1980s by the recognition of AIDS as a major hazard for the years ahead. While the number of reported cases is still small everywhere, they are incresing rapidly in Zaïre, Congo, Burundi, Rwanda, Uganda, Kenya, Tanzania, Malawi, Zambia and Zimbabwe, while many cases go unreported. Even more disturbing are the vastly greater numbers of people who have been found to be HIV-positive, and who are therefore likely to be afflicted by AIDS within the next ten years (Miller and Rockwell 1988, Panos Institute 1988). WHO estimates that 3 million people in Africa were HIV-infected by 1990. It is quite possible that by the late 1990s the disease will be responsible for millions of deaths each year in eastern Africa, and that it will have spread to all other parts of the continent.

In addition to the resulting suffering for the individuals and families involved, there are long-term economic implications. Those struck down with AIDS are mainly young adults, who have just ceased to be dependents and joined the labour force. A disproportionate number are well educated, with skills that these countries cannot afford to lose. At present, infection is heavily concentrated in the cities, but if it spreads widely into the countryside it will intensify the problem of falling per capita food production.

If AIDS does begin to kill vast numbers of people this is bound to have wider ramifications. People from the countries in question may be refused entry into other countries, and it may become much more difficult to recruit high-level workers from overseas – or more expensive. The tourist industry may be threatened, which would mean a serious loss of revenue for Kenya in particular. Perhaps the most direct economic impact would come from the extra strain on the health care budget: a rapid spread of AIDS would reduce spending on prevention and cure of other diseases, while itself exacerbating some of these.

In the short run, some slowing of population growth can be expected, especially if most AIDS deaths are of people who have recently entered their reproductive years. The death rate will be boosted and the birth rate suppressed almost simultaneously. However, the rising mortality is likely to encourage many parents to try to guarantee their security in old age by having even more children than they do now. This could happen in countries where the disease has not yet taken hold, if there is widespread fear that it is coming.

AIDS will intensify poverty in Africa. It will damage national economies, and will drive some families into destitution. A cure must somehow be found, but this is likely to come from outside Africa, and may be expensive. Meanwhile, many African governments are making strenuous efforts to check the spread of the disease, and this is largely a matter of education – for children and adults, in and out of school.

Conclusions

Low levels of education, like low standards of health, are both a consequence and a cause of poverty in Africa. Many children receive little or no schooling because governments cannot afford to provide it for all at no cost, and because parents cannot afford to pay for it or even to forgo the child's contribution to household income. There has, however, been a vast improvement in the situation in most countries over the past thirty years, at least in quantitative terms. Most governments have allocated a large share of their budget to education, and most plans have been fulfilled to a far greater extent than in other sectors. It is very doubtful that more should have been set aside for education, either by governments or by parents, though some priorities within education might have been different, and might usefully change even now.

The overall health situation in tropical Africa is to a greater extent a disgrace to mankind, even though here too there has been some improvement, and it can be seen as a major casualty of the global system of nation–states. An 'inverse care law' has been suggested with respect to the distribution of health care within rich countries: it is far more evident at a global scale. Vast sums are spent on health care in the countries where the incidence of most diseases is lowest, while very much less is available for spending in those where it is highest, and where the needs are incomparably greater. With Ghanaian doctors now practising in the United States, and with Sudanese doctors practising in Saudi Arabia, we have quite literally good health in rich countries secured at the expense of continuing ill health in poor countries.

11
Aid

The main international response to poverty in Africa and elsewhere is a flow of financial and other aid, either direct from government to government or through international agencies such as the European Community or the United Nations. This aid should do something to compensate for the various forces in the world economy that work against the poorer countries, though there are critics who consider that most aid does more harm than good to the recipients. It is encouraging to note that three recent studies of world-wide aid (Cassen 1986, Mosley 1987, Riddell 1987) all come to the opposite conclusion, though all have some criticisms of how aid is handled.

Arguments about aid are much affected by problems of definition. Here the term will be taken to cover financial grants, the free supply of goods and services other than for military purposes, and loans made at less-than-commercial rates of interest. A narrower definition would include only the grant element in such loans. Broader definitions often include both military assistance and loans for development purposes provided at commercial rates, such as those made by the World Bank. This institution itself doubts the wisdom of providing such loans to any but the richest African countries, and the poorer countries instead receive no-interest loans through the International Development Association arm of the Bank, which are certainly appropriately included in aid. Conversely, finance provided at high interest rates by the International Monetary Fund should certainly not be considered as aid, especially since there has been a net flow from Africa to the IMF in several recent years.

In addtion to government funds, aid flows to Africa also include funds provided through voluntary agencies such as OXFAM, Save the Children Fund and Christian Aid (Poulton and Harris 1988). The total amount of such aid is small – little more than one-tenth of the level of government aid in most years – but it is thought by many to be more effective in terms of reaching the poor. To some extent it can by-pass African governments, and there are cases where this is clearly an advantage.

The mid 1980s brought a massive expansion of voluntary aid and some expansion of government aid for a year or two, in response to the famine in large parts of Africa. Emergency aid of this nature is rather distinctive, and while some attention will be given to it later in the chapter the main concern here is with longer-term development aid. This has been maintained at a more or less stable level through the past decade. Many calls for a substantial expansion, as in the Brandt Commission reports of 1980 and 1983, have been ignored. The flow of aid from certain countries, notably the USA, has in fact shrunk, but this has been offset by increased flows from Scandinavia, Japan, Italy, and for a while from the Middle East oil exporters.

More data are available, and these are more reliable, for aid flows than for most topics considered in this book. The spatial distribution of aid is relatively easily documented. What is far more difficult to establish is its impact, especially as a long time-lag may be involved. It is always impossible to say just what the situation would have been in the absence of aid, while the benefits of aid investments in fields such as education are extremely hard to measure.

The volume and spatial pattern of aid

The total net flow of official development assistance to Africa south of the Sahara in 1988 amounted to about $14 billion (OECD 1989). The increase from $9 billion in 1980 is more or less in line with inflation, so the flow has remained very constant in real terms. About $9 billion was provided directly in 1988 by western governments, about $1 billion by other governments including the USSR, and about $4 billion through multilateral agencies. To this should be added $1 billion provided by voluntary organizations.

Although much the largest bilateral government aid programme is that of the United States, only 10 to 12 per cent of this, around $¾ billion a year, is destined for tropical Africa. Various other parts of the world, including Egypt as well as Latin America and South East Asia, are perceived as far more politically significant to the USA, which sees Africa to some extent as Western Europe's area of responsibility. The British aid programme is also very widely spread around the world, and India is the largest individual recipient; but the share allocated to Africa has been increasing in recent years and this flow reached $½ billion in 1988. French aid has always been much more heavily concentrated on tropical Africa, and it is still much the largest

Table 11.1 Aid inflows, 1978–88 (*Net disbursements of Official Development Assistance from all sources in $ million at constant prices and exchange rates.*)

	1978	*1984*	*1988*	*1988 $ per head*	*1988 as % of GNP*
Tanzania	686	804	975	38	16
Sudan	570	908	923	39	12
Ethiopia	238	748	912	20	16
Mozambique	174	432	882	60	31
Kenya	395	593	808	35	9
Zaïre	505	450	580	17	12
Senegal	344	530	566	80	13
Zambia	296	350	477	60	23
Ghana	182	306	474	34	8
Somalia	313	505	447	63	32
Côte d'Ivoire	209	184	439	38	4
Mali	262	484	427	49	22
Niger	249	232	371	55	18
Uganda	57	235	353	20	8
Malawi	157	228	335	42	27
Burkina Faso	254	272	297	35	15
Cameroon	287	269	286	27	2
Zimbabwe	15	430	270	30	5
Chad	199	166	264	49	28
Guinea	104	116	262	40	13
Rwanda	200	237	247	36	12

Note: All others were below $200 million in 1988.

Source: OECD, 1989 Report, *Development Co-operation in the 1990s*

supplier of aid to the region, contributing $2 billion in 1988. Italy has recently become the second largest supplier, providing over $1 billion in 1988. Flows from Arab countries have dropped markedly since the early 1980s, as their oil revenues have fallen.

The main multilateral sources of aid are the IDA, which provided $1¼ billion in 1988, and the European Community, which also provided $1¼ billion. The share of IDA funds going to tropical Africa had risen over the previous ten years from 15 to 35 per cent. In the case of the EC the share remained almost 60 per cent throughout. The proportion of aid from all sources going to tropical Africa rose from around 20 per cent in the early 1970s to 30 per cent in the early 1980s, and has stayed about that figure.

The primary question with regard to the geography of aid in Africa

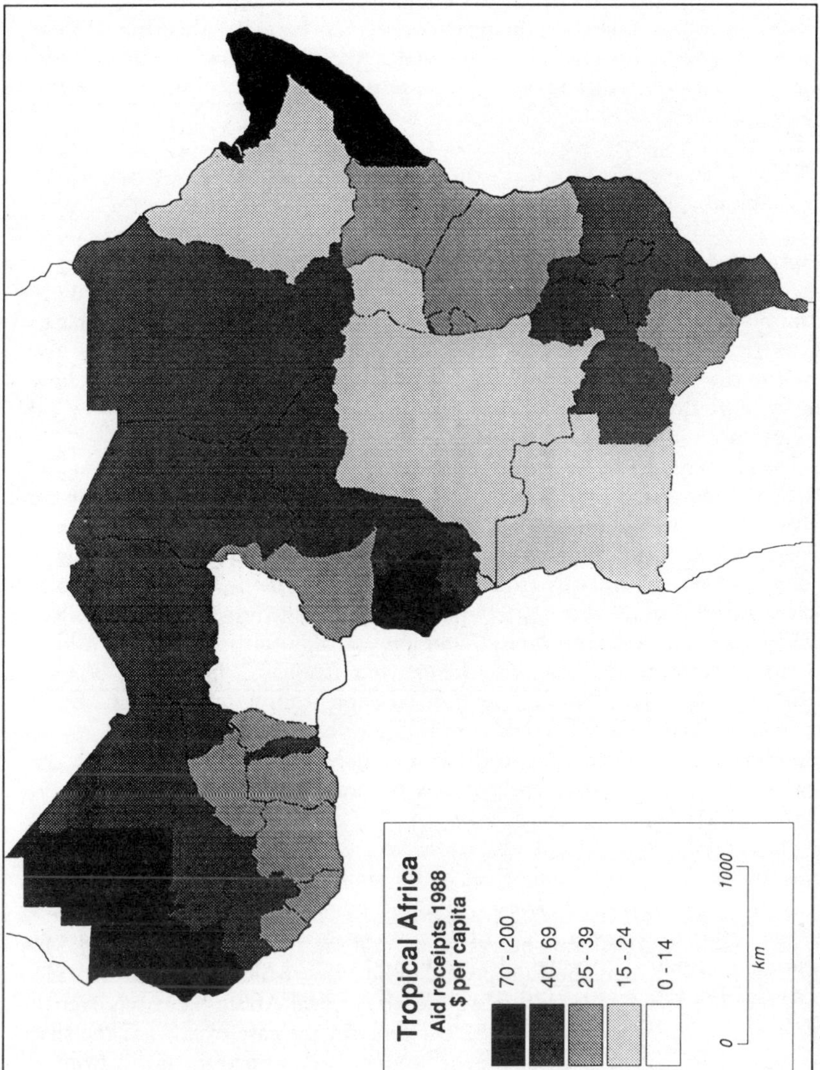

Map 11.1 Aid receipts, 1988

concerns where it goes, and the broad picture is indicated in Table 11.1 and Map 11.1. The distribution of aid is clearly very uneven. In per capita terms very little aid, strictly defined, has been supplied to Nigeria throughout the 1980s, since the country's oil revenues seemed to make this unnecessary. Nigeria's own ambitious plans did make loans necessary, but these were obtained from both official and private sectors mainly at commercial rates – leading to the present huge burden of debt.

Relative prosperity also helps to explain why only moderate amounts of aid have been provided for Cameroon and Côte d'Ivoire, and especially why they rank low in aid receipts as a proportion of GNP. Internal conflict rather than lack of need has been the main reason for low flows over many years to Angola and Uganda, and more recently to Liberia also. A combination of internal conflict and the nature of the regime contributed to a feeble flow to Ethiopia up to 1984, since when emergency food aid has brought it nearer to the African average. The flow to Ghana has also increased from very low levels in the early 1980s, which were due in part to lack of confidence in how the state would use the aid. The same factor contributes to relatively low aid receipts per capita in Zaïre.

The greatest inflow in per capita terms in the mid 1980s was to drought-stricken Mauritania and Somalia. As deeply Islamic countries, both were favoured recipients of aid from oil-rich Middle Eastern governments. Senegal, Mali and Niger also received, and continue to receive, large quantities of aid, primarily from France which was the former metropolitan power in each case. Among Commonwealth countries, Tanzania has for many years received the largest amount of aid, with the Scandinavian countries prominent among the donors; but recently Zambia has become even more dependent on aid in relation to population numbers and GNP, as its economy has suffered severely from low prices for the copper exports on which it is so heavily reliant. Aid has long played an even larger role in the Malawi economy; and recently it has become vital to Mozambique also (Table 11.1).

The spatial pattern of aid allocations across the world has been frequently criticized as reflecting the motives of the donors far more closely than the needs of the recipients. However, it could be argued that tropical Africa's share of total aid receipts is a fair reflection of its needs (whereas the share of South Asia might be thought too low, and that of various middle-income countries far too high). And in general the pattern within Africa bears a reasonable relationship to needs. Kenya might be regarded as reasonably typical in terms of needs, and it is also about the African average in terms of per capita aid inflow. The same is true of Sudan in most years, while there was a notable increase in the inflow of aid there in the crisis years of 1985 and 1986. The most serious anomaly is Ethiopia, which continues to be starved of aid – both from the USSR which has concentrated on supplying military equipment, and from the West which has concentrated on emergency food aid.

Where the aid is used within countries is also important, but much less information is available on this. The general indications are that whereas some success has been achieved in directing more aid to the poorest countries, the same cannot be said of the poorest regions within countries. Aid projects are often heavily concentrated in and around the capital cities, and many remote rural areas are hardly reached at all. Tanzania is a partial exception, for strenuous efforts have been made there to involve aid donors in plans for every region – but not with great success. Emergency aid is very definitely an exception, for this has been directed explicitly to impoverished and especially famine-stricken areas, with relatively little syphoned off in the capital cities.

The question of directing more aid to the poorest regions within countries is closely related to that of directing more to the poorest people – on which the 1970s brought much rhetoric but little action. The problem is that in one country after another the most viable projects relate to the less poor areas and people. Funds allocated to agriculture in a region with erratic climate, infertile soils and a low level of infrastructure are bound to bring a poorer return than funds spent in a more favourable environment. Probably the least successful aid projects around the world have been those concentrated with livestock in semi-arid Africa. In a situation where no-one knows how to bring about economic improvements in the poorest regions, it may not really be appropriate for a larger share of aid to be directed there.

Evaluating the aid

Some of the difficulties of evaluating aid were indicated at the start of the chapter. Should we consider only the economic impact, or try to assess social and political impact also? Is a consequence such as increased political stability always to be seen as a benefit? How do we view aid that benefits large sections of the population but widens disparities between these sections and the remainder? It is hard to know what time-scale we should adopt in any assessment, for clear benefits can rarely be expected instantly. Many brave attempts at calculating the benefits of investments in education, health care and even family planning have been made: but some of the benefits, and some of the costs, are in no way quantifiable.

It certainly cannot be argued that aid to Africa in general, or even specific projects and programmes, have 'failed' just because poverty persists or because particular situations have not improved. The aid might have helped to prevent a massive deterioration. Very rarely can we determine precisely how things would have been different if the aid had not been provided, but no doubt virtually all aid has brought a mixture of gains and losses. All we can hope is that the gains do generally outweigh the losses.

Most of the criticisms of aid apply universally rather than just in Africa, and some are based on a particular ideological stance. Peter Bauer (1981) is the most eloquent spokesman of those who dislike aid because it increases the role of the state rather than private enterprise. Teresa Hayter (1985) speaks for those who dislike aid because it helps to preserve the largely capitalist status quo. The most ardent supporters of aid tend to fall more within the middle of the ideological spectrum.

It is very doubtful whether much aid to Africa has been on balance economically harmful, although even no-interest loans do contribute to a country's debt burden, and even though many local costs are always involved, including the time spent by officials dealing with the donor agencies. Possibly certain roads cost more to maintain than they save in reduced transport costs, and no doubt there are some other 'white elephants': but most aid has done something to increase productivity, to provide employment and to raise living standards. In general, people are materially better off than they would have been without aid. However, in very many cases the economic benefits have been far smaller than was anticipated. The Cassen study (1986) suggests that the record has been more disappointing in tropical Africa than in most other parts of the world.

The negative side of aid lies mainly in the dependence that it creates and reinforces. It gives outsiders power over the lives of people in Africa, and often leads to the imposition of inappropriate alien ideas. Barbara Harrell-Bond (1986) is highly critical of this even in the case of United Nations emergency assistance to Ugandan refugees in Sudan. It is surely a far more disturbing aspect of long-term bilateral aid, and applies just as much to the provision of services through technical assistance and scholarships as to the provision of finance. Both political and cultural dependence must be regarded as a heavy 'cost' of aid, perhaps especially in francophone Africa. The influence of France on countries such as Senegal and Niger through its aid programme is much stronger than the influence of Britain on countries such as Ghana or Tanzania.

Political, cultural and economic dependence are all intensified by the widespread tying of aid to expenditure in the donor country, and this is one of the main disadvantages of the fact that more aid is still bilateral than multi-lateral. Naturally, Britain wants its aid money spent on British goods, but this is not helpful to Tanzania if the goods could be obtained more cheaply from Japan, or even from Kenya.

The availability of aid for certain projects may affect priorities in most unfortunate ways, and lead to neglect of important matters that are not currently in fashion. But this argument is sometimes overplayed. With regard to health care, for instance, there is no evidence that most aid agencies have any greater bias towards specialist hospitals as against rural dispensaries than do most African governments. No doubt there is some bias towards intercity highways rather than local feeder roads, but again many African governments have shown a similar bias in their own spending. It is in fact difficult to point to specific wrong turnings that African countries have taken as a result of the availability of aid. The charge might be more justified for some of the conditions currently being imposed by the IMF, and for some of the advice offered by the World Bank, than for actual provision of aid.

Discussions of aid are often much concerned with the motives of the donors. These are never wholly altruistic, and are usually very mixed, but it is not clear how this normally affects the value of the aid. Most aid agencies are set up on the premise that what they do will be of mutual benefit to both donors and recipients. The alternative view, that one party can only gain at the expense of the other, could only lead to the conclusion that Africa would be better off without aid. An intermediate position is taken here. Donor countries have generally gained from their aid to Africa, directly or indirectly, and a group of extremely well paid international civil servants gain immensely from the operations of various UN bodies and the European Development Fund. The people of Africa have also gained, but may well have had a much smaller share of the gains when all aspects are taken into account.

The balance of advantage is probably quite different in the case of national and international voluntary agencies, and also in the case of emergency aid provided by governments. But in most years both these categories account for only a small proportion of the total aid flow, and therefore our assessment must be based mainly on long-term official aid.

Perhaps the most compelling reason for believing that most aid is of some benefit to Africa, albeit of far less benefit than it might be, is that African countries continue to seek it. Those who regard it as predominantly harmful must consider most African governments to be composed of either fools or crooks. African governments are, of course, highly diverse in nature, and no doubt in the extent of both their wisdom and their integrity, but *all* are keen to receive at least some types of foreign aid. However, such is the complexity of the issue that even the effects of aid on these governments themselves are ambivalent. In some ways it strengthens their power, and is sought partly for this reason; but in other ways it shifts power from them to the donor governments or agencies.

Most aid certainly does not bring 'power to the people' in the short run, but nor does the poverty that it is in part intended to relieve and even overcome. To suggest that in general it undermines people's capacity and will to look after themselves is surely unduly disparaging. Most people in Africa will continue to be very largely self-reliant even in the unlikely event of a great increase in aid.

Recent trends in aid to Africa

While the total volume of aid to Africa has remained almost constant in real terms for twenty years, there have been some important changes in its nature. And while there is much to criticize in many aid programmes, most recent trends do constitute improvements, with some evidence of learning from experience.

One trend that is particularly welcome to the recipients is an increase in the proportion of aid that is channelled through multilateral institutions, such as the European Community and the World Bank's International Development Association. In the early 1970s only 15 per cent of all aid to Africa passed through such institutions, but by the late 1980s this had risen to almost 30 per cent. This may not actually reduce the extent of African countries' dependence, but it does diffuse it somewhat. Whereas these countries are not represented in any way in the aid administrations of France or the USA, they do have a small representation in the administration of the World Bank and the IDA and of all United Nations bodies that provide aid.

An even more important trend has been towards an increasing proportion of outright grants rather than loans, as a response to the mounting debt problems of most African countries – discussed in the next chapter. This may not represent pure altruism on the part of the donors, but just a realization that there is no alternative. However, it certainly constitutes an improvement for the recipients. It is particularly good to note that there has been an almost complete shift to either grants or no-interest loans in the case of the poorest countries. For instance, these now receive no funds from the main section of the World Bank, but are supplied instead through the IDA.

There is some evidence of increased thought and sensitivity in the administration of aid. More attention is given to the diversity of local cultures than twenty years ago, with fewer attempts to impose a standard package often formulated in some other part of the world. Efforts are increasingly being made to consult local leaders with regard to their perceived needs and possible ways of fulfilling these. There is greater appreciation of the possible negative consequences of various innovations. And almost every aid administration has begun in the 1980s to take more account of the environmental impact of development projects. Many examples are provided in the recent books by Paul Harrison (1987) and by Czech Conroy and Miles Litvinoff (1988).

Another welcome trend in ways of thinking about the world that is beginning to be reflected in aid programmes is a recognition of the significance of gender issues. Some aid programmes are directed specifically to the needs of women, especially in the field of maternity health care. Others are at last acknowledging that tackling many issues, from basic agriculture to water supplies, involves direct contact with women as much as, or in some cases even more than, with men.

Undoubtedly, many African governments have gained valuable experience in dealing with aid agencies, and are coming to realize some of the ways in which badly-managed aid can be counterproductive. In particular, they are more aware of the ways in which programmes may incur substantial local costs. Partly at the insistence of these governments, some steps have been taken to improve co-ordination among rival donors – though of course too close a liaison among all the donors would not be welcome if this weakened the recipients' bargaining position.

Food aid

This is perhaps the most controversial form of aid. Some critics see it merely as a means of dumping surplus food produced by the highly protected agricultural systems of Europe and North America, and argue that it tends to undermine agriculture in the receiving countries. However, the most substantial recent academic study of the topic (Singer et al. 1987) is cautiously favourable.

Until recently such food aid was directed mainly at South Asia and North Africa, but during the 1980s the share taken by tropical Africa greatly increased. In 1984–6 some of this was emergency famine relief, considered below, but since 1986 most has been more orthodox food aid, amounting to over 3 million tons a year, and directed especially to Mozambique, Sudan, Ethiopia and Somalia. Much is grain provided by the European Community from its surplus stocks, and undoubtedly the need for it is far greater in the Horn of Africa.

A large proportion in normal years is used to feed the urban population, since they would otherwise be very short of food. Farmers have not been able to produce sufficient surpluses to feed the cities, and transport to move even small surpluses there is often not available. In the absence of food aid the urban dwellers would have to rely very largely on food imported commercially, which some countries simply cannot afford. The result would be either severe hunger for many people or a further increased burden of debt.

In the long run, increased productivity in African agriculture would be far preferable to continued food aid; but until this can be achieved food aid,

Table 11.2 Leading tropical African recipients of food aid, 1985–8 (*volume in thousands of tons*)

	1985	*1986*	*1987*	*1988*
Ethiopia	869	793	554	825
Mozambique	378	252	309	466
Somalia	248	126	145	152
Sudan	813	904	864	604

Source: UNDP/World Bank, *African Economic and Financial Data* (1989)

carefully handled, has a contribution to make to the welfare of people in Africa. This was the final conclusion of a very critical study of the topic by Philip Raikes (1988) in the specific context of the EEC and Africa.

Emergency aid

Emergency aid to Africa suddenly became highly significant in the mid 1980s in the wake of the famine crisis discussed in Chapter 7. The story has been told in several books (Gill 1986, Jansson et al. 1987, Fraser 1988) and will not be repeated here. It received so much publicity in the West, that for many people there, 'aid to Africa' would probably mean famine relief of this nature, even several years after it largely ended. Voluntary agencies played a leading role in the early stages, before national governments and the United Nations system belatedly creaked into action.

The aid took the form mainly of food and transport equipment, the largest flows being in 1985. At one stage twenty-five African countries were involved, but much the most important destinations were Ethiopia and Sudan. The total volume of emergency food supplied to these two countries alone from overseas in 1984–5 exceeded 2 million tons. In addition, large quantities were rushed from eastern Sudan into Ethiopia in the early part of 1984, when Sudan still appeared to have surplus grain. In early 1985 famine relief food was being distributed to more than 7 million people in Ethiopia, and it is generally thought to have saved several million lives. The needs were so great, and transport conditions so poor, that much of the food had to be flown into the areas that needed it – a very costly operation, even if a better use of military aircraft than that for which they are designed.

There are those such as Alex De Waal (1989) who doubt whether the emergency food did save many lives, at least in Sudan. He claims that most deaths were from disease rather than from lack of food, and that the emergency supplies should have been of medical equipment and drugs. However, it is also arguable that it is precisely because food aid did arrive just in time that mass starvation was avoided, and that these food supplies eventually checked the movements of people which had contributed to the spread of infectious diseases.

Various parts of Africa certainly needed some forms of international emergency aid in the 1980s, and we must expect this need to recur in the 1990s. Reporters such as Michael Buerk and Peter Gill, photographers such as Mohammed Amin, and entrepreneurial individuals such as Bob Geldof played extremely valuable roles in demonstrating the need to those in the rich world with the means to assist, and eventually in galvanizing governments into action. The issues involved in maximizing the benefits of such aid, and in minimizing its inevitable harmful side-effects, are unfortunately highly complex, as Randolph Kent (1987) has ably demonstrated. It seems particularly churlish to criticize people who are clearly sacrificing their own welfare and safety to assist others in need, but errors of judgemment are bound to occur, especially when decisions are taken in great haste. And since further emergencies are highly likely, it is vitally important that lessons are learned (Anderson and Woodrow 1989). There is perhaps an emerging consensus that the most important lesson from the 1980s experiences concerns the need to obtain a clearer picture of what those afflicted by disaster consider to be their greatest needs. This lesson must be learned by both governments and non-governmental organizations, and by both foreign donors and those within African countries with the power to assist.

It must be remembered, however, that emergency aid represents only a very small proportion of all overseas aid to Africa, and an infinitesimally small proportion of all forms of economic interaction between Africa and the rest of the world. Ideally, its importance within the total aid picture should shrink even further if real aid for long-term improvements in welfare can somehow be increased, and if, partly as a result of this, the need for emergency relief can be reduced.

Conclusions

The governments of all the countries of tropical Africa consider that foreign aid can be of benefit to them and to their people, and most will continue to feel the need for aid for the foreseeable future. Most probably the need will itensify in some countries as various pressures increase, including the pressure of population on the land.

There is little doubt that aid has indeed brought material benefits to Africa over the past twenty years, including improved communications, purer water supplies, better health care and an expanded educational system. During both the mid 1970s and the mid 1980s, emergency aid certainly saved the lives of millions of people who would otherwise have starved. At the same time, all types of aid have maintained and even increased the dependence of African countries on the richer nations, subjecting them to strong political and cultural influences.

There is much scope for the improvement of aid. It would be to Africa's advantage if more consisted of grants rather than loans, if more passed through multilateral institutions, if more of the bilateral aid were untied, and if there were better co-ordination among donors. The poor majority would benefit if more were directed specifically to their needs, and if there were a better understanding of these needs. In this regard African governments may be as much to blame as the aid agencies. It might be helpful for the poor of some countries if more aid could be channelled through voluntary agencies, which have some scope for by-passing governments. The impact on poverty might also be increased if some redirection of aid were to take place. There is a particular need, for instance, for long-term development aid to Ethiopia.

Aid is a very poor substitute for international responses to African poverty involving fundamental changes in global power structures, but there is absolutely no prospect of such changes. Even the idea of some global form of taxation is still generally regarded as absurd by those who would lose from it. As long as most people in Europe and North America remain ten, twenty or even fifty times richer than most in Africa, and there is no other mechanism for redistribution, an aid system in some form must continue. It is even likely that emergency aid of the type required on a massive scale in 1984–5 will again be needed at some stage in the 1990s.

The continuation of aid at the present level would surely be better than nothing, especially if its quality can be improved. However, if it is to do more than assist survival, for people and countries, the flow must be greatly increased. If it were doubled in real terms worldwide, to reach the level of 0·7 per cent of the rich countries' GNP, as recommended long ago by the United Nations and restated in the Brandt reports, and if the share allocated to Africa were maintained, then it might begin to have a substantial impact on poverty. Sadly, at present there is nothing to indicate that such an increase will take place.

12 Debt

Until very recently, a mention of 'the problem of debt' in Africa would normally have referred to debt at the individual or family level. This is an important matter, discussed by Polly Hill (1986) and a few others, but ignored by many writers on African societies and economies. It is neglected partly because little is known about it except by the people involved, and partly because it is perceived to be less of a problem than in some other parts of the world. Over most of tropical Africa moneylenders are much less in evidence than, say, in India; and most people incur only small debts to neighbours or to local traders. Even so, we probably ought to know much more than we do about debt at this level if we are properly to understand African poverty.

In the 1980s 'the problem of debt' in Africa came to refer mainly to the problem at national level (Parfitt and Riley 1989). At this level it is now a more serious and intractable problem in Africa than in any other part of the world; and the extent and effects of it are widely recognized. Whereas the aid situation has really changed little since the 1960s, debt as an aspect of Africa's external relations has changed out of all recognition. From being a minor and manageable issue, it has emerged as a major element in the widely-perceived 'economic crisis' in Africa. It has played a part in directing world-wide attention to the continent, and international bodies such as the IMF (International Monetary Fund) and the World Bank are becoming deeply involved in what seems an almost unmanageable situation.

The degree to which external debt is a new feature of tropical Africa is indicated by the fact that the size of the debt increased in real terms by over 25 per cent annually between 1972 and 1982. From a total of about $5 or 6 billion in the early 1970s it had risen to around $100 billion in the early

1980s. Fortunately, the rate of increase has now slowed very substantially, but the total size of the burden is still becoming greater every year, while the means to deal with it are not. Unless new means can be found to tackle the problem, it is expected that tropical African debt will grow further, from its 1988 level of $135 billion, to reach $200 billion by the year 2000.

In countries such as Sudan, external debt compounds other critical problems such as famine. In some countries that have been spared widespread famine, notably Zaïre, the government probably now sees debt as its greatest economic problem. Even there, of course, it is part of a complex of problems, so that it can be argued that the fundamental issue is not so much the debt itself, which countries trying to develop are almost bound to incur, as the failure to generate the income needed to pay it off (SCF/ODI 1988). In so far as debt is one element in a multiplicity of problems, it is very difficult to be specific about its consequences, but it has certainly contributed to the deterioration in the quality of life for many people in many African countries in the 1980s. So also, in the short term, has the 'medicine' that has been prescribed to treat the disease, especially in IMF structural adjustment packages (George 1988, Onimode 1989); and in many cases it is impossible to separate the effects of the disease from those of the medicine.

The size and nature of the debt

In absolute terms tropical Africa's external debt does not match that of Latin America, and it may therefore seem less important in the major centres of world finance. Africa's influence on global financial affairs is far less than that of Latin America as a result. The $140 billion involved by the late 1980s was comparable to the amounts owed just by Brazil or by Mexico. Figures of $200 to 250 billion are sometimes quoted, but these include the debt of Egypt, the Maghreb countries and South Africa.

This debt burden is, however, more crippling to tropical Africa than to Latin America since it represents a higher proportion of total GNP – over 90 per cent compared with under 60 per cent. For several individual countries the figure is well over 150 per cent (Map 12.1) and still rising. The equivalent figure for India is a mere 15 per cent, and relatively stable.

The most widely quoted figures are those for the debt service ratio, which relates scheduled annual payments of interest and capital to annual export earnings. The ratio has worsened not only due to increased payments but also due to falling export earnings in the 1980s. In many African countries it is now between 40 and 50 per cent, comparable to that in both Brazil and Mexico: but in certain countries it has risen above 100 per cent, and therefore payments could not possibly be made on schedule. Rescheduling

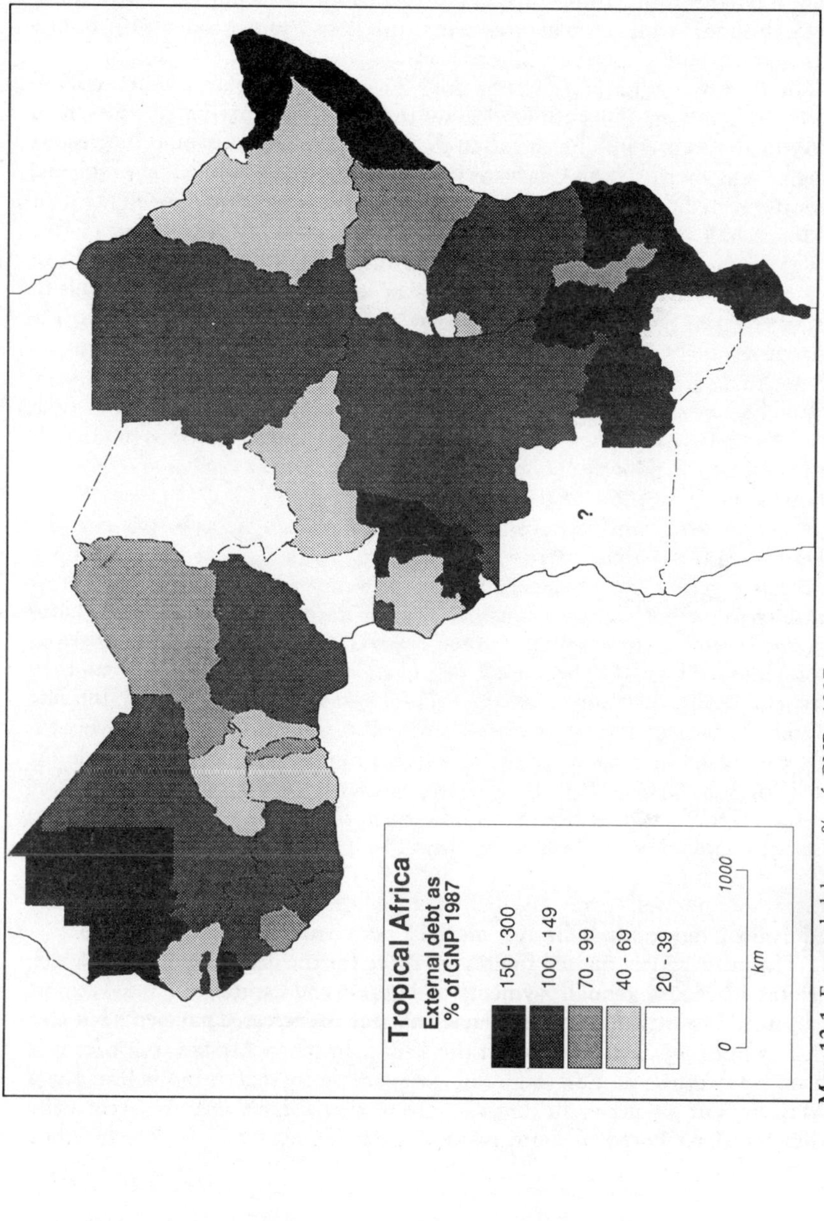

Map 12.1 External debt as % of GNP, 1987

has to be negotiated, often annually, and even after this has been done many countries must pay out over a quarter of their export earnings as debt service. Total payments due from tropical Africa in both 1988 and 1989 were about $21 billion, while actual payments in 1988 were about $10 billion (compared with exports of $38 billion).

In contrast to Latin America, only 20 per cent of the debt is owed to private banks in the rich world, so the African situation has not been considered to present any threat to the world banking system. A further 15 per cent is owed to other private firms, such as those which have supplied goods on credit – especially to Nigeria whose oil made it seem credit-worthy. Almost half the debt is owed by African governments to governments in the West, some as a direct result of past aid inflows in the form of loans – most of which involve repayment of interest as well as capital, even if at below-market rates. Further large sums are owed by some of the more prosperous countries, such as Nigeria and Côte d'Ivoire, to the European Community on loans that carried quite high interest rates, while some of the debt of Sudan, Somalia and Mauritania is to the oil-rich countries of the Middle East. Almost every African country has debts to the World Bank (or to the IDA in the case of the poorest countries), while a final 10 per cent or so represents borrowing from the IMF.

It is doubtful whether most of the debt arises from aid as it was narrowly defined in the last chapter, so we should be cautious about using indebtedness as a general argument against the provision of aid. Much arises from inter-government arrangements such as export credits provided by rich countries to boost their own exports. Nigeria in particular imported massive quantities of goods in the late 1970s and early 1980s using such high-interest official credit, assuming that oil revenues would maintain their high levels. Other large-scale recipients were Zaïre and Sudan. Military equipment has also been supplied to many countries both by the West and, notably in the case of Ethiopia, by the USSR. These armaments have not normally been gifts, yet few countries have been able to pay for them outright: their cost is a major component in the debt burden.

The distribution of the debt

Although the problem of debt is now widespread in Africa, it is by no means identical from country to country either in its nature or in its intensity. Many published accounts of African debt give far too little attention to the geography of the phenomenon, but comparative country data are provided in various World Bank and IMF publications. A summary is provided in Table 12.1, and the broad picture is shown in Map 12.1.

Table 12.1 Extent of external debt in selected African countries, 1987

	Total external debt ($ millions)	*Long-term debt as % of GNP*
Nigeria	28,700	111
Côte d'Ivoire	13,500	124
Sudan	11,100	102
Zaïre	8,600	140
Zambia	6,400	230
Kenya	5,900	64
Tanzania	4,300	144
Senegal	3,700	69
Ghana	3,100	45
Somalia	2,500	237
Zimbabwe	2,500	37
Uganda	1,400	30

Sources: World Bank publications

Despite its oil revenues, and even to some extent because of them as indicated above, Nigeria has incurred much the largest debts in absolute terms. There are, of course, no entirely reliable figures, but by 1987 its debts amounted to at least $28 billion. In per capita terms this is not far off the African average, while Nigeria's debt-service ratio is also not untypical. The size of its debt very largely reflects the size of its population and its economy. The most distinctive feature of Nigeria's debt is that half of it is owed to private banks and other firms, and much of this is owed by the Nigerian private sector. Timing and interest rates have been such that over 80 per cent of the debt-service due in 1986–7 was due to private lenders. This means that the nature of the debt problem in Nigeria has much in common with some Latin American countries rather than with most countries in Africa.

Sudan's debt is smaller in absolute terms, but is similar in relation to GNP and to annual exports. It is in fact about ten times the annual value of exports, and the debt-service ratio in terms of payments due in the late 1980s exceeded 120 per cent. Very little is owed to banks, the main lenders having been foreign governments, including those of Kuwait and Saudi Arabia which poured money into large-scale development schemes when Sudan was perceived as the future 'breadbasket' of the Arab world.

Zaïre and Côte d'Ivoire are probably the two other largest debtors, with accumulated debts larger than annual GNP, and with scheduled debt-service ratios of 40 to 50 per cent – comparable to Nigeria's. Money has been lent to

Côte d'Ivoire with some confidence, by private banks as well as governments: it has been lent to Zaïre more often in desperation to keep its economy afloat, with the IMF playing a larger role there than in most African countries.

Zambia is another of the most indebted countries, and it shares with Mauritania and Somalia the distinction of having debts that exceed 200 per cent of GNP. It borrowed heavily when copper prices fell, assuming that it would be able to repay when they rose again: unfortunately no such revival has occurred. Lower than expected mineral export earnings have also contributed to intense debt problems in Liberia and Togo, while efforts to maintain government spending in drought-stricken Mali and Niger have pushed them too deeper into debt. However, the most extreme position in terms of the ratio between debt and exceptionally small recorded exports is shared by Somalia and Guinea-Bissau.

It would be wrong to direct attention only to those countries where the debt crisis is particularly severe. Tanzania might be taken as a country where the level of debt in relation to population, GNP and exports is very typical of tropical Africa as a whole. It is fitting, therefore, that its former president, Julius Nyerere, has on many occasions acted as spokesman for Africa on the debt issue (e.g. Nyerere 1985). Kenya, Senegal and Ghana are among the countries whose situation is somewhat better than average, though in Ghana debt-service payments were increasing sharply in the late 1980s just as cocoa export prices were falling, and in both Senegal and Kenya debt constitutes a very severe burden – for the government and for the people.

Cameroon, Burundi, Rwanda, Uganda, Malawi and Zimbabwe are among the more favourably placed African countries in respect of external debt. In some cases this is because they have been cautious about incurring it: in others it is because few lenders have favoured them. Very few loans have been made to Uganda, for instance, in view of the political turbulence that has prevailed throughout the 1970s and 1980s. Similar considerations also apply to Angola, Mozambique and Ethiopia. For all three the data available are very incomplete, but we know that few loans have been made to any of these countries by governments of the West or the East, or by international bodies such as the World Bank and the IMF. It has been suggested, however, that Ethiopia's debt to the USSR for military equipment now exceeds $3 billion, though it must be very unlikely that this will ever be repaid.

The causes of the debt problem

At one level it is easy enough to explain why most African countries are in debt. They have borrowed money and have been increasingly unable to pay it back. Most also have a chronic balance of payments deficit, with the value of imports greatly exceeding that of exports. The gap is only partly filled by other transfers, notably aid in the form of outright grants. It is not so easy to explain why the debt has increased so rapidly in recent years, nor why it is so much greater than in regions such as South and South East Asia.

There is no doubt that a whole series of factors have contributed to the situation, and as in the case of the more general economic crisis, some are internal to Africa while others are external. Various African countries have formulated overambitious development plans, with a high import content, and some of the spending must be regarded as extravagant. In many cases corruption has increased costs and reduced social benefits. These may be regarded as primarily internal factors, although of course many plans have been prepared by advisers from outside, and foreign firms often play a part in the corruption. The debt of a country such as Zaïre is greatly increased by the diversion of billions of dollars from government funds into private Swiss bank accounts.

Basically, the debt has built up through the spending of borrowed money on projects and activities which have failed to yield positive financial returns. Some, such as re-equipping the military with everything from weapons to uniforms, could never be expected to do so. Others, such as building new schools and universities, could only do so in the long term. Yet others, such as new factories, should have created income almost immediately, but have in fact operated at a loss ever since they were opened. Irrigation schemes, tourist hotels and intercity highways are among the projects which have sometimes failed to generate enough revenue to allow repayment of the loans with which they were built. In a more general way, the debt crisis has intensified because exports have not expanded even in line with population growth, so that boosting exports has occupied a prominent place in the prescriptions of the World Bank and the IMF for easing the problem.

Export earnings are, of course, a function of prices as well as volume, and this wholly external factor has contributed greatly to the debt crisis. The terms of trade have moved against Africa during the 1980s, and the prices obtainable for many of its exports have been lower than might reasonably have been expected. Occasional booms, as for coffee in 1977, have encouraged spending, but have proved very short-lived. Meanwhile, prices for most imports have risen inexorably, whether they be luxury consumer goods for the élite or basic inputs to development projects.

Two other external factors of fundamental importance have been the availability of funds and the interest rates charged. The late 1970s brought vastly increased access to credit and loans, partly through the recycling of massive oil revenues through the 'Eurodollar' market. Both governments and banks in the West now acknowledge that funds were at times provided without sufficient attention to the prospects for repayment. At the same time the Middle East oil producers themselves became a supplementary source of loan finance on what then seemed generous terms. However, by the early 1980s a massive world-wide rise in interest rates has occurred, largely as a result of the domestic financial policies of the United States. Few of the loans had been offered at fixed rates, so African countries which had borrowed when interest rates were 7 or 8 per cent were soon faced with annual charges of 15 per cent. Here is a situation where dependency is contributing very directly to poverty – a relationship which in more general terms is far more often asserted than effectively demonstrated.

The rise in interest rates has, of course, been much more significant for countries such as Nigeria or Côte d'Ivoire than for those such as Tanzania or Mali whose borrowing has been mainly at highly concessional rates. Possibly more significant for the poorest countries has been the fact that grant aid has not flowed as freely as was anticipated. In per capita terms such aid has been shrinking, and while this might in theory be seen as reducing dependency it has often actually led African governments to borrow in order to make good the shortfall. There are clearly very close links between aid and debt, which demonstrate the critical importance of the form of aid. Aid in the form of loans has directly contributed to the debt problem, whereas aid in the form of grants can do much to relieve it.

The causes of Africa's debt problem thus lie partly in policies pursued by African and overseas governments, which can sometimes be changed. But they lie partly in structures which cannot easily be changed, some inherent in African economies and some inherent in the global economy.

The consequences of the debt

The most immediate consequence of the debt problem has been the amount of time and energy that African governments have had to devote to national finances. This has included both the rescheduling of official debt through what is known as the Paris Club and negotiations for short-term assistance from the IMF. Fresh arrangements often have to be made after just one or two years, and the process absorbs much very scarce skilled manpower.

A second consequence has been the need to accept the strict conditions now imposed by the lenders. The IMF is particularly significant in this respect, since an agreement with the IMF is often a prerequisite for rescheduling with other lenders. The debt situation has thus greatly curtailed African countries' freedom of manoeuvre, and given the IMF a great deal of power over them (George 1988, Onimode 1989). Nearly all observers agree on that, however much they differ on the appropriateness of the conditions imposed. It has been argued that debts the size of Brazil's actually give such countries a form of power, but the debts of African countries simply weaken their bargaining power in international affairs.

One of the most devastating results of the debt crisis in many African countries has been a dramatic cut in imports. In Nigeria the annual import bill was cut from $17 billion in 1982 to under $5 billion in 1985 and 1986; and while this included what some would consider a long-overdue restriction on luxuries for the élite, it also included reduced supplies of raw materials and spare parts for industry, basic transport equipment and so on. In other countries, such as Sudan, there have also been massive cuts in imports of fuel. What has been called 'import strangulation' causes industrial enterprises and transport systems to work far below capacity, and it has often also contributed to the stagnation or even decline of exports. This type of vicious circle is proving very hard to break.

In so far as the debt is owed by governments, it also leads to cuts in public spending on everything from health care to road maintenance. Again, some of this expenditure was very wasteful or was geared only to the élite, but the cuts are not necessarily made in these areas. Many of them have brought hardship for the poor majority, and UNICEF is among the organizations which have highlighted their impact on the welfare of children. Adults and children are dying because debt repayment is having to take priority over basic medical services or safer water supplies.

Debt is contributing to food shortages as agricultural extension services are cut, supplies of fertilizers and insecticides are restricted, transport bottlenecks hamper marketing, and schemes for better food storage cannot be implemented. It has long been recognized that research on food crops has been neglected as energies have been directed to export crops; but debt is causing the concentration on export crops to be reinforced. Even from the perspective of rural families, giving priority to increased exports makes good sense in certain areas, such as highland Kenya, but in many other areas it distorts the local economy and puts basic food supplies at risk.

To pick up an early theme of this book, incurring debt in the 1970s helped to relieve slightly the poverty of many people (and made a few very rich), but in a sense made the countries poorer. The measures taken in the 1980s to resolve the debt crisis may in this sense be relieving national poverty, but they have intensified the poverty of millions of individual families.

Prospects

Some African countries may continue to avoid a severe debt crisis by incurring few debts, but generally at the cost of continued extreme poverty.

Some more affluent countries, such as Côte d'Ivoire, may find a period of austerity sufficient to reduce their debt to manageable proportions. However, most countries in tropical Africa are likely to remain heavily in debt throughout the 1990s.

Rescheduling has brought short-term relief to many countries and will no doubt continue to do so, but it certainly does not resolve the problem. It merely increases the amount that has to be repaid at a later stage. Certain debts have been cancelled, generally by redesignating loans as grants, but this is often at the expense of fresh grants that would otherwise have been made. It is clearly unrealistic to expect widespread outright cancellation of debt, and it would surely be inappropriate in some cases, notably where the borrowed money has been used to swell the fortunes of corrupt leaders. A particular problem arises where a government inherits a massive debt from a very corrupt previous regime. No African government has yet simply refused to pay, and in view of the sanctions that would be imposed on it, none is likely to do so. The most that any of them could do would be to put a ceiling on the proportion of export earnings that can be used for debt repayment in any year.

In so far as accumulated debts will in the main have to be paid off, they inevitably mean intensified poverty in Africa for years to come. The options concern matters such as the timing and incidence of the impact. Should there be extreme austerity for a few years in order to cast off the burden, or should every effort be made to spread it out over a longer period? Can the cutbacks be directed at the rich, or is there no chance of that happening – so that the impact is bound to be felt at least in part by those already desperately poor? Should those to whom the debt is owed try to influence the incidence of the hardship? Can they discriminate between those countries where they need to exert great influence and those where this is not necessary? Can they single out those countries for which a substantial degree of debt 'forgiveness' is either justified by the past record or essential if widespread suffering to the point of starvation is to be avoided?

It is unlikely that a clear-cut answer to any of these questions will emerge over the next decade. The picture will probably remain very confused. However, we can be fairly sure that without incurring massive new debts most African countries will find themselves increasingly indebted despite great efforts to repay. Debt is likely to intensify both their dependence and their poverty, although a combination of actions by those in power both inside and outside Africa could do much to reduce the suffering resulting directly from it.

13 Conclusions

This book has painted a grim picture. A book concerned explicitly with poverty in Africa could not do otherwise. There are many very much more positive features of the continent, but these are increasingly being overshadowed by the curse of material poverty. The intensity of the poverty is not the same everywhere, but across the whole of tropical Africa there is a remarkable degree of similarity – certainly sufficient to take this region as the frame of reference for this book. In the preceding chapters attention has been drawn both to the similarities among tropical African countries and to some of the important variations from one to another. At the same time we should note that there are great differences even within countries; and that these incipient nation–states resulting from the colonial experience, with which many people do not yet identify at all strongly, are far from ideal units for the discussion of poverty.

It is in the nature of poverty that precise data are very rarely available. Poor countries cannot afford to collect accurate statistics, and poor people have much more important concerns than filling in forms, which many could not in fact read. The poverty of families who depend very largely on subsistence production is inherently unmeasurable: but that does not make it any less real. Although we lack any form of precise information on most of the topics discussed in this book, broad orders of magnitude are very well known in many cases, and are profoundly disturbing.

There are pockets of poverty in every country in the world, including the richest. In most Latin American and Middle Eastern countries large sections of the population must be considered as poor, although there is sufficient wealth elsewhere in these countries for such extensive poverty to be a national disgrace. In China poverty is even more widespread, though its intensity has been much reduced in recent years and inequality is much less evident. But only in South Asia and parts of South East Asia is poverty comparable to that in tropical Africa both in its intensity and in its extensiveness.

Regardless of the measure that we attempt to use, most of the countries of tropical Africa are among the world's poorest, and this poverty extends to most people within these countries. It is really almost meaningless to speak of 'the poor' in Sudan or Zaïre as if they constituted a distinct group, although it is possible to identify groups who are even poorer than the rest. It is far more meaningful to speak of the very small groups who are not poor, and the even tinier minority who can be considered rich. Perhaps a book will sometime be written about them. This book has been concerned with all the 400 million or more who must be regarded as poor by world standards, though with some special attention to the poorest 50 to 100 million threatened with, and in some cases suffering, starvation.

In some ways the most disturbing feature of poverty in Africa, and one which distinguishes it even from poverty in South Asia, is that it has been intensifying over the past two decades, and that no improvement of the situation is in prospect. Average incomes have been declining in real terms, and the absolute numbers of people below any given threshold have been rising rapidly. Even the widespread improvements in social welfare which continued through the 1970s and into the early 1980s seem to have halted in many countries, and gone into reverse in some. Death rates have continued to fall, so far as we know, but even this may be reversed in the 1990s if AIDS takes a firmer grip on large parts of Africa.

These trends and prospects are all the more distressing to observers of the African scene, as well as far more importantly to the millions of families experiencing the poverty, because of the optimism that prevailed in the 1960s. Despite severe political problems, first in Zaïre and then in Nigeria and elsewhere, the departure of the colonial powers had brought widespread euphoria, and rapid improvement in material well-being was thought to be almost inevitable. Export prices were high, rainfall was (as it turns out) exceptionally plentiful, industrialization was beginning, and in every way 'development' was the order of the day. In some places economic growth was more evident than true development, but higher incomes and improved social welfare were not always confined to the fortunate few: in most countries large sections of the population enjoyed some benefits from the changes taking place. Then gradually, first in one area and then another and eventually almost everywhere, the picture changed to the one portrayed here.

Any academic study, even one as basic as this, should attempt to go beyond mere description, towards explanation. Many writers do this by means of theoretical propositions which are applied to the situation in question. Often there is just one grand theory which is considered to provide a large part of the explanation. This book has not been based on such a single theoretical formulation. It is based on the belief that many approaches have a contribution to make to the explanation of poverty in Africa, and on the very firm belief that there is rarely a single, or even one primary, explanation for poverty in a particular area, never mind across a whole continent. It is suggested here that the basic poverty of Africa, and the current deterioration of its condition, are both due to a combination of many factors. The factors are far too diverse, and the combinations far too complex, for any single fundamental cause to be identified.

The causes lie both in the past and in factors still operating today. They lie both within Africa and beyond it in the global economic and political system. The internal factors include both elements in the physical environment and human failings – most of them universal but some particularly virulent in Africa at the present time. Furthermore, the relative importance of past and present, internal and external, physical and human, differs considerably from place to place within tropical Africa.

Drought is not *the* cause of poverty in Africa, or even of widespread famine, but it has certainly contributed in large measure. Disease is not *the* explanation that some are seeking, but its huge importance has often not been fully recognized. Rapid population growth is not *the* culprit, but it is very hard to see how it can be totally irrelevant as some have suggested. The colonial experiece is also clearly relevant, although it is very difficult to understand how it can be the primary reason for poverty intensifying in the 1980s. It is arguable that the worst result of colonial rule was not impoverishment through economic exploitation, but the legacy of a political framework which survived for a few years but then to a large extent collapsed. Lack of national integration, and outright civil war, have contributed much to poverty, and indeed to famine, in Africa. So also have political leaders concerned far more with, firstly, their own survival and, secondly, their personal and family fortunes than with the welfare of their peoples. Specific government policies have often been extremely unhelpful, as institutions such as the World Bank have stressed, but so has some of the advice and intervention of those same institutions. External factors certainly include deteriorating commodity prices and terms of trade, and also rising interest rates on borrowed money. At the same time it can be argued that regions such as Africa have to stay poor so that others can stay rich, since there is no possibility of even the present world population (much less its future population) living at a European/North American level of consumption. In the short term, economic boom in the rich countries might help Africa, but in the long term their command of a grossly and increasingly disproportionate share of world resources can be seen as one fundamental cause of African poverty.

Once all these, and many more, causes are considered, Africa's present condition ceases to be surprising. Perhaps the greater mystery is why there was such widespread improvement in the 1950s and 1960s. Perhaps also those in, and concerned with, Africa should also be enquiring why the situation seems to be improving in China and even in India. Some might even suggest that since poverty has been the norm for most of humanity throughout history, it is always cases of advance towards affluence that require explanation.

However, there is no way that the present situation is acceptable to the people of Africa, especially when world communications are improving and awareness of far more favourable situations and trends elsewhere is spreading. Nor should it be acceptable to anyone else, though it is quite unrealistic to expect most people outside Africa to show much concern except in extreme cases such as well-publicized famines. It is, of course, also quite unrealistic to consider how Africa might advance along a path to prosperity in the near future. The immediate issue is how to halt decline in many respects in many areas, and then how to work for some improvement in at least some aspects of life. To a very large extent these things can only be done by people within Africa for themselves, but outsiders may even have some part to play in influencing internal circumstances, as well as having primary responsibility for the external factors.

This is not the place to make policy recommendations, even if I were competent to make them. All that is proposed here is that, just as the causes of African poverty are many and complex, so must be the solutions to the problem – or rather, the ways in which it might be alleviated, since 'solutions' are not in sight. The present situation is very mixed, but in comparison with most of the world, it is grim. The prospects vary from place to place, and family to family, but in comparison with most of the world, they are bleak. The fact that *many* factors contribute to this means that *many* things must change before there is much hope of substantial and widespread improvement. But it also means that there are many possible changes, each one of which might be of some benefit, and therefore worth striving for.

Nothing can be done in the foreseeable future about how much rain falls in each part of Africa. But with regard to rainfall and drought, as also to other aspects of the physical environment, there is much scope for increased *understanding* on the part of both African rural dwellers and those advising or assisting them, sometimes through the sharing of their respective and complementary knowledge. Equally important are many forms of *adjustment* to the environment, such as breeding drought-resistant crop varieties, hopefully through the combined efforts of local farmers and exponents of 'western' science. Thirdly, there is clearly a need for improved *management* of the environment, such as through both large-scale and micro-scale control of surface water, though it is often very hard to say who should be responsible for the managing.

There is probably little that can be done in the near future about some forms of disease, such as malaria. Bilharzia might even spread more widely as a consequence of the surface water management mentioned above. But low-cost methods of curing, or preventing, some very widespread types of diseases are available. Both 'western' and indigenous medicine have important roles to play in reducing poverty through improved health, and in reducing the awful impact of poverty on health, especially that of children. The great unknown with regard to health in the next century is, of course, AIDS. Here medical science, local or international, has as yet little to offer; so effort must be concentrated on prevention through education. This will not stop a horrific spread of the disease, but we must hope that it will help to slow the process and reduce its impact.

Rapid population growth is a fact of life in Africa whatever one's attitude to it, and only an unthinkable spread of a disease such as AIDS could stop it within the next generation. It is absurd to assume that increased prosperity will reduce birth rates when no such increased prosperity is anticipated. However, there are *some* parents in Africa who want no more children, especially once they already have six or seven; and family planning has some role to play in alleviating poverty, particularly in certain densely-populated parts of Africa, both at the national level and at the individual family level.

Blaming the colonial experience for African poverty is much more popular in some quarters than others, but all must agree that nothing can now be done about this fact of history. On the other hand, something *must* be done about the political turmoil that affects the resulting non-nations such as Sudan and Mozambique, and also largely non-colonized Ethiopia. Certainly no recipe for that can be offered here, though it should be noted that an ending of external support for warring factions could make a very positive contribution in certain cases.

There seems to be an emerging consensus that in many African countries there needs to be both a strengthening of the state, in terms of its effectiveness and accountability, and at the same time a reduction in the range of activities that it aims to undertake. Opinions differ widely, both within Africa and outside, on the role that the state should ideally play in the economy, but most agree (some very reluctantly) that few African states have the capacity to play a large role very effectively. However, to what extent private enterprise can be more effective, especially in assisting the poor majority, is an open question. In saying opinions differ, I was thinking of those observing from afar or 'above'; but no doubt those suffering the poverty also have diverse opinions on these matters.

For someone writing from outside Africa, it would be good to think that however little outsiders could affect the factors internal to Africa, there was at least some prospect of their modifying the 'external' factors. Certainly every individual has the option of making a minute contribution to the welfare of Africa by donations to organizations such as OXFAM. These, of course, might operate in such a way as to do more harm than good, but I do not believe this to be generally the case, with respect either to disaster relief or to long-term development assistance. However such organizations cannot have more than a marginal impact on a continent-wide situation.

Government aid, both bilateral and multilateral, could have a far greater impact, and it was suggested in Chapter 11 that while the balance may be less clear than for NGOs, even this does more good than harm. Furthermore, the quality of such aid could be greatly improved, so that one could then argue more confidently for its expansion. However, even in the unlikely event of this happening, the total impact on African poverty within the next ten or twenty years would be small.

There is a dire need for changes in so many other aspects of the global economy, most of which are highly unlikely without changes in the global distribution of political power. With regard to the external debt of African countries there are real prospects that some relief may be forthcoming, and this would be of great assistance in the short term. However, some of this relief will merely extend the burden into the future, while the prospects of African countries being able to borrow in the future at rates they can really afford are as remote as the equivalent prospects for most poor families in Africa. With regard to commodity prices, the prospects of improvement are very poor indeed. The African farmer should not receive a mere pittance for his or her cocoa, coffee or cotton; but consumers in the rich countries are not prepared to pay more, especially when there are always alternative sources of supply, or the possibility of synthetic substitutes. One consequence of world patterns of population growth is, of course, that increasing numbers of producers in Africa are competing to supply an almost fixed number of consumers in Europe and North America, while conversely those regions gain from increasing numbers in Africa requiring their products. In this regard the greatest hope for Africa must lie in greater links with other parts of the world. On the other hand, the very substantial recent changes in the spatial patterns of the global economy, involving many parts of Asia, and often labelled The New International Division of Labour, have been of very little direct benefit to Africa.

Most people in Africa will remain very poor unless and until a whole series of internal circumstances can be altered. The prospects for this must now be left for the reader to judge. Most will also remain very poor unless and until some basic shifts in thinking take place elsewhere in the world, so that for instance 'we' in the West begin to think of people in Africa less as 'them' and more as 'others of us', in other words, to think more globally. The prospects for this must equally be left for the reader, whether in Africa or elsewhere, to judge.

Bibliography

Abdel-Ati, H. (1988) 'The process of famine: causes and consequences in Sudan.' *Development and Change*, 19 (2), 267–300.

Adams, W. M. and Grove, A. T. (eds.) (1984) *Irrigation in Tropical Africa*. Cambridge, African Studies Centre.

Adeniyi, E. O. and Bello-Imam, I. B. (eds.) (1986) *Development and the Environment*. Ibadan, Nigerian Institute of Social and Economic Research.

Amis, P. and Lloyd, P. (eds.) (1990) *Housing Africa's Urban Poor*. Manchester, Manchester University Press.

Anderson, D. and Grove, R. H. (eds.) (1987) *Conservation in Africa*. Cambridge, Cambridge University Press.

Anderson, M. B. and Woodrow, P. J. (1989) *Rising from the Ashes: development strategies in times of disaster*. Boulder, Westview; Paris, UNESCO.

Andrae, G. and Beckmann, B. (1985) *The Wheat Trap: bread and underdevelopment in Nigeria*. London, Zed.

Bates, R. H. (1981) *Markets and States in Tropical Africa*. Berkeley, University of California Press.

Bauer, P. T. (1981) *Equality, the Third World and Economic Delusion*. London, Weidenfeld & Nicolson.

Bell, M. (1986) *Contemporary Africa*. London, Longman.

Berg, R. J. and Whitaker, J. S. (eds.) (1986) *Strategies for African Development*. Berkeley, University of California Press.

Bienen, H. S. (1989) *Armed Forces, Conflict and Change in Africa*. Boulder, Westview.

Borton, J. and Clay, E. (1988) 'The African food crisis of 1982–1986' in Rimmer, D. (ed.) *Rural Transformation in Tropical Africa*, London, Belhaven.

Brandt, W. et al. (1980) *North–South: a programme for survival*. London, Pan.

Bray, M. et al. (1986) *Education and Society in Africa*. London, Edward Arnold.

Brokensha, D. et al. (1980) *Indigenous Knowledge Systems and Development*. Washington, University Press of America.

Brundtland, G. et al. (1987) *Our Common Future*. Oxford, Oxford University Press.

Bulcha, M. (1988) *Flight and Integration: causes of mass exodus from Ethiopia and problems of integration in Sudan*. Uppsala, Scandinavian Institute of African Studies.

Cairncross, S. (1988) 'Domestic water supply in rural Africa' in Rimmer, D. (ed.) *Rural Transformation in Tropical Africa*, London, Belhaven.

Caldwell, J. and P. (1987) 'The cultural context of high fertility in sub-Saharan Africa.' *Population and Development Review*, 13 (3), 409–37.

Cassen, R. et al. (1986) *Does Aid Work?* Oxford, Oxford University Press.

Chambers, R. (1983) *Rural Development: putting the last first*. London, Longman; New York, Wiley.

Chambers, R. (1985) *The Crisis of Africa's Rural Poor*. Brighton, Institute of Development Studies.

Chambers, R. et al. (1981) *Seasonal Dimensions to Rural Poverty*. London, Pinter.

Chazan, N. and Shaw, T. M. (eds.) (1988) *Coping with Africa's Food Crisis*. Boulder, Lynne Rienner.

Chazan, N. et al. (1988) *Politics and Society in Contemporary Africa*. Boulder, Lynne Rienner; London, Macmillan.

Cheru, F. (1989) *The Silent Revolution in Africa*. Harare, Anvil; London, Zed.

Clapham, C. (1987) 'Revolutionary socialist development in Ethiopia.' *African Affairs*, 86 (343), 151–65.

Clay, E. and Shaw, J. (eds.) (1987) *Poverty, Development and Food*. London, Macmillan.

Cliffe, L. and Davidson, B. (1988) *The Long Struggle of Eritrea*. Nottingham, Spokesman.

Collier, P. and Lal, D. (1984) 'Why poor people get rich: Kenya 1960–79.' *World Development*, 12 (10), 1007–18.

Commins, S. K. et al. (1986) *Africa's Agrarian Crisis*. Boulder, Lynne Rienner.

Conroy, C. and Litvinoff, M. (eds.) (1988) *The Greening of Aid*. London, Earthscan.

Cornia, G. A. et al. (1987) *Adjustment with a Human Face, Vol. I*. Oxford, Oxford University Press.

Court, D. and Kinyanjui, K. (1986) 'African education: problems in a high growth sector' in Berg, R. J. and Whitaker, J. S. (eds.) *Strategies for African Development*, Berkeley, University of California Press.

Curtis, D. et al. (1988) *Preventing Famine: policies and prospects for Africa*. London, Routledge.

Davison, J. (ed.) (1988) *Agriculture, Women and Land: the African experience*. Boulder, Westview.

Dawit Wolde Giorgis (1989) *Red Tears: war, famine and revolution in Ethiopia*. Trenton, Red Sea Press.

De Waal, A. (1989) *Famine that Kills: Darfur, Sudan, 1984–85*. Oxford, Oxford University Press.

Dodge, C. P. and Raundalen, M. (eds.) (1987) *War, Violence and Children in Uganda*. Oslo, Norwegian University Press.

Dodge, C. P. and Wiebe, P. D. (eds.) (1985) *Crisis in Uganda: the breakdown of health services*. Oxford, Pergamon.

Dumont, R. (1966) *False Start in Africa*. London, Andre Deutsch. Re-issued by Earthscan, London, 1989.

FAO (annual) *Production Yearbook*. Rome, FAO.

FAO (annual) *Trade Yearbook*. Rome, FAO.

Fieldhouse, D. K. (1986) *Black Africa, 1945–1980: economic decolonization and arrested development*. London, Allen & Unwin.

Findlay, A. and A. (1987) *Population and Development in the Third World*. London, Methuen.

Fraser, C. (1988) *Lifelines for Africa still in Peril and Distress*. London, Hutchinson.

George, S. (1988) *A Fate Worse than Debt*. London, Penguin.

Gill, P. (1986) *A Year in the Death of Africa*. London, Paladin.

Gish, O. (1975) *Planning the Health Sector: the Tanzanian experience*. London, Croom Helm.

Glantz, M. (ed.) (1987) *Drought and Hunger in Africa*. Cambridge, Cambridge University Press.

Good, C. M. (1987) *Ethnomedical Systems in Africa*. Hove, Guilford.

Gorman, R. F. (1987) *Coping with Africa's Refugee Burden*. Dordrecht, Nijhoff.

Goyder, H. and C. (1988) 'Case studies of famine: Ethiopia' in Curtis, D. et al., *Preventing Famine*, London, Routledge.

Green, R. H. et al. (1987) *Children on the Front Line*. New York UNICEF.

Griffin, K. (1987) *World Hunger and the World Economy*. London, Macmillan.

Griffiths, I. L. (1984) *An Atlas of African Affairs*. London, Methuen.

Grove, A. T. (1989) *The Changing Geography of Africa*. Oxford, Oxford University Press.

Guyer, J. I. (ed.) (1987) *Feeding African Cities*. Manchester, Manchester University Press.

Hake, A. (1977) *African Metropolis: Nairobi's self-help city*. London, Chatto & Windus.

Hancock, G. (1985) *Ethiopia: the challenge of hunger*. London, Gollancz.

Hanlon, J. (1986) *Beggar Your Neighbours: apartheid power in southern Africa*. London, James Currey.

Hansen, H. B. and Twaddle, M. (eds.) (1988) *Uganda Now: between decay and development*. London, James Currey.

Harrell-Bond, B. (1986) *Imposing Aid: emergency assistance to refugees*. Oxford, Oxford University Press.

Harrison, P. (1987) *The Greening of Africa*. London, Paladin.

Haswell, M. (1975) *The Nature of Poverty*. London, Macmillan.

Hayter, T. (1985) *Aid: rhetoric and reality*. London, Pluto.

Hill, P. (1977) *Population, Prosperity and Poverty: rural Kano 1900 and 1970*. Cambridge, Cambridge University Press.

Hill, P. (1986) *Development Economics on Trial*. Cambridge, Cambridge University Press.

Hill, A. G. (1988) 'Population growth and rural transformation in tropical Africa' in Rimmer, D. (ed.) *Rural Transformation in Tropical Africa*, London, Belhaven.

Hinderink, J. and Sterkenburg, J. (1987) *Agricultural Commericalization and Government Policy in Africa.* London, Kegan Paul.

Hjort, A. and Salih, M. (eds.) (1989) *Ecology and Politics: environmental stress and security in Africa.* Uppsala, Scandinavian Institute of African Studies.

Hodd, M. (ed.) (1988) *Tanzania After Nyerere.* London, Pinter.

Hogg, R. (1978) 'Development in Kenya: drought, desertification and food scarcity.' *African Affairs*, 86 (342), 47–58.

Hunt, D. (1984) *The Impending Crisis in Kenya: the case for land reform.* Aldershot, Gower.

Hyden, G. (1980) *Beyond Ujamaa in Tanzania.* London, Heinemann; Berkeley, University of California Press.

Hyden, G. (1983) *No Shortcuts to Progress.* London, Heinemann; Berkeley, University of California Press.

Iliffe, J. (1987) *The African Poor: a history.* Cambridge, Cambridge University Press.

ILO (1972) *Employment, Incomes and Equality: a strategy for increasing productive employment in Kenya.* Geneva, ILO.

Jackson, R. H. and Rosberg, C. G. (1982) *Personal Rule in Black Africa.* Berkeley, University of California Press.

Jamal, V. and Weeks, J. (1988) 'The vanishing rural–urban gap in sub-Saharan Africa.' *International Labour Review*, 127 (3), 271–92.

Jansson, K. et al. (1987) *The Ethiopian Famine.* London, Zed.

Johnson, D. H. and Anderson, D. M. (eds.) (1988) *The Ecology of Survival: case studies from Northeast African History.* London, Lester Crook; Boulder, Westview.

Kent, R. C. (1987) *The Anatomy of Disaster Relief.* London, Pinter.

Lappe, F. M. and Collins, J. (1988) *World Hunger: twelve myths.* London, Earthscan.

Last, M. and Chavunduka, G. (eds.) (1986) *The Professionalization of African Medicine.* Manchester, Manchester University Press.

Lawrence, P. (ed.) (1986) *World Recession and the Food Crisis in Africa.* London, James Currey.

Leach, G. and Mearns, R. (1988) *Beyond the Woodfuel Crisis: people, land and trees in Africa.* London, Earthscan.

Lewis, L. A. and Berry, L. (1988) *African Environments and Resources.* Boston, Unwin Hyman.

Lindskog, P. and Lundqvist, J. (1989) *Why Poor Children Stay Sick: the human ecology of child health and welfare in rural Malawi.* Uppsala, Scandinavian Institute of African Studies.

Lipton, M. (1977) *Why Poor People Stay Poor: a study of urban bias in world development.* London, Temple Smith.

Lipton, M. and Longhurst, R. (1989) *New Seeds and Poor People.* London, Unwin Hyman.

Livingstone, I. (1986) *Rural Development, Employment and Incomes in Kenya.* Aldershot, Gower.

Mabogunje, A. L. (1989) *The Development Process*, second edition. London, Unwin Hyman.

MacGaffey, J. (1983) 'How to survive and become rich amidst devastation: the second economy in Zaïre.' *African Affairs*, 82 (328), 351–66.

Makinwa, P. K. and Ozo, A. O. (eds.) (1987) *The Urban Poor in Nigeria.* Ibadan, Evans.

Maliyamkono, T. L. and Bagachwa, M. S. D. (1990) *The Second Economy in Tanzania.* London, James Currey.

Mazrui, A. A. (1979) *The African Condition.* London, Heinemann.

Meadows, D. et al. (1972) *The Limits to Growth.* Washington, Potomac; London, Pan.

Mellor, J. W. et al. (1987) *Accelerating Food Production in Sub-Saharan Africa.* Baltimore, Johns Hopkins Press.

Mesaroviç, M. and Pestel, E. (1975) *Mankind at the Turning Point.* New York, Dutton; London, Hutchinson.

Mesfin Wolde Mariam (1985) *Rural Vulnerability to Famine in Ethiopia 1955–77.* New Delhi, Vikas; London, Intermediate Technology Publications.

Miller, N. and Rockwell, R. C. (eds.) (1988) *AIDS in Africa: the social and policy impact.* New York, Edwin Mellen.

Momsen, J. H. and Townsend, J. (eds.) (1987) *Geography of Gender in the Third World.* London, Hutchinson.

Monod, T. (ed.) (1975) *Pastoralism in Tropical Africa.* London, Oxford University Press.

Moris, J. (1988) 'Failing to cope with drought: the plight of African ex-pastoralists.' *Development Policy Review,* 6 (3), 269–94.

Mortimore, M. J. (1989) *Adapting to Drought: farmers, famines and desertification in West Africa.* Cambridge, Cambridge University Press.

Mosley, P. (1987) *Overseas Aid: its defence and refrom.* Brighton, Wheatsheaf.

Munslow, B. et al. (1988) *The Fuelwood Trap: a study of the SADCC region.* London, Earthscan.

Nafziger, E. W. (1988) *Inequality in Africa.* Cambridge, Cambridge University Press.

Ndegwa, P. (1985) *Africa's Development Crisis.* Nairobi, Heinemann.

Nyerere, J. (1968) *Freedom and Socialism.* Nairobi, Oxford University Press.

Nyerere, J. (1985) 'Africa and the debt crisis.' *African Affairs,* 84 (337), 489–97.

O'Connor, A. M. (1971) *The Geography of Tropical African Development.* Oxford, Pergamon.

O'Connor, A. M. (1978) *The Geography of Tropical African Development*, second edition. Oxford, Pergamon.

O'Connor, A. M. (1983) *The African City.* London, Hutchinson; New York, Holmes & Meier.

OECD (1989) *Development Co-operation in the 1990s.* Paris, OECD.

Onimode, B. (ed.) (1989) *The IMF, the World Bank and the African Debt.* London, Zed.

Pacey, A. and Payne, P. (eds.) (1985) *Agricultural Development and Nutrition.* London, Hutchinson.

Panos Institute (1988) *AIDS and the Third World.* London, Panos Institute.

Parfitt, T. and Riley, S. (1989) *The African Debt Crisis.* London, Routledge.

Poulton, R. and Harris, M. (eds.) (1988) *Putting People First: voluntary organizations and Third World development*. London, Macmillan.

Raikes, P. (1988) *Modernising Hunger: famine, food surplus and farm policy in the EEC and Africa*. London, James Currey.

Ravenhill, J. (1986) *Africa in Economic Crisis*. London, Macmillan.

Richards, P. (1985) *Indigenous Agricultural Revolution*. London, Hutchinson.

Richards, P. (1986) *Coping with Hunger*. London, Allen & Unwin.

Riddell, R. C. (1987) *Foreign Aid Reconsidered*. London, James Currey.

Rimmer, D. (ed.) (1988) *Rural Transformation in Tropical Africa*. London, Belhaven.

Rogge, J. R. (1985) *Too Many, Too Long: Sudan's twenty-year refugee dilemma*. Totowa, Rowman & Allenheld.

Ross, D. H. (1988) *Educating Handicapped Young People in Eastern and Southern Africa*. Paris, UNESCO.

Sada, P. O. and Odemerho, F. O. (eds.) (1988) *Environmental Issues and Management in Nigerian Development*. Ibadan, Evans.

Sandbrook, R. (1982) *The Politics of Basic Needs: urban aspects of assaulting poverty in Africa*. London, Heinemann.

Sandbrook, R. (1985) *The Politics of Africa's Economic Stagnation*. Cambridge, Cambridge University Press.

SCF/ODI (1988) *Prospects for Africa*. London, Hodder & Stoughton.

Sen, A. K. (1981) *Poverty and Famines*. Oxford, Clarendon Press.

Shepherd, J. (1975) *The Politics of Starvation*. Washington, Carnegie Endowment.

Singer, H. et al. (1987) *Food Aid: the challenge and the opportunity*. Oxford, Oxford University Press.

Stren, R. and White, R. (eds.) (1989) *African Cities in Crisis*. Boulder, Westview.

Swindell, K. (1985) *Farm Labour*. Cambridge, Cambridge University Press.

Timberlake, L. (1985) *Africa in Crisis*. London, Earthscan.

Twose, N. (1985) *Fighting the Famine*. London, Pluto.

United Nations (1989) *South African Destabilization: the economic cost of frontline resistance to apartheid*. New York, UN.

UNICEF (annual) *The State of the World's Children*. Oxford, Oxford University Press.

UNICEF (1985) *Within Human Reach: a future for Africa's children*. New York, UNICEF.

United States (1980) *The Global 2000 Report to the President*. Washington, US Government. (Abridged version published by Penguin Books, London, 1982.)

Watts, M. (1983) *Silent Violence: food, famine and peasantry in northern Nigeria*. Berkeley, University of California Press.

Watts, M. (ed.) (1987) *State, Oil and Agriculture in Nigeria*. Berkeley, Institute of International Studies.

Williams, R. (1987) *Political Corruption in Africa*. Aldershot, Gower.

Wisner, B. (1988) *Power and Need in Africa*. London, Earthscan.

World Bank (annual) *World Development Report*. Oxford, Oxford University Press.

World Bank (1981) *Accelerated Development in Sub-Saharan Africa*. Washington, World Bank.

World Bank (1986) *Population Growth and Policies in Sub-Saharan Africa.* Washington, World Bank.

World Bank (1988) *Education in Sub-Saharan Africa.* Washington World Bank.

World Bank (1989) *Sub-Saharan Africa: from crisis to sustainable growth.* Washington, World Bank.

Yeager, R. (1989) *Tanzania: an African experiment*, second edition. Boulder, Westview.

Young, C. (1982) *Ideology and Development in Africa.* New Haven, Yale University Press.

Zayd, A. et al. (1988) *War Wounds: development costs of conflict in southern Sudan.* London, Panos Institute.

Zolberg, A. R. et al. (1989) *Escape from Violence: conflict and the refugee crisis in the developing world.* New York, Oxford University Press.

Index